'RACE' IN BRITAIN TODAY

'Race', Education and Society

'Race' in Britain Today

RICHARD SKELLINGTON

WITH PAULETTE MORRIS

WITH AN INTRODUCTORY ESSAY BY PAUL GORDON

This is a resource book for the Open University course ED356 *'Race', Education and Society*.
The following three volumes, also published by SAGE Publications, are Readers for the course.

Racism and Education

Structures and strategies

EDITED BY DAWN GILL, BARBARA MAYOR AND MAUD BLAIR

'Race', Culture and Difference

EDITED BY JAMES DONALD AND ALI RATTANSI

Racism and Antiracism

Inequalities, opportunities and policies

EDITED BY PETER BRAHAM, ALI RATTANSI AND RICHARD SKELLINGTON

(Details of the course are available from Central Enquiry Service, PO Box 200, The Open University, Walton Hall, Milton Keynes MK7 6YZ.)

For Ray Serrano

'RACE' IN BRITAIN TODAY

RICHARD SKELLINGTON

WITH PAULETTE MORRIS

WITH AN INTRODUCTORY ESSAY BY PAUL GORDON

Second Edition

SAGE PUBLICATIONS
London • Thousand Oaks • New Delhi

in association with

The Open
University

This edition published 1996

First edition 1992

SAGE Publications Ltd
6 Bonhill Street
London EC2A 4PU

SAGE Publications Inc
2455 Teller Road
Thousand Oaks, California 91320

SAGE Publications India Pvt Ltd
32 M-Block Market
Greater Kailash – I
New Delhi 110 048

British Library cataloguing in publication data

Skellington, Richard
'Race' in Britain Today
I. Title II. Morris, Paulette
305.800941
ISBN 0 7619 5049 4
ISBN 0 7619 5024 9 pbk

Library of Congress catalog card number 92–50116

Designed by the Graphic Design Group of The Open University

Typeset by The Open University

Printed in Great Britain by Galliards, Great Yarmouth

C ONTENTS

List of figures, maps and tables

FOREWORD TO THE FIRST EDITION

The authors would like to thank the Runnymede Trust, the Commission for Racial Equality, the Child Poverty Action Group and the Radical Statistics Race Group, particularly the authors of *Britain's Black Population* (Bhat *et al.*, 1988) for their valuable assistance. Within the Open University special gratitude is due to Kate Hunter, who edited the book, Lesley Passey, who designed it, Sally Baker, the School of Education liaison librarian who worked so hard obtaining illustrations and original newspaper cuttings and photographs, and to Aileen Lodge, who typed the material and coped heroically with the many changes.

We also want to thank James Donald for the contribution he made to the production of the final draft, June Evison, Sheila Gilks, Chris Golding, June Humphreys, Riz Sharma and Marie-Claude Bovet for their help with previous drafts and artist Alison George and designer Sian Lewis.

FOREWORD TO THE SECOND EDITION

For the second edition Richard Skellington would like to thank Maud Blair, Clive Harris, Peter Braham and Maria Francis-Pitfield for their unyielding support and academic input; Allan Cochrane, Stuart Hall, Diane Bailey, Alison Kirk, Helen Howard, Kate Hunter and Paulette Morris for their encouragement; Hazel Coleman (editor), Jonathan Davies (designer), Hannah Brunt (designer), and June Evison (secretarial support) for their skilled contributions, the Runnymede Trust, the Commission for Racial Equality and the Institute of Race Relations, and the Board of the School of Education for keeping the faith.

How to use this book

This is a work of reference. It is designed for two kind of reader: those who are searching for evidence on specific issues related to 'race', and those who might wish to read through a range of contemporary evidence on black and Asian life chances.

The book is essentially a resource for readers to use as they wish. This second edition covers data, information and events until mid-August 1995; this material can be found at the end of *each* section under the heading 'Developments since 1992'. There are also new sections, on politics and sport, and a new introduction and conclusion. All this material has been authored by Richard Skellington. Paul Gordon's introductory essay on ethnic minority monitoring has also been revised.

INTRODUCTION: FOUR YEARS FURTHER ON A LONG JOURNEY

▼ ▓▓▓▓▓▓▓▓▓▓▓▓▓▓▓▓▓▓▓▓▓▓▓▓▓▓▓▓▓▓▓▓ ▼

Looking ahead, we should be able to set our work of eliminating racial discrimination in education, housing services and the administration of justice within a firmer context of information and data during the 1990s – these sources of data will open up opportunities to identify patterns of disadvantage and possible discrimination, and will pinpoint, for the benefit of service providers as well as service customers, the policy, training and resource needs that must be met to overcome any discrimination that is identified.

(Commission for Racial Equality, 1990a, p. 19)

The biggest lie is it doesn't matter what race, creed, nationality you are – the colour of your skin doesn't matter, it's the person that you are and if you do a good job, you can succeed. Bullshit! Race has everything to do with everything.

(Spike Lee, quoted in Crawley, 1994, p. 216)

▲ ▓▓▓▓▓▓▓▓▓▓▓▓▓▓▓▓▓▓▓▓▓▓▓▓▓▓▓▓▓▓▓▓ ▲

'Race' matters. This book was designed in the first instance to be used by students taking the Open University third level course, ED356 'Race', Education and Society. This second edition expands both the breadth of information available, and its relevance for people concerned about black people's life chances.[1] It constructs a UK profile across a wide range of institutional areas – in education, the labour market, the criminal justice system, health, welfare and housing, politics and sport – and places this profile in demographic and historical perspective. The profile is also illustrated in relation to key issues confronting Britain in the 1990s, for example, other inequalities in society, immigration policy, poverty and racism. It has sought evidence which allows controls to be established across a range of factors: for example, in relation to age, class, gender and location. A particular emphasis has been placed upon the experiences of young black and Asian people, especially with regard to racism, racial harassment, and across the breadth of institutional contexts negotiated in daily life.

Paul Gordon's article, 'The racialization of statistics', examines the ways in which statistics about minority ethnic groups are defined, analysed and interpreted in British society. The article has been substantially revised in the light of growing evidence from monitoring minority ethnic group outcomes. He shows how the collection of data is not a neutral exercise, but is inevitably conducted from particular ideological perspectives. He also raises fundamental questions about the relationship between data collection and policy implementation, and highlights some of the key implications for minority ethnic groups as knowledge about their life chances and relative status increases.

Part 2 has been expanded from eleven inter-related sections to thirteen. These sections draw together the results of an extensive survey of existing research and statistical findings. They include relevant material available up to spring 1995. The review contains new sections on politics and sport, and a short conclusion.

The Commission for Racial Equality (CRE) has long argued for the need to monitor and evaluate in order to measure how racial discrimination is being combated. Statistical information can enable organizations to tackle problems that arise in implementing policy strategies, to keep policies under review, and to overcome internal resistance to change. However, some members of minority ethnic groups have expressed doubts and concerns about the need for and the use to which these 'new' statistics will be put. Why are more statistics necessary when there is already sufficient official and independent research evidence documenting both the extent of racial inequality and the processes which produce it? Why have decades of monitoring and evaluation, however partial, failed to produce effective policy implementation in areas particularly designed to remedy the historic consequences of racial discrimination and disadvantage? These questions raise sensitive issues and complex debates. Robert Moore's evidence to the Home Affairs Committee still rings true: 'statistics have seldom been used to the advantage of the black population, but have been the basis for abuse and for building a climate of opinion in which "the numbers game" proclaims that blacks are intrinsically a problem' (Home Affairs Committee, 1983, p. 138).

I have tried to avoid this 'numbers game' approach to 'race' statistics. In attempting to produce as representative a profile as possible, I have no wish to reify dubious categories. As Ahmed and Sheldon (1991) have argued, data collection is not an end in itself, and neither should the rising mountains of research into the life chances of black people provide the illusion of progress; evidence is no substitute for action. It must also be recognized that many of the disadvantages described in this profile also apply to white British people. The focus here, however, is on black British people. The emphasis is not to project black people as victims, but as survivors of a range of experiences, living in a changing and evolving multi-ethnic society, where nothing is permanent or fixed.

In producing this profile of Britain's black and Asian population, I have been aware of two important issues that arise from the survey of existing research and statistical findings. One is the problem of categorization and terminology; the other is the range and variety of sources used.

There is no one agreed set of terms in use among researchers in this field for the different minority ethnic groups. Sometimes differences in terminology reflect the use of different words for the same or similar groups (such as 'West Indian' and 'Afro-Caribbean'). At other times, different sets of terms refer to different classifications and different ways of classifying. For example, a classification may be based on skin colour, or country of origin, or descent. Terminology is also problematic because, over time, the terminology itself shifts: some terms fall into disuse and disrepute, while others change. Many terminological usages are controversial, and probably none is without its drawbacks. What was broadly acceptable in the 1980s may not be acceptable in the 1990s, and so on. I have generally adopted the analytical categories used by our sources.

But here we confront a second important issue: the type of data source used. It is axiomatic that all sources should be treated with degrees of caution. As Gordon's analysis of the 'racialization' of statistics shows, the 1970s and 1980s revealed a relative dearth of consistent minority ethnic group monitoring across many areas of institutional life in Britain. Gordon also emphasizes how the official statistics have changed, and how shifting definitions, for example in the context of our discussion of the labour market in Section 10, have rendered analysis problematic. Sometimes governments have dropped a particular measure altogether, making trend analysis impossible to sustain, for example in relation to the discussion of poverty in Section 4.

Apart from the work by the Runnymede Trust and the Radical Statistics Race Group (RSRG) in the 1980s, there have been few attempts to produce the kind of profile presented here. In the introduction to the first study of Britain's black population, compiled in the late 1970s, Usha Prashar, then director of the Runnymede Trust, reflected that in some areas there was a complete 'statistical vacuum' and in others 'a partial vacuum' (Runnymede Trust and RSRG, 1980, pp. xii–xiii). Fifteen years later, the situation has improved, especially in the early 1990s, but the range of sources quoted in this book bears testimony to the need for more official and effective monitoring that permits analysis over time by using a smaller range of agreed categories and terminology. We are still at the mercy of our sources.

It is important to recognize, too, that what is presented here is a selection from an enormous flow of information. A diverse range of sources has been used: for example, official government statistics, national and local surveys of circumstances, attitudes and opinions, studies of one ethnic group in more than one locality, comparative research into black, Asian and white outcomes, experiential research studies, newspaper and journal articles, television and radio broadcasting, policy statements from individuals involved in particular institutional contexts, personal statements from individuals in particular institutional contexts, and statements from individuals reflecting their own experiences.

Legislative reform is also needed. The CRE has argued for tougher laws to challenge entrenched forms of discrimination that still persist after 30 years of race relations legislation (CRE, 1991a). The role and power of organizations such as the CRE may also require radical overhaul and proper funding.

The 1980s witnessed, according to Gordon, a deepening of the division in British society along the lines of 'race' and skin colour. He argues that minority ethnic groups continue to experience a different reality:

> Black and white people, as the writer Salman Rushdie remarked some years ago, inhabit different worlds – it is black people who suffer the degradations, the injustices and the threats to their security of the immigration control system. They who are required to produce their passports to establish their immigration status and the legality of their presence here when they claim benefits or seek services. They who are attacked in their homes, schools and public places because of their physical appearance. They who are regarded by people in authority, and portrayed in the press, as an alien threat from which the rest of society must be defended. This is the reality of racism in Britain in the late 1980s, a reality which contradicts any rhetoric of equality or equal opportunities.
>
> (Gordon, 1989a, p. 26)

Young people, and young black people in particular, have become increasingly vulnerable. In June 1991, Michael Day, then chair of the CRE, observed:

> We have come a long way since 1966 but there are still too many token gestures. The achievements of many from the minority ethnic communities are impressive, but young black people in particular do not feel valued. Many of the social factors which contributed to inner city disturbances of 10 years ago are still apparent.
>
> (*Independent*, 15 June 1991)

Will the 1990s see these 'token gestures' transformed into effective policies? Will the 'social factors' underlying the profile presented here be radically changed?

The 1993 Policy Studies Institute (PSI) survey on minorities concluded that despite racial discrimination some minority ethnic groups had made progress since 1984, notably those of Indian origin, while others (those of Pakistani, Bangladeshi and Afro-Caribbean origin) had not. The PSI reported a growing gap in education, employment and socio-economic background between Indian and Chinese groups on the one hand and Pakistani, Bangladeshi and Afro-Caribbeans on the other. The survey also revealed sharp contrasts in relation to gender, with Pakistani and Bangladeshi women worst affected in terms of educational qualifications held compared with all other groups (Jones, 1993). Modood has argued that race relations, discrimination and disadvantage should not be analysed in black and white terms: 'aggregate statistics about "black" unemployment or, say, under-representation in a particular occupation or economic section are blunt tools for analysis' (Modood, 1994).

'Race' in Britain Today acknowledges the multi-ethnic diversity of the UK. This book, however, remains essentially a descriptive account of black and Asian life chances in an unequal society.

In the period since the first edition several factors have significantly affected minority ethnic groups. First, the recession deepened, exposing more black and Asian people, in particular the young, to unemployment, homelessness, hardship and disadvantage. The possible beginnings of a national recovery cannot disguise the high levels of unemployment and housing shortages that continue disproportionately to affect black people. Second, racial violence and racist attacks continue to rise and could be as high as 170,000 a year, according to the Home Office's 1994 British Crime Survey. The Home Secretary, Michael Howard, insists that existing laws are adequate. Third, there is growing concern about the extent to which black and Asian households are suffering from acute levels of poverty. Fourth, more young Afro-Caribbean and Bangladeshi pupils are being subjected to exclusion from our educational institutions. Fifth, a disproportionate number of Afro-Caribbeans inhabit our prisons. Sixth, increasing evidence of police racism has emerged, amid growing concern about the vulnerability of black and Asian people in the criminal justice system. For example, Metropolitan Police Force (MPF) Commissioner Sir Paul Condon's claims in July 1995, supported by Home Secretary Michael Howard, that 80 per cent of recorded 'muggings' (street thefts and robberies) in high areas of black and Asian minority ethnic group concentration were committed by young 'black' (Afro-Caribbean) men, caused much debate, consternation and concern in Afro-Caribbean, Asian and African communities. By singling out 'black' communities, Sir Paul was accused of destabilizing progress made in police–community relations (*Independent*, 8 July 1995, 14 July 1995; *Guardian*, 8 July 1995; *Independent on Sunday*, 9 July 1995). The Home Secretary's public support for Sir Paul's 'Eagle Eye' campaign was criticised by the United Nations Human Rights Committee: 'In a multi-racial state that Britain has become such comments do not contribute to a climate of racial harmony', the Committee observed (*Independent*, 21 July 1995). Seventh, disturbances in Manningham, Bradford, in June 1995 witnessed the most significant urban unrest in the 1990s. British-born children of poor Pakistani Mirpuri migrants were involved in violent clashes with West Yorkshire Police. The disturbances raised further the extent to which black and Asian youth may be increasingly alienated by a range of cultural, economic and societal factors, especially if triggered by perceived insensitive policing. Finally, new calls for increased immigration and asylum controls, and a growing support for far right organizations especially among the working class, add to this complex picture of multi-ethnic Britain.

A PSI study on Britain's ethnic minorities has identified some improvement for some minorities and the growth in the black and Asian middle class (Jones, 1993), whilst Modood's research into higher education revealed that some minorities were making significant progress (*The Times Higher Education Supplement*, 16 July 1993). But the persistent levels of racial discrimination in the labour market, and related high black and Asian unemployment, the squeeze on rights and benefits, the climate of resource underfunding and the substantial growth in relative poverty have, if anything, made the situations of many black and Asian people more vulnerable than they were at the end of the 1980s. Further cuts in the urban programme and Section 11 funding (aimed specifically at meeting the special needs of minority ethnic groups), and more reductions in state welfare provision will hit black and Asian minorities hard. Khurshid Ahmed, secretary of the National Association of Race Equality Advisors, commented:

> It is a recipe for disaster that cuts are falling on the black community at a time when there is a rising tide of racism and fascism across Europe. These cuts are devastating.

> (P. Gosling, 'Poor relations in race for government cash',
> *Independent*, 10 December 1992)

Black and Asian minorities are still being denied a representative and influential political base, although there is evidence of increasing political awareness and participation at local level. Black and Asian people are increasingly recognizing the need to establish their own political platforms, and to pressure for relevant shifts in legislative change.

In his inaugural address the first black chair of the CRE, Herman Ouseley, called for the eradication of racial intolerance and prejudice, and the freeing of our society from racial discrimination by the end of the century. His words were echoed by the new black chair of the Runnymede Trust, Trevor Phillips, who expressed his dismay at the divided, directionless and feeble response of those who say they want to improve 'race' relations in Britain. There is still, four years on, a very long way to go.

Richard Skellington
August 1995

Note

1 The definitions and terms used by the authors of the research projects and official statistics have been used. I wish to respect people's self-definitions. I have used the phrase 'black and Asian' to broadly follow the Office of Population Censuses and Surveys' (OPCS) use of this term as it applies to 'Caribbean', 'African' and 'Black other'. Sometimes 'Caribbean' and 'Black other' are collapsed into a single 'Afro-Caribbean' category. The term 'South Asian' or 'Asian' is used where Bangladeshi, Indian and Pakistani people cannot be isolated. Where known, the 'Chinese' category has been isolated from the general 'Asian' category. The term 'minority ethnic group' has been used where it has not been possible to distinguish between groups, or to isolate black and Asian people. Paul Gordon uses the word 'black' to mean Afro-Caribbean or Asian unless otherwise stated (see Part 1, p. 21).

THE RACIALIZATION OF STATISTICS

Paul Gordon

A personal prologue

'There are three kinds of lie', the American writer Mark Twain is reputed to have observed; 'lies, damned lies and statistics.' Twain's scepticism towards statistics is reflected in the common observation that 'you can do anything with statistics'. And yet, despite such scepticism, we all at some point in our lives make use of statistics, usually to support an argument that we are putting forward or, indeed, one that we are opposing. Statistics seem to us to be 'hard facts', unlike, say, moral or political positions which are, after all, only 'our views' or other people's opinions. Statistics can seem unchallengeable or, at least, they demand that an opponent come up with a more convincing argument. If I say, for instance, that a certain proportion of the population is living below the poverty line, an adversary has to challenge the basis of my facts, perhaps by disputing the methods used to collate the information or the definitions involved.

Statistics are particularly beloved by the communications media: television, radio and newspapers. Again, they are seen as 'hard facts' as opposed to opinions, and are much more likely to be quoted, at least when reporting on people or organizations whose opinions are seen as requiring support from facts. Thus, a pressure group is much more likely to have a story published in a national newspaper or reported on radio or television if it can support it with, or, better, if it can base it on, statistical evidence. A number of organizations working in the field of 'race' relations have traditionally sought to base their argument on statistical evidence, believing that only by their doing this will serious attention be paid by those whom the organization hopes to convince, whether these be groups of parliamentarians (Members of Parliament or peers), key civil servants in important departments or sections of the general public. Only by presenting 'facts', as opposed to opinion, such organizations might argue, can the argument for more effective action be won. There is, indeed, considerable truth in this. Most people in Britain today would probably agree that racial discrimination is wrong and should not be tolerated. But they would probably disagree about the existence and the extent of such discrimination, and many would have to be convinced that it did indeed exist in certain areas of life and would have to be shown proof of its extent.

During the years that I worked at the Runnymede Trust, the 'race' relations research and information body, a common response from people to whom the organization was trying to put a case was that they wanted statistics as proof of what was being said. It was not enough to claim, for instance, that there was discrimination by the police or by employers or by the courts. Hard evidence had to be produced to substantiate such charges. Statistics, it should be said, are not the only form of evidence used. The 'case study' is also frequently adduced. Here, instead of statistics which might not be available or in addition to such statistics, examples of actual cases are cited in order to support an argument. In the area of 'race' relations, this is very common in arguments about police practice. In both these examples, as in others, statistical information is either not available or would not really be appropriate. I should like to give an actual example from my experience of this reliance on statistics and the problems which can arise.

Some time in early 1992, I took a telephone call at the Runnymede Trust from a television journalist who was thinking about making a short film on racial attacks in East London. She was, I might say, unclear about what the Runnymede Trust actually was, but she had heard from a colleague that we 'collected statistics' and wanted to know what statistics we had on racial violence in the London Borough of Tower Hamlets. I explained that, while we did indeed have much statistical information, this was only a small part of the material we held in our library and files. As for racial attacks, I went on to explain, we probably did have some figures but there were a number of serious problems with these. First, the only ones available were those collated by the Metropolitan Police and it was widely accepted, both by the police and by those campaigning on the issue, that they represented but a small fraction of all incidents; the vast majority, perhaps as much as 90 per cent, were not reported to the police. Second, there was the problem of definition. The concept of racial attacks, as it is most commonly understood, refers to attacks which are in some way racially motivated (which does not rule out other motives). In the context of Britain, this means overwhelmingly attacks by whites on blacks since few attacks on whites by blacks (and by this I mean Asian or Afro-Caribbean unless otherwise stated) could be said, in any meaningful sense, to be motivated by racism. The definition used by the police, on the other hand, refers to 'inter-racial incidents'; by which they mean incidents in which aggressor and victim come from different *ethnic* groups and which could, and did, include attacks by blacks on whites. Third, there were problems in interpreting statistics such as these since increases or decreases were as likely to reflect tendencies to report incidents as they were to reflect the actual prevalence of the problem.

I could sense a growing impatience, possibly irritation, on the part of the caller. After all, I seemed to be standing in the way of some information that she wanted. So, she asked, how was one, how were they, to measure any rise or fall in racial attacks in the area? I suggested that they might talk to people in the area, local residents and workers, for instance, or to community organizations, the police, and so on. That way they might get a better picture of what was happening. To the journalist, however, this would not provide *facts,* only impressions, opinions. What she needed was facts and these could only come in statistical form.

I offer this story because it provides an example, typical in my experience, of the way in which many people look at statistical information. Here was someone committed to an idea of journalistic objectivity, looking for objective factual information and seeing in statistical data the most factual and objective kind of information available. The lived experience of human beings, while undoubtedly interesting was, as far as this journalist was concerned, simply not factual enough. In effect, she was defining reality in terms of what could be measured. This, of course, is not something that is peculiar to journalists. As I have said, we all, at some point or another, want some kind of factual information to support cases we are making, and to many people there is nothing as factual and objective – and incontrovertible – as a statistic.

Until the mid-1980s relatively little statistical information about minority ethnic group people in Britain was collated at a national level or, indeed, in any systematic way. The three main categories of such information were: those of the national population census held every ten years, which, in 1971 and 1981, had asked a question about the country of birth of heads of households; the Labour Force Survey (LFS) carried out every two years on people in the workforce; and the statistical data collected on a continuing basis in connection with immigration control, such as the number of people accepted for settlement or making short-term visits. There were virtually no data collected nationally and regularly in the fields of education, health, housing, welfare, social services, the criminal justice system, policing or racial violence. It was therefore impossible to know, for instance, how many black pupils there were in schools or local education authority areas; how many black teachers and at what grades; the number and position of black doctors and nurses; the extent of racial violence; or the proportion of black people going through the criminal courts. This presented considerable problems for both academics and policy-makers who could obtain such information only through specific research projects and, sometimes, through locally-based surveys.

A decade or so later, the situation has changed considerably. Now data are collected on a range of areas including the ethnic origins of school pupils and school teachers, students in higher and further education, people on probation, the prison population, and on racial incidents (using the police's definition mentioned above). In addition, and of great importance both symbolically and practically, the census in 1991 was the first to ask a question about the ethnic origins of respondents. (As mentioned above, previous censuses had asked a question about the birthplace of the heads of households. This was used to calculate the population of minority ethnic origin but became increasingly useless as a growing proportion of the minority population were born in Britain.)

What has brought about these changes? How are we to understand what seems to be a greater acceptability of 'racial' monitoring of one kind or another? Why is information being collected on some aspects and not on others? To what uses will this information be put? These are some of the questions that I shall try to answer in this introductory essay. At the same time, I want to look critically at the statistics that are collected on black people, in the same way that I tried to do with the journalist, although in more detail and by looking at a number of different areas. By looking at the way in which statistics are defined and analysed and the decisions which lie behind whether or not to collect information, I hope to illustrate some of the problems of official data on matters related to 'race'. A case history of the development of ethnic statistics in education helps me to suggest some answers to the questions just posed in relation to that field of policy.

The construction of racialized data

First of all, what do we mean when we speak of ethnic or racialized statistics? When thinking about such data, it is important to keep in mind that they are not just a reflection of objective reality which is 'out there', as it were, and which simply has to be recorded, counted or measured. Rather such data have been *racialized*, that is, 'race' has been introduced into the definition or data-collection exercise as a factor of some importance and the subjects have been defined, at least partly, in racial terms. Thus, for instance, people in a particular group being measured, say, in schools, are not just seen as men, women and children but as men, women and children who belong to particular racial, ethnic, linguistic or religious groups. Such an approach to data depends on a decision being taken that these are, or at least may be, factors of importance in explaining performance or status (as opposed, say, to whether people have short or long hair or wear spectacles, which may, of course, be considered important by others in a different context). The use of racial categories assumes racial difference and implies the existence of some degree of inequality that is based on such assumed racial difference and that can be quantified.

Once a decision has been made to collect racialized data, a further decision has to be made, about the categories to be used. Particularly as the collection of such data has become more common, it is easy to lose sight of the fact that the categories used are terms that have to be decided. Although we talk of 'race' and 'race relations', often without thinking, 'races' – racial categories or racial groups – do not exist as objective biological facts in any meaningful way. The study of human beings has been unable to identify significant characteristics that can be found in some groups of people but not in others that would allow us to define and delineate distinct racial groups. Nor has such study found any difference of ability or intelligence. The differences that do exist between peoples from different parts of the world, particularly the physical characteristics of skin pigmentation, bone structure, hair type and so on, are, in themselves, of no importance. Such characteristics *become* important only when values are attached to them and when physical differences are seen as outward signs of other character traits or personality types. For example, Jews may be seen as devious, clannish and mean; Afro-Caribbeans as lazy, disorderly and prone to criminal activity; Asians as dishonest; Latins as volatile and emotional; Scots as mean and dour; Germans as humourless and efficient; English as formal and averse to washing too much; and so on. But these are always *ascribed* by one group to others.

'Race', racial groups and categories, in other words, are not things that are given – objective facts waiting to be used – but concepts that have to be *constructed* and constructed by *someone*. This construction involves a number of stages: differences of a certain kind between people have to be discerned; these differences have to be considered consequential; and these perceived shared attributes, such as skin colour, nationality, or regional or ethnic origins, have to become the basis for defining groups or categories of people. This has considerable importance for the collection of racialized data, which can use a wide range of categories, as shown in the following examples of the major surveys which involve differentiation along ethnic lines:

1   From 1990, schools have been required to collect data on the ethnic origins of pupils and teachers, as well as on their religious and linguistic backgrounds. (This is dealt with in more detail in the case study of education statistics given later.) The categories used are the same as those developed for the 1991 census (see 3 below).

2   The 1971 census asked respondents about the birthplaces of their parents. The size of the black population was calculated by subtracting the estimated number of people born in the New Commonwealth (all Commonwealth countries except for Australia, Canada and New Zealand) but of non-New Commonwealth origin, from the total number of British residents of New Commonwealth origin, plus those with at least one New Commonwealth-born parent.

3   The 1991 census asked people to select one of nine categories – white, black-Caribbean, black-African, black-other, Indian, Pakistani, Bangladeshi, Chinese or other.

4   The Labour Force Survey, which looks extensively at patterns of employment and unemployment, uses yet another classification scheme, currently asking respondents if they are white, West Indian or Guyanese, Indian, Pakistani, Bangladeshi, Chinese, African, Arabian, mixed or other.

5   From 1970 to 1982 the Department of Employment monitored what it referred to as 'coloured' unemployment using the categories of East Africa, other African countries, West Indies, India, Pakistan, Bangladesh (after 1973) and other Commonwealth countries. This monitoring was carried out by staff who identified those considered 'coloured' who were then asked about their country of birth. This scheme was abandoned in 1982 when the responsibility for producing unemployment statistics moved from job centres to unemployment benefit offices. Plans to introduce a new method of monitoring by visual assessment by staff were blocked by unemployment benefit staff. The new scheme would have used three categories – Afro-Caribbean, Asian and others.

6   The General Household Survey, a survey of various social policy issues such as health, marriage and leisure, has since 1983 asked a

question on ethnic origin in addition to the questions previously asked on country of birth. The categories are those used in the LFS.

7 The Metropolitan Police has used its own 'identity code' since 1975 involving six classes: IC1 – white-skinned European types – English, Scottish, Welsh, Scandinavian and Russian; IC2 – dark-skinned European types – Sardinian, Spanish, Italian; IC3 – Negroid types – Caribbean, West Indian, African, Nigerian; IC4 – Indians and Pakistanis; IC5 – Chinese, Japanese, Mongolians, Siamese; IC6 – Arabians, Egyptians, Algerians, Moroccans and North Africans.

8 The British Crime Survey, which investigates actual as distinct from reported crime and victimization patterns, seeks information on ethnic origins of respondents and, where known, alleged perpetrators of crimes. Categories used are white, black (West Indian or African), Indian, Pakistani or Bangladeshi, and other. (For respondents the last are replaced by 'other non-white' and 'mixed or uncertain'.)

9 Since 1988 all police forces have been required to record details of 'racial incidents' and submit these for central collation.

10 The Prison Department's ethnic monitoring of the prison population uses the same categories as the LFS and is based on self-assessment by prisoners.

11 The Hospital In-Patient Enquiry, completed for all admitted patients, has requested information on the place of birth of patients since 1969, as has the Mental Health Enquiry since 1970.

These examples show that the ethnic or racial categories used in a census or survey are not fixed or given (if they were, the same categories would be used all the time) but have to be decided upon and have to be constructed. It is important to note that 'race' and ethnicity are generally conceptualized as interchangeable categories in the various areas of data collection. Indeed the category 'white' is a good example of this in that it is regarded as a fixed and unchanging category whereas 'black' is generally broken down into different 'ethnic' groups. The only truly objective category in this respect is that of legal nationality. The fact that someone is British, Pakistani, Canadian or Jamaican is a fact of law and verifiable according to established procedures. Even these categories are not fixed. A person can, in certain circumstances, change her or his nationality. So too new nationalities can come into existence, as they have done notably since the collapse of the Soviet Union and the division of Czechoslovakia and Yugoslavia. It is, of course, something quite different from other categories, racial or ethnic, and may not be considered the most important. A person may not wish to be identified in terms of where they were born or what kind of passport they hold but in some other way. A woman who is a Pakistani national living in Scotland, for example, may think of herself as black, or Asian or Muslim or Scottish. A British-born black girl may think of herself as West Indian or black or British or Afro-Caribbean. Probably such people would think of themselves as each of these things at different times and in different situations, just as I think of myself at different times to be white, male, an inhabitant of London, Scots, Glaswegian, British, European and so on, depending on the circumstances in which I find myself.

The problems of devising suitable categories, other than legal nationalities, have been discussed by several academics in relation to the question of whether information on ethnicity should be sought in the census. Dr Roger Ballard, for example, has said that it is 'virtually impossible to pose askable or answerable questions about "race"' (Home Affairs Committee, 1983), while another writer has stated that the 'the search for "races" ... has been shown to be a fool's errand' (White, 1979). Frequently, the categories used in a survey are a mixture of racial, national and ethnic classifications. To take the categories for the 1991 census as an example, white and black are pseudo-racial categories, referring, rather inaccurately, to perceived skin colours, but Indian, Pakistani and Bangladeshi are all legal nationalities although they may also be regarded as ethnic categories. Chinese is a nationality, but also an ethnic description as well as a linguistic group, and so on.

A further complication arises in that people do not have fixed views of themselves. It is not just that people think of themselves in different ways in different circumstances, but also that their self-perception or self-description changes. In the United States, for instance, only 65 per cent of the population categorized themselves by the same racial or ethnic description *from a fixed inventory* as they had done the previous year, showing that racial or ethnic identities are not simple or straightforward (Leech, 1989).

Rather than ask about ethnic origins, critics have suggested, a question should be asked directly about colour, although here again problems arise. The description 'black' might be used by some people of Asian origin but not by others, and so on. Similarly, 'white' can include people who are quite different not only in actual skin colour but also in national or ethnic origins, from fair-skinned north Canadians to darker-skinned Slavs or people from Mediterranean countries. And when skin colour is used, how are people such as Chinese, Japanese, native Americans and Arabs to be designated? (We might note here, too, that the catch-all concept 'non-white' is equally unsatisfactory since it asserts the superiority of the category 'white' in that it defines its subjects in terms of this, of what they are not.)

There is no system of categorization which will please everyone. What is important to remember is that involved in any system of categorization are choices and decisions.

The various censuses and surveys described above also illustrate matters which, by their absence, are not considered sufficiently important to be subject to some kind of racialized data collection. Thus there is no racialized data collection on the numbers of people claiming welfare benefits, using some form of personal social services, or seeking health care (other than as in-patients). These gaps are important because they mean that basic information about important questions is lacking. For example, are particular ethnic groups less or more likely than others to make use of personal social services? It is difficult, therefore, for academic researchers and others to make any meaningful comparisons between the experiences of people of different ethnic origins and point to any desirable policy changes.

Even where something is regarded as worthy of being recorded, it may be defined in a way that is problematic. Many people, for instance, argued for a long time that there should be central monitoring by the Home Office of the extent and nature of racial attacks. This is now being done, but the definition used is not that of attacks on people because of their colour or ethnic origin – that is, attacks motivated at least in part by racism – but of 'racial incidents' in which victim and assailant are of different ethnic groups and where a racial motive is either suggested by the victim or inferred by a police officer. This means that attacks on white people where the offender is alleged to be black can be and are recorded as 'racial incidents' even if these are, in reality, purely criminal acts and there is no evidence of racial hostility but simply an allegation by the victim or the officer to whom it is reported. The specifically *racist* nature of many white attacks on black people is therefore denied and racial violence is redefined as just another aspect of inter-racial crime.

A final problem to be considered here is the isolation of 'race' or ethnicity from other factors. Obviously, any human being or group of human beings is not defined by any one characteristic. We are not just, for example, men or women. We are men and women who are also of particular age groups, in different parts of the country, with different educational backgrounds, of different ethnic origins, different family responsibilities, with different physical abilities and much more. Any of these may be important in itself in explaining our position in the job market, for example, or educational achievement, but a more accurate explanation is likely to flow from a cross-fertilization of factors. In many cases where data have been racialized, gender difference is also monitored and account may also be taken of age. So, for instance, if we look at the statistics produced by the Prison Department of the Home Office we can see that, while Afro-Caribbean men are disproportionately represented in the prison population, Afro-Caribbean women are even more disproportionately represented. Here gender and ethnicity appear to interact, suggesting that for an explanation of the numbers of black female prisoners we must look not just at 'race' or ethnicity but also at gender.

There is, however, a major gap in every case of racialized data and that is the absence of any consideration of social class, even though this has been shown in many cases to be a prime explanatory factor for comparative success (or failure). One example of this is that the high achievement of some school pupils of Asian origin compared with their counterparts can be explained to some extent by their social class position. To put it crudely, children from middle-class families on the whole do better in school than those from working-class families. Similarly, the British Crime Survey found relatively high criminal victimization rates among Afro-Caribbeans and Asians but said that this could be explained by the related factors of geographical location and social class. In other words, Asians and Afro-Caribbeans were more likely to be victims of certain crimes than whites not because of their colour but because they were more likely than whites to live in areas of high crime. It is important to bear this in mind, as an emphasis on the single factor of 'race' or ethnicity can lead to social class – or indeed other factors – being ignored and wrong conclusions being drawn.

The collection of racial or ethnic statistics is not then a neutral exercise involving the simple collection of objective facts. Rather, from the start, it involves decisions of a political nature about what to record, in what terms and in what way, stemming from a particular ideological position. To illustrate this more concretely, let us look at two examples of racial statistics: the Government statistics on the control of immigration and the more specific example of the crime statistics released by the Metropolitan Police in 1982.

Immigration statistics

Until the mid-1980s, immigration statistics were one of the three main categories of racialized statistics collected in the UK on a systematic basis. Indeed, immigration statistics have been collected for longer than any other category of ethnic data, since the first restrictions were placed on the immigration of Commonwealth citizens in the Commonwealth Immigrants Act 1962. These statistics, collated by the Home Office, are published annually and provide extensive information on, for example, the numbers and countries of origin of people admitted to the United Kingdom (and the purpose of their visits); those refused admission; people accepted for settlement; and applications for entry clearance from the Indian subcontinent. They also provide some information on the number of people deported each year or removed as alleged illegal entrants.

Why is this information considered sufficiently important that it should be collated and published each year? It may be answered that governments need to know how many people enter and leave the country each year so that they can plan for significant increases or decreases in population and allocate resources to assist the settlement of new immigrants. This is a plausible answer, but it does not hold in this case. The immigration statistics do not record those who left the country. (This is done on a completely different basis, the International Passenger Survey, which uses a different system of definition and categories which makes it impossible to compare its findings with the immigration figures.) Therefore, the purpose of these figures is not to determine loss or gain of population through migration, nor is it to assist the allocation of resources for new immigrants since the figures are concerned only with where people have come from, not where they may be settling. They are thus useless in ascertaining areas of the country where particular social or educational needs might arise.

The answer to why the immigration statistics are collected would appear to have more to do with the commitment of successive governments since the 1960s to policies of strict controls on immigration of black and Asian people. The annual immigration statistics are evidence of how such policies are working. Thus Government statements will frequently point to the decline in the numbers accepted for settlement as proof of the Government's fulfilment of its manifesto commitments or to a rise in deportations as evidence both of more effective 'after-entry' controls and of the greater extent of law-breaking. In other words, the statistics seem to be there to appease anti-immigration sentiments. This is not to say that the immigration statistics do not have other uses. Critics of British immigration policies can and do use them to argue that Government policies are becoming increasingly harsh, that they have a disproportionate impact on black people, and so on. But their main purpose, it would appear, is to support the Government of the day in indicating the effectiveness of government policy.

Crime statistics

My second example is of a particular set of data produced in a particular year, rather than, as with the immigration statistics, continuously over a period of years. In March 1982, the Metropolitan Police issued its statistics on crimes recorded in London in 1981. The figures highlighted two things. First, an 8 per cent rise in serious crime over the previous year and, second, an increase in 'mugging' and the alleged disproportionate involvement of black people in this crime. The figures stated that the 'appearance of the assailant' had been described as white by just under 5,000 victims, but as 'coloured' by more than 10,000. This was the first occasion on which police statistics had been racialized in this way.

What was the point of collating and then publishing such information? If, as was claimed at the time, this was simply a disinterested exercise on the part of the police, would we not have expected the statistics to have presented details of the 'racial' or ethnic origins of alleged victims and offenders in relation to all categories of crime? As it was, the category of 'robbery and other violent theft' was the only category to be racialized in this way. We might also have expected the police statistics to have highlighted other interesting features, for example that the number of homicides had fallen by 36 per cent on the previous year, that assaults had scarcely increased, and that the clear-up rate for reported serious crime had fallen to only 17 per cent. When asked why the police had highlighted this category of offence and done so in this way, Metropolitan Police Deputy Assistant Commissioner Gilbert Kelland said that it had been done in response to 'public opinion and pressure'. When asked how such public opinion was ascertained, he said it was done through the media. A closer analysis reveals, however, that the media, especially sections of the popular press, were not so much reflecting public opinion as constructing it, and that this was done partly through the use of statistics leaked by the police. This shows that in the construction of policy agendas, statistics are a powerful tool indeed, precisely because people regard them as indisputable 'facts'. Against the police claim that they were only responding to public opinion, it has been argued that in choosing to link 'race' and crime in the way they did and then highlighting this, the Metropolitan Police were seeking to establish a firm correlation between black people, especially young black males, and street crime. If this were so, one interpretation could be that the police were seeking public support for the introduction of a tactical offensive in areas of significant black settlement. In particular, it has been argued that the police hoped to deflect the criticisms of their operations and methods made by Lord Scarman in his report, published only a few months before, on the Brixton disorders. In other words, it is arguable that the police had *chosen* to racialize these statistics and had done so for their own political reasons. (For more detailed accounts of this episode see Bentley, 1982, and Sim, 1982.)

Arguments for collecting data on ethnicity

Why should ethnic data be collected at all? What purposes do they serve? Broadly speaking we can identify three main reasons used to justify collecting data on an ethnic basis; first, 'fact-finding'; second, to inform government policy; and third, to bring about social reform. These can, of course, overlap, but the distinctions may be useful for descriptive purposes.

Fact-finding

There is a tendency in all bureaucratic societies to collect a great deal of information about its citizens. Such data may not be collected with any apparent aim in mind and once collated may not be used for any obvious purpose. In relation to data on ethnicity this would be true in Britain, for example, of the data from the 1971 and 1981 censuses and the Hospital Enquiries mentioned earlier. Here, information was collected on the country of birth of respondents (and in the case of the hospital surveys continues to be collected) without any obvious purpose. It was also true of the data on 'immigrant' school pupils which was collected between 1966 and 1973 when the then Education Minister, Margaret Thatcher, admitted that no use was made of the data. (This is dealt with in more detail in Section 9.) Such information *may*, of course, be used at some point in the future, either by the government department that collects it or by someone else, but this is almost incidental. The main reason for its collection in the first place would appear to be a tendency in bureaucratic societies to gather information for its own sake, but this nevertheless shows the salience of 'race' as an administrative concern, particularly since the racialization of public debate since the 1960s.

Informing government policy

It is more common, of course, for information to be gathered for the reason that it will somehow assist in the exercise of some government policies. The most important example of this in Britain with regard to racialized data lies in the provision of funding under Section 11 of the Local Government Act 1966. Section 11 allows local authorities with substantial minority ethnic group populations to apply to central government for funding to meet the 'special needs' of such populations. If such applications are successful, central government contributes 75 per cent of the funding. (Originally, local authorities qualified if more than 2 per cent of the school population had parents who were born in the New Commonwealth and Pakistan (NCWP) and who had arrived in the UK in the previous ten years. In 1982, the 2 per cent and ten year criteria were abolished.) Before the 1991 census, data from the 1981 census was used to estimate the numbers and proportion of minority ethnic group populations in particular local authority areas, although this is less important than hitherto as the Home Office, which is responsible for the administration of Section 11 funding, has expanded discretion to fund even authorities with relatively small minority populations. Another example of this kind of data collection relates to expenditure under the Urban Programme. The size of local minority ethnic group populations is one of the criteria used by central government in determining the level of support grant payable under this scheme to local authorities and in allocating expenditure for alleviating urban poverty and promoting regeneration.

Although racialized data is used for these purposes, it should be borne in mind that expenditure under these headings is comparatively limited. In addition, minority ethnic groups do not necessarily benefit directly from it. Even Section 11 funding, which is supposed to be aimed specifically at meeting the needs of minority populations, has been widely abused by some local authorities who have used such funding for general spending. One result of this was an extensive review by the Home Office of the whole Section 11 spending.

Social reform

The third argument put forward for the collection of racialized data is that it is necessary for the purposes of social reform; that is, that such information is necessary to identify areas where minority ethnic groups may be subject to discrimination and to assist in the implementation of policies aimed at ensuring equal opportunities. Organizations such as the Commission for Racial Equality (CRE) and the Runnymede Trust have argued that without such data it is impossible to identify and locate discriminatory practices, while equal opportunities will remain no more than paper policies and good intentions. In the 1970s, the Runnymede Trust, for example, used census and other data in two influential but very different studies which pointed to systematic discrimination against black people. In 1975, the Trust used information from the 1971 census on the size of the 'coloured' population along with information from the Greater London Council's (GLC) housing department to show that the department's allocation procedures were discriminating against black families (Runnymede Trust, 1975). This led to an investigation by the GLC itself and a revision of allocation procedures (Parker and Dugmore, 1976). A few years later, the Runnymede Trust again used census data along with statistics gathered by the Metropolitan Police to show that young black men were disproportionately at risk of being arrested and prosecuted under the Vagrancy Act 1824. Often known as the 'sus' law, this Act made it an offence to be a 'suspected person' loitering with the intent to commit a criminal offence, a charge which could be substantiated on the evidence of two police officers and which, many contested, was used by the police in some areas as a means of controlling the movements of young black people. This study played some part in the successful campaign to have the law repealed (Demuth, 1978).

Not only can racialized data be useful in proving discrimination, but the collection of ethnic statistics is effectively required by law. Since 1968, it has been unlawful to discriminate against someone on 'racial' grounds in employment and housing. Thus, in either field, it is unlawful to give a white person (or a black person for that matter) preferential treatment because of the colour of their skin. This is what the law calls direct discrimination. But since 1976, the law has also prohibited indirect discrimination; that is, practices or procedures that may not be discriminatory themselves but which have the effect of discriminating against a particular racial or ethnic group. An example would be a requirement that workers be of a minimum height, which could not be met by, say, most Bengalis or Chinese, and which could not be justified by the nature of the job in question. The concept of indirect discrimination would be quite unworkable in the absence of ethnically-based data about local and national populations, as well as particular workforces. By extension, such data are also essential to the work of the CRE, which is charged with implementing the Race Relations Act 1976 and which carries out formal investigations of institutions and organizations to identify possible discriminatory procedures. In the absence of accurate data about the ethnic composition of a local workforce, for example, it would be impossible for the Commission to argue that a workplace where only 2 per cent of staff were black was in fact discriminating in some way. (This, of course, is only part of the story as the Commission has to identify mechanisms that might be excluding workers from a particular group, but it is an essential part.) So, too, the Commission has argued that ethnic monitoring is essential if local authorities are to discharge their responsibilities under Section 71 of the Race Relations Act 1976 to eliminate unlawful racial discrimination and to promote equality of opportunity in all their functions.

Such arguments for collecting racialized data were given considerable impetus in the early 1980s when they were supported by Lord Scarman in his report on the Brixton disorders of 1981 (Scarman, 1981) and, the same year, by the Parliamentary Home Affairs Committee in its wider-ranging enquiry and report on 'racial disadvantage' (Home Affairs Committee, 1981). Both were concerned at the continuing extent of what they saw as racial 'disadvantage', which, as the 1980 and 1981 urban disorders showed, and as Lord Scarman had accepted, had been at least contributory factors to the most serious public disorder seen in Britain for a long time. The Home Affairs Committee strongly supported the idea of an ethnic question in the census, complaining that:

> it is impossible to discover the simple factual truth about some of the most significant and apparently straightforward matters ... As matters stand we know neither the total ethnic minority population nor their true rate of unemployment ... Inspired guesswork and extrapolation from old and often unreliable national figures is reflected on a local scale.

(Home Affairs Committee, 1981, pp. viii–ix)

The Committee also called for ethnic monitoring by local authorities, employers and others and recommended the production of national figures on the performance of what it called 'West Indian' children.

Arguments against collecting racialized data

It should not be assumed that everyone favours the idea of racialized data collection. Some such opposition comes from people who argue that there is no real problem of racial discrimination and that collecting such statistics is in itself discriminatory. Some employers, for instance, have strongly opposed ethnic monitoring in the workplace, maintaining that this is an unwarranted intrusion into the freedom of employers to employ whom they like. Such voices are, at least publicly, relatively rare as more and more people have come to accept that there is discrimination in society and that this should be tackled. But even among those who share an opposition to racial discrimination there has been disagreement about the value of collecting racialized data. This debate has in the past often focused on the issue of the ethnic question in the census. (Leech, 1989; Booth, 1988).

The political context

First, critics of racialized data collection have questioned the political context in which such information is gathered and the uses to which it might be put. Many people have drawn attention to the context of racially discriminatory immigration controls, the successive withdrawal of rights from Commonwealth citizens (including an automatic right to British citizenship and to be joined in Britain by their families), and the fears of many black people about their status in the UK. Thus Professor Robert

Moore, a sociologist who has done a great deal to reveal the existence and operation of racism in Britain, has argued that there has never been a real programme aimed at 'racial' equality in Britain which might support the inclusion in the census of an ethnic question. He has said that while, as a social scientist, he has found the absence of certain data from the census a nuisance, 'given the record of governments since 1961, I would nonetheless advise the black population not to collaborate in the provision of such data in the present circumstances' (Home Affairs Committee, 1983, p. 139). Similarly, another prominent academic in 'race' relations, Professor John Rex, has questioned the value of racialized data:

> The benefit which immigrants have had from statistics has been confined largely to help on technical matters, like language instruction. Otherwise, the presence of immigrants has been used as an index of pathology, justifying increased payments to particular local authorities who have all too often used such increased payments for the benefit of their native British citizens.

> (*The Times*, 28 January 1980)

Such criticisms reflect the attitude of many black people who have pointed to the extensive research, including statistical analyses, which has been carried out in a number of areas but which has resulted in little by way of action to improve the material lives of the people researched and counted. It is also argued that racialized statistics have invariably been used, not in the interests of black people but, as with immigration figures and police statistics on crime, against them.

Abuse of statistics

Second, some critics have claimed that information gathered for one purpose, the census for example, might be used for other, less acceptable purposes. In the 1970s, for example, many people referred to fears of repatriation or expulsion as one of their reasons for opposition to an ethnic question which was to be included in the 1981 census, or to other forms of ethnic data collection. They pointed to the fact that one firm supporter of an ethnic question in the census was the fascist National Front, which advocated a policy of expulsion of all 'non-white' people from Britain. (The Front's support for an ethnic question illustrates how different people can support the collection of data for very different reasons.) It should be remembered that this was a time not only when electoral and other support for the National Front was considerable, but when the Conservative Party was developing a new tougher immigration policy, aimed in part at winning back supporters lost to the far right. There were, in other words, good grounds for the fears of black people about their security in Britain. It is worth saying, though, that a programme of forced expulsion would not require census data if it were based on the obvious physical attribute of skin colour, although census data would certainly facilitate the planning of such a programme. In this respect, it is also worth noting that discrimination against people on racial grounds is easy without statistics, as the CRE found when it investigated the allocation of housing by the London Borough of Hackney. At the time there was no ethnic record-keeping but the ethnic origin of tenants was relatively easy to ascertain, for instance, through their names or other references (CRE, 1984a).

Problems of definition

Finally, critics have pointed to the difficulties in formulating suitable questions in collecting racialized data, a point looked at earlier in the discussion of how racialized data are constructed. Some have argued that it is impossible to devise a meaningful set of categories and have pointed to the problems arising from existing definitions – that people may define themselves in different ways at different times and in different contexts, and that some categories may mean different things to different people. For example, Chinese is a language as well as legal nationality but it may also be regarded as an ethnic category.

Although there is now widespread support for various forms of ethnic monitoring and an ethnic question in the census, it should be remembered that critics of such data collection have had some impact. The ethnic question that was to be included in the 1981 census, for example, was dropped after just over half the households in a 1979 test census in the London Borough of Haringey returned their forms. Similarly, in 1980 the Rampton Committee on the education of minority ethnic group children was forced to abandon plans for research into the reasons for under-achievement among Afro-Caribbean children when it became clear that there was considerable disquiet amongst black and Asian parents about such research, which they felt would stigmatize them. In 1983, opposition from community organizations prevented research into patterns of crime in the London boroughs of Hackney and Camden. In both cases it was argued that the research was wrongly focused and misguided and would result in the blaming of black people rather than produce any gains for them. Many of the issues discussed above have arisen in relation to the collection of ethnically-based statistics in the field of education, which provides a useful case study of how these matters are experienced in practice.

Education and racialized statistics: a case study

In 1966 the Department of Education and Science (DES) began to collect statistics on the numbers of 'immigrant' pupils in schools in England and Wales. An immigrant, for the purposes of these statistics, was someone who had been born outside the UK or who was born in the UK to parents who had been in the UK less than ten years. (As was later to be noted by the Swann Committee in its report *Education for All* (DES, 1985), this definition implied that after ten years an immigrant family would cease to suffer from any educational difficulties that could be attributed to immigration and racial difference.)

There were two main reasons for the collection of these statistics. The first was to assist central and local government in making provision for the teaching of English to those whose first language was not English. As a 1965 DES circular put it: 'From the beginning the major educational task is the teaching of English' (DES, 1965). The same year that the collection of 'immigrant' statistics began, provision was made, through Section 11 of the Local Government Act 1966, for local authorities with substantial minority ethnic populations to apply to central government for funding to help with special provision.

The second reason for the collection of the statistics had to do with the policies of dispersal of black children advocated by central government and pursued by some local education authorities. In 1963, the then Minister of Education, Edward Boyle, said in Parliament that, where possible, it was 'desirable on education grounds' that no one school should have more than about 30 per cent of immigrants (*Hansard*, 1963). In promulgating what became known as 'Boyle's law', the Minister was responding to a row in Southall, West London, where a group of white parents had protested against the large number of black children at a particular school. This was now, Boyle said, 'irretrievably an immigrant school'. The important thing, he said, 'is to prevent this happening elsewhere'. The policy of dispersal was confirmed by DES Circular 7/65 (ibid.) which said that the chances of assimilating 'immigrant children' became more remote as their numbers increased and that 'serious strains' arose when the proportion went over one-third in a school or class. Catchment areas of schools should be drawn to avoid such concentrations and, where this was impracticable, physical dispersal should be arranged. It is not hard to see that this policy confirmed for many white parents what they already believed – that black pupils *per se* were a problem in schools and a barrier to progress in education. The collection of ethnic data was therefore contributing to the definition of black people as a problem. (The question of dispersal and all-black or all-white schools has, of course, been a recurring concern of minority ethnic communities as some white parents have complained about sending their children to schools where the majority of pupils are of Asian or Afro-Caribbean origin and where parental choice of schools has raised the prospect of this development – described by some as educational apartheid – continuing.)

Within a few years, however, the definition used in the statistics was criticized as unsatisfactory by the House of Commons Select Committee on Race Relations and Immigration. The Select Committee said that the statistics gave only an 'indirect indication' of colour and recommended the keeping of statistics on the numbers of 'coloured people' (Select Committee on Race Relations and Immigration, 1969). As a result of the Committee's report, the DES undertook to revise its definition. In 1973, however, the Select Committee found that the definition was still in use and was contributing to a considerable underestimate of the numbers of black children in schools. Furthermore, the then Secretary of State for Education and Science, Margaret Thatcher, told the Committee: 'My department makes no use of them whatsoever except to publish them. They do not form the basis of any grant from my department.' The Committee concluded that the statistics had served 'little or no practical purpose' and recommended that their collection should cease forthwith (Select Committee on Race Relations and Immigration, 1973). The collection of the information was stopped the same year.

After 1973 there was no systematic collection of data on the numbers of black, that is Asian or Afro-Caribbean, children in schools or their progress and experience in school, including performance in examinations. No data were collected on the numbers of black teachers or their promotion (or lack of it). Nor were any data collected on what happened to black pupils after they left school. Did they go on to university or polytechnic, or to colleges to improve their school qualifications? Were they more likely to follow certain paths than others, more or less likely to take certain routes than their white counterparts? Without data it was impossible to answer these questions.

Calls for the reintroduction of ethnic monitoring in schools by bodies such as the Select Committee on Race Relations and Immigration (see 1977a), the CRE, the Inner London Education Authority (ILEA) and the National Union of Teachers, went unheeded. In addition, the lack of data was a problem which faced the Committee of Inquiry into the Education of Children from Ethnic Minority Groups set up in 1979 as a result of increasing disquiet about the relative under-achievement of many black pupils in schools. This was chaired initially by Anthony Rampton, and then by Lord Swann. In its interim report, *West Indian Children in Our Schools*, the Rampton Committee said that, while some schools collected ethnic data, there was little uniformity in the classifications used and it was difficult to make any meaningful comparisons between schools, let alone gain an overall picture. The Committee argued that ethnically-based statistics could be of use to central government in determining national education policy; to local education authorities in quantifying and locating particular needs; to schools so that they could take full account of the cultural and linguistic backgrounds of pupils and see whether any groups were under-achieving or were disproportionately represented in any subject or class; and to parents so they could assess their children's performances in relation to their peers. The Committee recommended the ethnic monitoring of pupils, trainee and qualified teachers. It also recommended ethnic monitoring in higher education, an area in which information on the ethnic composition of student populations (apart from overseas students) and staff and their progress was even more sparse than in schools (Rampton, 1981; DES, 1985).

It should also be noted that the Rampton Committee had originally wanted to carry out a study of the performance in schools of children of 'West Indian' origin, a study which would inevitably have involved the collation and analysis of a great deal of statistical data. This study was dropped after protests from black parents who objected that it could only succeed in shifting the blame for any apparent 'under-achievement' on to themselves and their children and away from the schools and the educational system – away, in other words, from the racism they believed was responsible for any failure by their children.

Following the Rampton and Swann Committees' recommendations, a working group was convened by the DES to consider how this might be put into practice and in 1989 the Government announced that, with effect from September 1990, all local education authority and grant-maintained schools would be required to collect ethnically-based data on their pupils (DES, 1989; Scottish Education Department, 1989). The Government accepted the working party's conclusion that the collection of such statistics would be of great benefit to schools and education authorities in making appropriate provision and in monitoring progress. The working party recommended, and the Government accepted, that information should be provided on a voluntary basis on three subjects: ethnic origin, categorized as white, black-African, black-Caribbean, black-other, Indian, Pakistani, Bangladeshi, Chinese and other; language, involving thirteen categories; and religious affiliations. It was proposed that this information be collected during interviews with parents about the admission of children. The circular anticipated that a full profile of the school population would take four years. After this, the Department of Education and Science said, it would also require returns to be made on the destinations of pupils leaving school and on examination results at ages 16 and 18.

In the same year, the DES announced that from January 1990, education authorities in England and Wales would be required to submit returns on the ethnic origins of school teachers. These use the same categories as used in relation to school pupils and also record details of seniority, pay and specialization. The collection of such data, Kenneth Baker, then Education Secretary, said, was essential to measure the success of efforts to increase the numbers of minority ethnic group school teachers. (There is no comparable monitoring in Scotland.) In the case of further and higher education, systematic ethnic monitoring was to start from November 1990 (the academic year 1990–1) for universities and polytechnics. Again this applies only to England and Wales and not the Scottish universities.

Such monitoring will reveal a great deal, not just about bare numbers but also about the progress of black children through school, the examinations for which they are entered, the results achieved and their destinations after leaving school. It will also show how these compare with their white counterparts. In identifying any significant differences such monitoring may also establish ways in which the treatment of black pupils in schools may discriminate against them. In the case of teachers, the monitoring will highlight not just the numbers of black teachers but their grades and positions and, again, will help to highlight possibly discriminatory mechanisms. This brief case study illustrates the point made earlier: that the collection of data involves decisions about what is being looked for, about the purpose of statistics. The experience of the collection of data on 'immigrant pupils' between 1966 and 1973, in particular, showed how the fact of collecting information could contribute to the definition of black people as a problem and how it could be used to their disadvantage in that it was the number of black pupils in individual schools that was officially regarded as the source of the social problem. It also shows that data collected for one purpose cannot always be easily transferred to another purpose. In this case, the problems related to the presence of Asian and Afro-Caribbean children in schools were initially seen as being related to the problems of immigration. But as an increasing proportion of such pupils were British-born, the problem could no longer be seen as one of immigration but one of colour. The basis of the monitoring system remained unchanged and became less and less accurate and increasingly useless as the years passed.

The reintroduction of ethnic monitoring in schools, of staff as well as pupils, coupled with the extension of monitoring into the areas of further education, teacher training, and universities and polytechnics, stemmed from a growing dissatisfaction among minority ethnic group communities. This was reflected in the reports of the influential Government-created committee into the education of minority ethnic group children (Rampton, 1981; DES, 1985). It stemmed also from a recognition among politicians and other policy-makers, particularly after the 1981 urban disorders, that continuing racial discrimination and inequality and the resultant exclusion from society of a section of the population, could have seriously disruptive effects.

Conclusion: the limits of statistics

Statistical information can play an important role in identifying patterns of inequality and the processes that produce them. The data which will emerge, for example, from ethnic monitoring in education ought to point to any ways in which black people, whether pupils or teachers, are treated differently from their white counterparts. It is important to keep in mind, however, that statistics do not just reflect facts which are 'out there' waiting to be discovered, but are the result of many decisions and, of course, can be open to very different interpretations.

While acknowledging the importance that statistical information can have, it is important to keep in mind the limitations of statistics. Statistics can, and perhaps have a tendency to, reify – that is, to turn human subjects and human problems into things. It is all too easy sometimes to forget that behind many statistics lies a human being or beings. This is particularly so, it seems to me, of statistics in the field of 'race', where what gets lost all too often is any sense of the human behind the number.

A second problem is that once one starts talking or thinking in statistical terms it can become difficult to stop, and so one can fall into the trap of thinking that because something is not statistically significant, or at least cannot be shown to be such, then there is no problem. Yet, the fact that there may not be a statistically significant difference between, say, a particular group of whites and a corresponding group of Asians does not mean that there is no problem, just that the problem does not lend itself readily to this kind of measurement.

A third point to remember is that statistical information is only one form of information among many. It is not necessarily superior to other forms of evidence and may, indeed, be inappropriate. The problems of human beings cannot always be quantified and, even when they can, they may not be best described in this way. The story I cited earlier about the journalist seeking information about racial attacks is a case in point. There is a sense in which attempting to quantify the problem of racial violence misses the meaning of such violence for those who are affected, whether they are actually victims or simply fear that they may be attacked. The case study or history or open interview may well yield more information and prove more illuminating of a particular problem than bare numerical data. This is why, for example, many studies of the problem of racial violence have sought to combine the existing statistical information with descriptive accounts of people's actual experience (see, for instance, Gordon, 1990). So, too, to give an example in another field, we might contrast the many papers and articles written on the number of black people in mental hospitals with a report on the *actual experiences* of black people in the mental health system (Westwood *et al.*, 1989). The former yield data which are, to be sure, important and necessary, but the latter goes behind the statistics to illuminate the human experience and thus adds to our understanding of the processes behind the patterns.

Statistics do not in themselves prove anything. They always require interpretation and, of course, they are always open to competing interpretations. For instance, when research has shown that young black men were considerably more likely to be arrested or stopped and searched by the police than their white counterparts there have been two immediate interpretations. For their part, the police would say that this simply showed that young black men were more likely to be committing offences or acting suspiciously. Against this, anti-racists and others would say that the statistics showed that the police were behaving in a racially prejudiced and discriminatory way. The statistics, in other words, do not settle the argument. They are the beginning of the debate, not the end.

A final point I want to make about the limitations of statistics is to offer a cautionary tale about how things can go wrong. At least since the 1970s, there has been serious concern among Britain's minority ethnic groups about the nature and extent of racially-motivated violence. Even though a Home Office report in 1981 recognized the existence of the problem, ten years later there was still no national collation of incidents reported to police forces. Individual police forces had, however, begun to collate their own statistics. Many saw this as an important step forward in combating racially-motivated violence. However, the definition used by the police (and approved by the Home Office and others) did not refer to racially-motivated attacks as usually understood – that is, as attacks by whites on members of minority groups motivated, at least in part, by racism. The police definition included the possibility of racist attacks on whites and required to be categorized as racial any incident alleged to be racial or considered by the police to be so. Although this definition was presented as recognizing the importance of the victim's perception of the incident, its effect was to allow for the recording of incidents involving black assailants and white victims as 'racial incidents' in just the same way as racist attacks. (The Metropolitan Police recorded 439 such incidents in 1990.)

Now, black people may attack white people for all sorts of reasons but racism is not among them, at least not if we understand racism as hostility towards people because of their skin colour or their ethnic origins in the context of a system of unequal power relations. While black people and white people may have equal power as individuals, black people in Britain lack the social, economic and political power of the white majority who are not considerably more numerous but have the power to define and determine the situation of others. So what has been lost in the police collation of statistics is the specificity of racist attacks, which become just another aspect of 'inter-racial incident' of the kind to be expected in any multi-racial society. The racism that informs and underlies such attacks is thereby denied. What therefore seemed to some as a step forward in the effort against racist violence has, in effect, been a diversion.

Central to any discussion of statistics is, of course, the uses to which they are put. There is little value in collecting information simply for its own sake (undoubtedly a tendency in bureaucratic societies) and this is particularly true when the subjects of such data collection are human beings. As we have seen, many people have objected to being the object of study, research or simply counting when they have been unable to see any benefits that might accrue. They have argued that a considerable amount of research has been conducted and a vast amount of data accumulated in the past 30 years, pointing to the existence of discrimination on a wide scale and to the continuing subordinate position of black people socially and economically, and that this has given rise to very little by way of action to alter the situation in any significant way.

The collection of ethnic data is not an end in itself but a means to an end: that of implementing equal opportunities and racial equality. The current support for ethnic monitoring in education, as well as in other areas, indicates a willingness to take at least the first steps in this process by identifying the ways in which minority ethnic groups may be discriminated against. But it must be remembered that these are first steps only. They will have to be followed, where the data show it to be necessary, by changes in policy and practice.

PART 2

MINORITY ETHNIC GROUPS IN THE UK: A PROFILE

Richard Skellington, with Paulette Morris

1 DEMOGRAPHIC TRENDS AMONGST GREAT BRITAIN'S MINORITY ETHNIC GROUP POPULATION

1.1 Introduction: a note of caution

In compiling this dossier, we hesitated before deciding to include a section on demographic trends. We did not want to reinforce stereotypes or exacerbate a sense of 'otherness' between ethnic groups. We did feel, however, that some population details about minority ethnic groups in Britain would leave readers better informed, particularly in relation to differences between the groups themselves, and to the importance of age differences between population cohorts.

Details about the British minority ethnic group population are best derived from Labour Force Surveys (LFS). In the summer of 1990, LFS figures summarizing the surveys of 1986, 1987 and 1988 were published. The three-year average represents a far more reliable estimate of the British minority ethnic group population than annual snapshots.[1]

1.2 Population size

According to the LFS, almost one person in twenty living in Great Britain belongs to a minority ethnic group. For the period 1986–8, the LFS estimated the minority ethnic group population to be 2.58 million, or 4.7 per cent of the total British population. This represented an increase of half a million on their estimate for 1981, and more than double the minority ethnic group population of 1971. Of these 2.58 million, about 1 million are Muslims.

The first edition of this book was written before minority ethnic group data from the 1991 census was known. (See Section 1.6 for information from this census.) *Figure 1.1* shows the age and place of birth of the black and Asian population of England and Wales enumerated by the census of 1981.

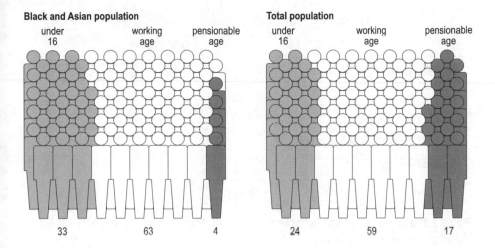

Black and Asian population

under 16	working age	pensionable age
33	63	4

Total population

under 16	working age	pensionable age
24	59	17

Place of birth of black and Asian population, England & Wales 1981

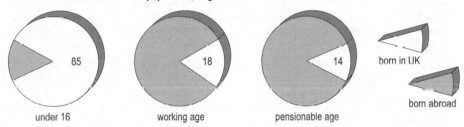

under 16	working age	pensionable age
85	18	14

born in UK

born abroad

Figure 1.1: age and place of birth of population, England and Wales, 1901
(Adapted from Fothergill and Vincent, 1985, p. 14)

A comparison of LFS estimates with census findings shows that the minority ethnic group population has grown from 0.4 per cent in 1951, 1 per cent in 1961, 2.3 per cent in 1971, to 3.9 per cent in 1981 (see *Figure 1.2*). During the 1980s the total British minority ethnic group population increased at around 80–90,000 per year (OPCS, 1986; Shaw, 1988). *Figure 1.3* provides a breakdown of the percentage of the total British population for different minority ethnic groups. *Figure 1.4* shows the percentage of the total minority ethnic group population belonging to each group. Over a half (51 per cent) of the total minority ethnic group population were of Indian, Pakistani or Bangladeshi origin, almost a fifth were of West Indian origin, while one in nine were of mixed ethnic origin. Between 1981 and 1988 the Pakistani population was estimated to have grown by a half and the Bangladeshi population to have doubled, whereas the West Indian population declined by 33,000 during the same period. *Table 1.1* analyses these trends. LFS findings show that West Indian families have fewer and Pakistani and Bangladeshi families more dependent children than the average minority ethnic group family (see Section 1.3).

45

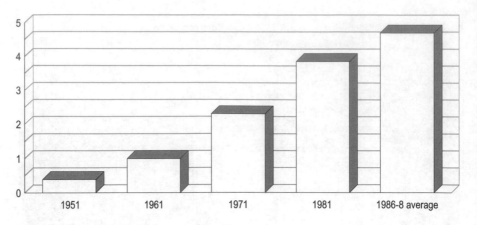

Figure 1.2: percentage growth in the British minority ethnic group populations, 1951–88
(Adapted from OPCS and LFS)

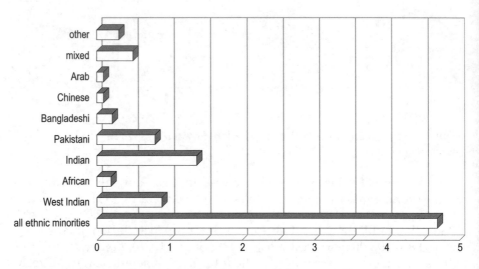

Figure 1.3: percentage of the total British population of each minority ethnic group
(Adapted from LFS, average 1986–8)

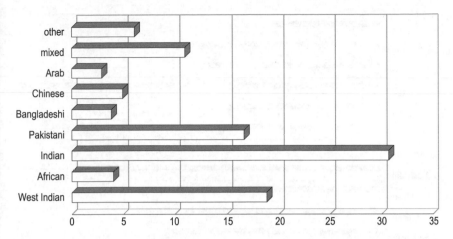

Figure 1.4: minority ethnic group populations as a percentage of the total minority ethnic group population of Great Britain
(Adapted from LFS, average 1986–8)

Table 1.1: estimated growth and decline in minority ethnic group populations

	1981	1986–8 average
West Indian	528,000	495,000
African	80,000	112,000
Indian	727,000	787,000
Pakistani	284,000	428,000
Bangladeshi	52,000	108,000
Chinese	92,000	123,000
Arab	53,000	73,000
Mixed	217,000	287,000
Other	60,000	164,000
All minority ethnic groups	2,092,000	2,577,000

(Adapted from LFS, 1981, 1986, 1987 and 1988)

Variations in the growth (or decline) of minority ethnic group populations are related to stages in the life cycle. *Figure 1.5* shows the LFS estimates of the British population aged under ten. Considerable variation is revealed: 30 per cent of the Pakistani population, 34 per cent of the Bangladeshi, and 40 per cent of those of mixed ethnic origin were children aged under ten (compared with 17 per cent for the West Indian population and 12 per cent for the white). The LFS estimates reveal that at least nine in every ten minority ethnic group children aged under five were born in the UK.

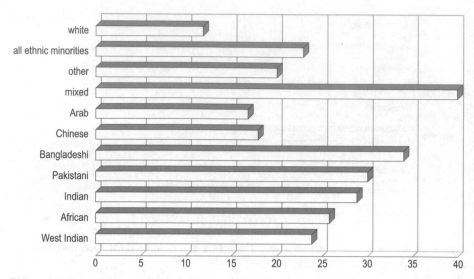

Figure 1.5: percentage of the population under 10
(Adapted from LFS, 1986)

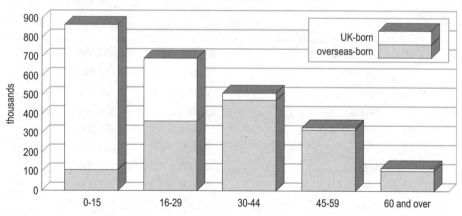

Figure 1.6: the minority ethnic group population in Great Britain, by age and whether UK-born or overseas-born
(Adapted from Central Statistical Office, 1991, p. 25)

Further analysis of the 1984–6 LFS averages showed that more than one in three of the British minority ethnic group population was younger than 16. *Social Trends 21* revealed marked differences in age structure between UK-born and overseas-born members of the minority ethnic group population (see *Figure 1.6*). Two-thirds of the minority ethnic group population born in the UK were aged under 16 and only one in twenty were aged over 29. In contrast, only 8 per cent of the overseas-born population were aged under 16, while almost two-thirds were aged over 29. Most of the overseas-born arrived in the UK as young adults, or as dependents, while those born within the UK were the first or subsequent generation of migrants (Central Statistical Office, 1991, p. 25). These distinct age distributions are related to length of residence in the UK and to the cycle of migration.

1.3 Household and family data: size and composition

LFS averages for 1985–7 showed that three-quarters of Pakistani and Bangladeshi households and three-fifths of Indian households contained four or more people, compared with a quarter of white households (Central Statistical Office, 1990a)[2] (see *Figure 1.7*). *Figure 1.8* reveals the average number of persons per household for each ethnic group.

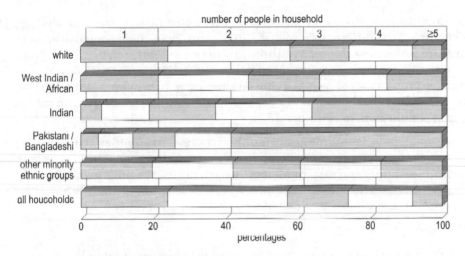

Figure 1.7: household size in Great Britain, by ethnic group of head of household, 1985-7 *(Adapted from Central Statistical Office, 1990a, p. 36)*

In 1988 over a quarter of all households in Britain contained only one person, compared to one in eight in 1961; the proportion was higher for white and West Indian/African populations than for Indian, Pakistani and Bangladeshi groups. During the same period the proportion of households containing five or more people has halved. In 1988 it was less than one in twelve, while the average household size reduced from 3.09 to 2.48 people.

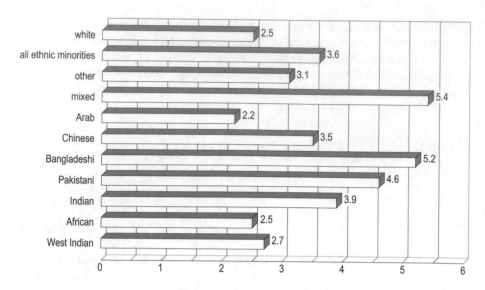

Figure 1.8: average number of persons per household in Great Britain, by ethnic group
(Adapted from LFS, 1985-7)

These data are crucially related to a variety of factors such as the age structure of the different groups, fertility rates, household composition and cultural influences. Minority ethnic group households, particularly Asian households, contain greater proportions of families with children and smaller proportions of people living on their own. LFS averages for 1985–7, for example, reveal over 40 per cent of Pakistani, Bangladeshi and mixed origin populations to be under 16.[3]

Analysis of minority ethnic group family sizes reveals significant differences between ethnic groups. For example, on average, there are three people in each white family and just under four in each minority ethnic group family.[4] *Figure 1.9* shows the mean family size by ethnic group of the family head and *Figure 1.10* the numbers of dependent children per family.[5]

The figures show that:

1   The proportion of lone-parent families was highest among West Indian families (44 per cent). For other groups the figures were: 33 per cent for 'mixed' ethnic origin, 27 per cent for African, 6 per cent for both Indian and Pakistani, 5 per cent for Bangladeshi and 11 per cent for white families. About every other West Indian family was a one-parent family compared with every third African and mixed ethnic origin family. The prevalance of one-parent families among Indian, Pakistani and Bangladeshi groups was well below that of white families (Haskey, 1991b, p. 39).[6]

    Three observations should be noted. First, West Indian families account for less than 1 per cent of all families in Britain. Second, in

1987, 14 per cent of all families with dependent children in Britain were headed by lone parents, which is twice the proportion found in 1971. Third, it is estimated that over six out of every ten one-parent families are living in or on the margins of poverty, compared with two out of ten two-parent families (Family Policy Studies Centre, 1986; Central Statistical Office, 1991, p. 35).

2   37 per cent of all West Indian families were headed by a female, compared with 9 per cent of white families.

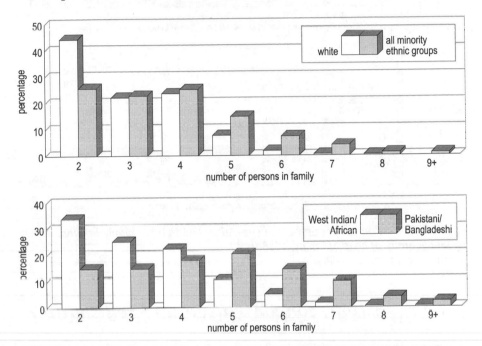

Figure 1.9: distribution of family size in Great Britain, by ethnic group of head of family, 1985–7
(Adapted from Haskey, 1989, p. 12)

Fertility rates fell in England and Wales between 1971 and 1981, and have since remained relatively stable. However, fertility rates for overseas-born women have in general continued to decline. The proportion of births to mothers born in the New Commonwealth and Pakistan (NCWP) fell during the 1980s, from 7.8 per cent in 1981 to 6.8 per cent in 1989.[7]

To summarize the LFS findings, West Indian, African, Chinese, Arab minority ethnic groups and the white majority population share several characteristics: smaller numbers of people and families per household, fewer dependent children per family, and a smaller proportion of households containing extended families. Indian, Pakistani and Bangladeshi populations have followed these broad trends but are still far more likely to live within extended families.

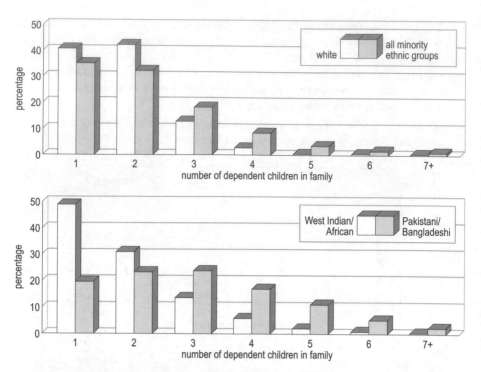

Figure 1.10: distribution of numbers of dependent children per family in Great Britain, by ethnic group of head of family, 1985–7
(Adapted from Haskey, 1989, p. 12)

1.4 Location, concentration and segregation

Britain's minority ethnic group population is largely urban and is characterized by residential segregation. Only 3 per cent of black and Asian residents (in contrast to the national average of 24 per cent) live in rural enumeration districts, while 75 per cent live in a set of urban enumeration districts which contain only 10 per cent of whites.[8] Half the white population in Britain live in towns and rural areas that have less than half of one per cent of their residents coming from minority ethnic groups. Only about one in sixteen white people live in an enumeration district with a black and Asian population of 5 per cent or more, although these areas accommodate 60 per cent of all minority ethnic group populations. The 1980s began with a higher proportion of black people living in the most segregated urban areas than did the 1970s (Brown, 1984, p. 20).

Maps 1.1 to *1.5* show the regional distribution of each of Britain's minority ethnic group populations towards the end of the 1980s.[9] The highest concentrations live in London and Birmingham, while the lowest are in non-metropolitan counties, especially in the South West, the North and Wales.

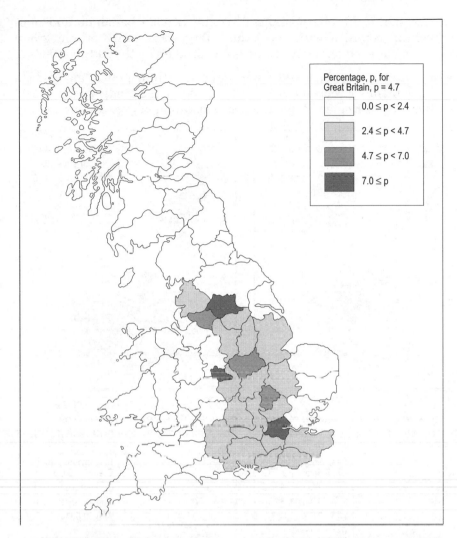

Map 1.1: estimated minority ethnic group population as a percentage of the total population, by county or region, 1986–8
(Haskey, 1991a, p. 28)

One in six residents in Greater London and the West Midlands is either Asian, Afro-Caribbean, Chinese or of mixed 'race', according to OPCS estimates (1991a). These estimates of minority ethnic group populations revealed that Birmingham has the largest populations of West Indians, Pakistanis and Indians, with 36,100, 39,700 and 49,800 respectively, the London borough of Lambeth the largest African population, with 7,700; Tower Hamlets the largest Bangladeshi population, with 18,100; Westminster the largest Chinese population, with 3,600; and Kensington and Chelsea the largest Arab population, with 3,500. The London borough of Brent has the highest proportion of minority ethnic group population – 27 per cent.

Table 1.2 shows the metropolitan districts, London boroughs and non-metropolitan counties with the twelve largest minority ethnic group populations for each minority ethnic group studied by the LFS in 1986–8.

The concentration of black and Asian minority ethnic groups also affects their parliamentary representation. Estimates in 1987 indicated that 100 constituencies in England have a black population of over 10 per cent: of

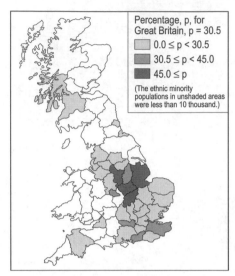

Map 1.2: estimated percentage of the minority ethnic group population of Indian origin, by county or region, 1986–8

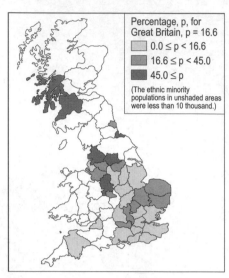

Map 1.3: estimated percentage of the minority ethnic group population of Pakistani origin, by county or region, 1986–8

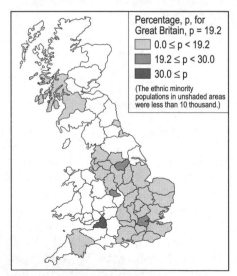

Map 1.4: estimated percentage of the minority ethnic group population of West Indian origin, by county or region, 1986–8

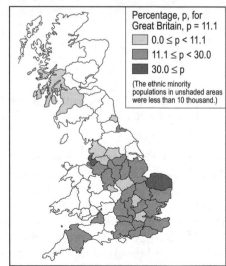

Map 1.5: estimated percentage of the minority ethnic group population of mixed ethnic origin, by county or region, 1986–8

(Haskey, 1991a, p. 30)

Table 1.2: metropolitan districts, London boroughs and non-metropolitan counties with the twelve largest minority ethnic group populations, 1986–8, in thousands

	West Indian/Guyanese		African		Indian		Pakistani		Bangladeshi		Chinese		Arab		Mixed	
	Area	Pop.	Area	Pop.	Area	Pop.	Area	Pop.	Area	Pop.	Area	Pop.	Area	Pop.	Area	Pop.
1	Birmingham	36.1	Lambeth	7.7	Birmingham	49.8	Birmingham	39.7	Tower Hamlets	18.1	Westminster	3.6	Kensington and Chelsea	3.5	Hampshire	7.1
2	Lambeth	23.9	Wandsworth	7.1	Leicestershire	41.6	Bradford	32.2	Birmingham	9.9	Hampshire	3.5	Westminster	3.5	Kent	6.9
3	Wandsworth	20.0	Haringey	6.0	Ealing	33.6	Lancashire	22.4	Bedfordshire	3.5	Barnet	3.2	Camden	2.5	Essex	6.7
4	Lewisham	19.9	Hackney	5.3	Brent	32.4	Leeds	17.5	Camden	3.0	Ealing	3.0	Barnet	2.2	Birmingham	6.4
5	Hackney	18.5	Southwark	4.8	Hounslow	21.7	Kirklees	16.3	Newcastle-upon-Tyne	2.8	Brent	3.0	Birmingham	1.8	Wandsworth	5.8
6	Southwark	17.9	Newham	4.6	Barnet	21.5	Manchester	10.5	Hackney	2.7	Camden	2.9	Liverpool	1.5	Lambeth	5.5
7	Haringey	17.7	Lewisham	4.4	Harrow	19.8	Glasgow	8.9	Sandwell	2.5	Essex	2.6	Haringey	1.5	Lewisham	5.4
8	Brent	16.5	Islington	3.9	Croydon	19.2	Newham	8.5	Bradford	2.4	Kent	2.6	South Glamorgan	1.5	Surrey	5.0
9	Newham	15.9	Westminster	3.5	Coventry	17.9	Berkshire	7.9	Westminster	2.4	Surrey	2.3	Wandsworth	1.4	Southwark	4.8
10	Hammersmith and Fulham	11.1	Brent	3.3	Wolverhampton	17.5	Calderdale	7.2	Southwark	2.3	Kensington and Chelsea	2.2	Lambeth	1.3	Newham	4.8
11	Islington	11.0	Camden	3.1	Sandwell	17.4	Wakefield	7.0	Wandsworth	2.3	Haringey	2.2	Hammersmith and Fulham	1.3	Hertfordshire	4.7
12	Westminster	9.7	Hammersmith and Fulham	2.9	Derbyshire	15.2	Staffordshire	7.0	Lambeth	2.2	Wandsworth	2.1	Hackney	1.3	Haringey	4.6

(Haskey, 1991a, p. 34)

these, half were considered marginal. Had Parliament been truly representative in the 1987 General Election, there would have been at least 30 black MPs elected, not six.[10]

1.5 Future trends

In 1979 projections indicated that by the year 2000 the NCWP-origin population of Britain would be in the region of 3.3 million (OPCS, 1979). This estimate was based on trends in births and deaths, and on the levels of immigration and emigration then current. This would mean that about 1 in 17, or 5.9 per cent, of the total population of Britain would be black. Further immigration restrictions would, of course, be expected to reduce the number of immigrants. However, even if all immigration of NCWP citizens were to cease, OPCS calculated that their estimate for the year 2000 would be reduced by only 0.6 million. After the year 2000, OPCS expected the proportion of black people in the total population of Britain to stabilize at around 6 per cent, because of low net migration and a gradual levelling out of demographic differences in age patterns and relative affluence between populations (Runnymede Trust and RSRG, 1980, pp. 27–8).

1.6 Developments since 1992

The 1991 census revealed that the minority ethnic group population of Britain was just over 3 million, or 5.5 per cent of the general population. Half of the total was made up of people of South Asian origin, representing 2.7 per cent of the population. Table 1.3 shows the ethnic composition enumerated (Runnymede Trust, 1994a; Pearce and White, 1994).

The 1991 census was the first to ask respondents to state their ethnic group. It is advisable to be cautious about both the census and LFS findings concerning the relative sizes of minority group populations. Over two million people were estimated to have been 'missed' by the 1991 census, while Charles Owen's analysis of LFS data (1989–91) showed a 0.9 per cent refusal rate for minority ethnic groups (Owen, C., 1993). Factors such as immigrant status, poll tax evasion and the classifications used, combined to persuade the OPCS to abandon the results of the 1991 census as the official population estimate. Instead, OPCS are currently updating the 1981 data, which were felt to be more plausible for some age groups, particularly young adults (Independent, 23 December 1994). Robert Moore's report on the 1991 census in Liverpool showed how respondents' self-descriptions were too complex for the classifications provided (Moore, 1995).

Owen and Teague's analyses of LFS data between 1989 and 1991 suggested some minority ethnic group under-enumeration as measured by the 1991 census (Owen, C., 1993; Teague, 1993). The LFS estimate for the ethnic minority population is 4.9 per cent (2.67 million people) compared with the

1991 census's estimate of 5.5 per cent (3.01 million). *Table 1.4* compares the 1991 census and LFS (1989–91) data.[11]

Data on country of birth in the 1991 census showed that 3.8 million residents (6.9 per cent) were born outside the UK (half a million more than in 1981).Of the 1991 total, 45 per cent were born in the New Commonwealth (Pearce and White, 1994). *Social Trends 25*, analysing data for the adult population over 16 years, showed that the minority ethnic group population constituted

Table 1.3: population, by ethnicity, 1991

Ethnicity	Number in thousands	Percentage of total population	Percentage of minority population
Black communities	891	1.6	29.5
African	212	0.4	7.0
Afro-Caribbean	678	1.2	22.5
South Asian communities	1,480	2.7	49.1
Bangladeshi	163	0.3	5.4
Indian	840	1.5	27.9
Pakistani	477	0.9	15.8
Other minority communities			
Chinese	157	0.3	5.2
Asian	198	0.4	6.6
Various	290	0.5	9.6
All minorities	3,015	5.5	100.0
Majority communities	51,874	94.5	–

(OPCS, 1991b; Runnymede Trust, 1994a, p. 12)

Table 1.4: comparison of results from the 1991 census with the LFS (1989–91)

Ethnic group	Percentage of total population		Percentage of population in other groups	
	Census	LFS	Census	LFS
White	94.5	94.2		
Other groups	5.5	4.9	100	100
Black*	1.6	1.1	30	23
Indian	1.5	1.4	28	30
Pakistani	0.9	0.9	16	18
Bangladeshi	0.3	0.2	5	5
Chinese	0.3	0.3	5	5
Other†	0.9	1.0	16	20
Not stated	n/a	0.9		

* Census categories: Black Caribbean, Black African, Black other.
LFS categories: West Indian or Guyanese, African.
† Census categories: Other Asian, Other other (non Asian).
LFS categories: Arab, Mixed origin, Other.
n/a Not applicable (not stated answers in the census are imputed).
(Teague, 1993, p. 17)

4.9 per cent of the population, with 25 per cent being born in the UK (CSO, 1995, p. 19). *Table 1.4* demonstrates the extent to which the census treats 'white' as a category of normality/universality and as a homogenous entity.

The 1991 census revealed that Greater London accounted for 45 per cent of the minority ethnic group population. Over one half of the minority ethnic population, but only one third of the total population, lived in the South East in 1991. London boroughs consistently housed the highest proportions of enumerated minorities, with the exception of Pakistanis, who were more geographically spread throughout the country. One third of the residents in Brent, Newham, Tower Hamlets and Hackney belonged to minority ethnic groups (see *Table 1.5*). The minority ethnic group population of London was 1.35 million, or 20 per cent of the total. One half of the London minorities were born in Britain (*Independent*, 16 August 1994).

Outside London, the main minority ethnic group concentrations were in Leicester, Bradford, the West Midlands and the Pennine conurbations (Teague, 1993). In 305 of the 459 local authority districts enumerated, less than 2 per cent of the population said that they belonged to an ethnic group other than white; in 211 districts less than 1 per cent did (Bailey, 1993).

Table 1.5: black and minority ethnic groups, by district, 1991

District	Thousands	Percentage of black and ethnic minority*	Percentage of total minority population	Largest minority (%)
1 Birmingham	206.8	21.5 (15)	6.87	Pakistani (6.9)
2 Brent	109.1	44.9 (1)	3.63	Indian (17.2)
3 Newham	89.9	42.4 (2)	2.99	Indian (13.0)
4 Ealing	89.1	32.4 (5)	2.96	Indian (16.1)
5 Leicester	77.1	28.5 (8)	2.56	Indian (22.3)
6 Lambeth	73.8	30.1 (6)	2.45	Afro-Caribbean (15.3)
7 Bradford	71.5	15.6 (27)	2.38	Pakistani (9.9)
8 Hackney	61.0	33.7 (4)	2.03	Afro-Caribbean (15.3)
9 Haringey	58.7	29.0 (7)	1.95	Afro-Caribbean (11.6)
10 Tower Hamlets	57.1	35.4 (3)	1.90	Bangladeshi (22.9)
11 Croydon	55.7	17.6 (24)	1.83	Afro-Caribbean (6.0)
12 Waltham Forest	54.3	25.6 (11)	1.81	Afro-Caribbean (8.5)
13 Barnet	53.7	18.3 (22)	1.79	Indian (7.3)
14 Southwark	53.4	24.4 (12)	1.78	Afro-Caribbean (10.6)
15 Harrow	52.6	26.3 (10)	1.75	Indian (16.1)
16 Manchester	51.2	12.6 (33)	1.70	Pakistani (3.8)
17 Wandsworth	50.9	20.2 (18)	1.69	Afro-Caribbean (7.7)
18 Lewisham	50.8	22.0 (14)	1.69	Afro-Caribbean (12.5)
19 Hounslow	49.9	24.4 (12)	1.66	Indian (14.3)
20 Redbridge	48.4	21.4 (16)	1.61	Indian (10.2)

*Number in brackets refers to national ranking.
(OPCS, 1991b; Runnymede Trust, 1994a, p. 15)

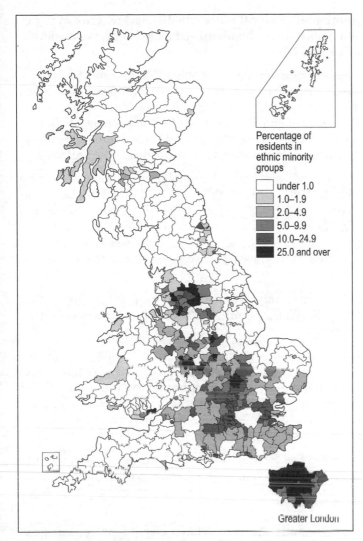

Map 1.6: minority ethnic population of Great Britain, 1991
(Runnymede Trust, 1994a, p. 14)

Table 1.5 shows the twenty districts with the largest numbers of black and minority ethnic residents. *Map 1.6* reveals the picture for Great Britain.

Map 1.6 shows that minority ethnic communities are concentrated in urban and industrial areas – Greater London (where just on a fifth of the population, 20.2 per cent, is of minority ethnic group background), Slough, Birmingham and the West Midlands (where the proportion is 8.2 per cent), Leicester, Greater Manchester and West Yorkshire. In Slough and in Leicester, and also in nine London boroughs, the minority ethnic population is more than a quarter. In mainly rural areas, however, the proportion is less than 1 per cent.

The ten minority ethnic groups identified by the 1991 census reveal distinctive geographical differences. When the groups are disaggregated only 2 per cent of Britain's population live in local authority districts where over 5 per cent of that district's population can be identified as belonging to a specific minority group (Dorling, 1994).

It would be wrong, however, to under-emphasise the spread of minority ethnic group settlement in rural Britain, since there is increasing evidence that these groups – the Chinese in Cornwall and Northern Ireland, and the Afro-Caribbean in Powys, face significant levels of racism (see Section 3) (L. Grant, 'Why don't they stay in Birmingham?', *Independent on Sunday*, 5 March 1995; D. Myers, 'Country matters', *Guardian*, 21 March 1995).

LFS data revealed that the minority ethnic group population increased by 25 per cent in the decade 1981–1990 (OPCS, 1992). The UK's black and Asian population, according to OPCS projections, is likely to stabilize in a generation. Projections made in 1993 indicated that it is likely to double from a 2.7 million base to 5.5 million, but is unlikely to exceed 10 per cent of the total UK population (Manchester University, 1994; *Guardian*, 20 January 1994).

Between 1981 and 1991 census analysis showed that the gender composition of Britain's minority ethnic group population has become more balanced (Runnymede Trust, 1993d).

OPCS research found that children formed a third of minority ethnic communities, compared with under a fifth of the 'white' population. Children accounted for a much larger proportion of Pakistani and Bangladeshi groups, with nearly a third of each minority of school age in 1991 (Owen, D., 1993). Minority groups also have a much smaller proportion of people over the age of 65 (Runnymede Trust, 1994a, p. 14; Pearce and White, 1994, p. 37).

LFS analysis has confirmed the census finding (see Amin and Oppenheim, 1992, p. 98). The younger age profile means that minority ethnic groups have become more vulnerable to Government cuts in income support and freezes in child benefit.

In 1988 there were approximately one million lone-parent families. Of these about one in ten were from minority ethnic groups. The proportion of families headed by one parent increased from 8 per cent in 1981 to 19 per cent in 1991 (HMSO, 1993). The 1991 census revealed that lone-parent rates varied considerably from 43 per cent in the 'Black other' group to 9 per cent in the Indian, 13 per cent in the white group, and 14 per cent for the country as a whole (Pearce and White, 1994). Nine out of ten of Britain's one million lone-parent families were headed by a woman. Amin and Oppenheim's analysis of family patterns and minorities showed that lone-parent household rates were: 8 per cent for Bangladeshi families; 8 per cent for Pakistani families; 6 per cent for Indian families; 49 per cent for West Indian families; 30 per cent for African families; 18 per cent for all minority ethnic families; and 15 per cent for white families (Amin and Oppenheim, 1992; *Employment Gazette*, May 1994; CSO, 1994, p. 36).

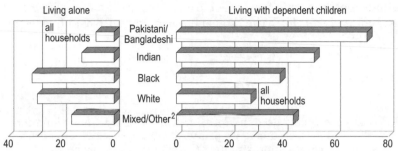

[1] Percentage of heads of households in each ethnic group living in each household type.

[2] Includes Chinese, other ethnic groups of non-mixed origin and people of mixed origin.

Figure 1.11: households, by ethnic group of head of household, 1994
(CSO, 1995, p. 31)

Figure 1.11 highlights differences between minority ethnic groups in household formation. Pakistani/ Bangladeshi households were most likely to live in families with children and least likely to be living alone.

More complex analysis has been conducted by Manchester University's Census Microdata Unit, focusing on the living arrangements of minority ethnic groups, based on the 1991 census findings. Heath and Dale, exploring variations between 16–35-year-olds, found that there were very significant differences in patterns in leaving the parental home between groups (for example, the greater likelihood of young Asian men and women with families of their own to live with their own parents or parents-in-law). Women and men under 20 years, however, were more likely to have left the parental home and to live away from their parents. The data point to the importance of the influence of cultural differences on new household formation (Heath and Dale, 1994).

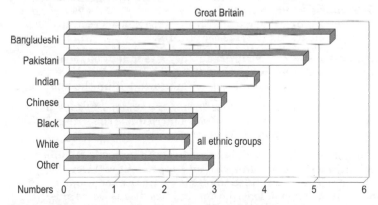

Figure 1.12: average household size, by ethnic group of head of household in Great Britain, 1991
(CSO, 1994, p. 34)

Variation in household size between minority ethnic groups confirms previous research. General Household Survey data show (see *Figure 1.12*) that white households contain fewer people on average than minority ethnic households; Bangladeshis form the largest households, with over five people on average in 1991.

Notes

1   Since LFS data are widely used in *'Race' in Britain Today*, an explanation of how the data are gathered is appropriate. The LFS is conducted each spring. The survey covers approximately 60,000 private households containing about 150,000 individuals. Respondents are shown a card listing a number of minority ethnic groups and asked to say to which group they consider they belong. The response rate is around 80 per cent each year, and approximately 7,000 of successful interviews are conducted with members of minority ethnic group populations. The LFS minority ethnic group definitions are: West Indian or Guyanese, Indian, Pakistani, Bangladeshi, Chinese, African, Arab, mixed origin, and other.

In this section on demographic trends, LFS definitions are used unless specified otherwise: the term 'white' comes from LFS. LFS data are presented from annual surveys between 1985 and 1989. For demographic trend data, *Social Trends 20* (Central Statistical Office, 1990a) remains the main source, backed up by detailed OPCS analyses of earlier LFS three-year averages, and the Haskey analysis published in spring 1991 (see below). Later sections have incorporated labour market data from the surveys of 1986–9, and from *Social Trends 21* (Central Statistical Office, 1991).

For a detailed analysis of the minority ethnic group population resident in private households in England and Wales only, based on LFS data from 1986 to 1988, see John Haskey's analysis of county and metropolitan data (1991a).

2   LFS definitions of a household are used here. A household refers to a group of co-resident individuals who share certain space within a dwelling.

3   A detailed discussion of the demography of minority ethnic group household and family data can be found in Haskey (1989). Haskey's data were based on rough estimates pending the outcome of the 1991 census results. For an analysis of lone-parent trends see Haskey (1991b).

4   Haskey's definition of a family comprised either a married couple on their own, or a married couple/lone parent and their never-married children, provided these children have no children of their own within the household.

5   Dependent children here refers to either those aged under 16 years, or those aged 16–18 (inclusive) who have never married and are either in full-time education or on a government scheme.

6   Haskey's definition of a lone parent is wider in scope than the standard definition and includes lone parents with non-dependent children. Neither his interpretation nor those included in official statistics mentions cohabitation: the proportion of lone-parent families discussed here is therefore an under-representation for *all* groups.

7   See Central Statistical Office (1991) pp. 28–9. These trends reflect changes in the number of women of childbearing age born in different parts of the world. But, increasingly, mothers from minority ethnic groups in the younger childbearing ages are themselves born in Britain and births to such women are now included in the category of mothers born in the United Kingdom. Categorized by country of birth of mother, the data for 1989 show that the estimated fertility rate for mothers born in the UK was 1.8 and for mothers born in NCWP 2.7.

8   Here 'black' and 'white' refer to the categories used by the Policy Studies Institute (PSI) in their 1982 national survey of multi-racial Britain (Brown, 1984).

9   See Haskey (1991a) pp. 28–31 and Smith (1989) p. 30. The 1991 census will clarify the extent to which Britain has become more segregated during the 1980s. Smith's definition 'black' merges LFS minority ethnic group categories used in 1985 to 1987.

Both Haskey and Smith exclude Northern Ireland from their maps and analyses.

10 Reported on BBC Radio 4, *The Black Vote in Britain*, 14 April 1990.

11 The 1991 census was estimated, in mid-1993, to have missed 2 per cent, or 1.1 million people, of the resident population of Great Britain. Validation research is being done in 1993–95, comparing LFS, General Household Survey and census data, to discover the extent to which ethnic groups may have been under-represented in the census.

2 IMMIGRATION

2.1 Introduction: the politics of control

Immigration policy is central to understanding racism in British society. British governments have long sought to control immigration. In 1985, reporting their formal investigation into immigration procedures, the Commission for Racial Equality (CRE) concluded:

> The way in which the [immigration] controls developed, and all the surrounding debate and controversy, made the issue as much one of race as of immigration *per se*, and there have been several opposing views about what are acceptable objectives for immigration control policies. At one extreme has been the view that the efficiency and effectiveness of the controls can be judged almost solely on their success in reducing and restricting the numbers of black people admitted for settlement. At the other has been the view that the legislation has been racist and that the governments responsible have pandered to racist attitudes in society, even encouraging and exacerbating them, rather than seeking to eradicate them.
>
> (CRE, 1985a, p. 126)

Politicians have focused on controlling entry to the United Kingdom by imposing restrictive legislation, particularly upon black Commonwealth migrants and their dependents. In 1989, the Runnymede Trust concluded:

> Black people are a problem and unwelcome here. That is the message which is restated and reaffirmed every time immigration policy is made more restrictive. It is a message not lost on 'our people' in Britain – on the employers who can ask, with reason, why they should have 'them' in their firm if the government does not want them in the country, on the tenants who do not want them in 'their' streets or housing estates, on the parents and pupils who do not want them in 'their' schools, on the 42 per cent of young white people who, according to the *British Social Attitudes Survey*, will now willingly admit to racial prejudice.
>
> (Gordon, 1989a, p. 13)

To most politicians, immigration controls have been a necessary corollary of 'good relations'. The political rhetoric justifying the necessity for immigration control can potentially have the effect of institutionalizing racism and, through the use of emotive language and imagery, reinforce the commonsense assumptions which have kept racism flourishing in British society. The extracts below represent a cross-section of mainstream political statements on immigration since the end of the Second World War:

An influx of coloured people domiciled here is likely to impair the harmony, strength and cohesion of our public and social life and to cause discord and unhappiness among all concerned.

(Letter to Clement Attlee signed by eleven Labour MPs, 1948)[1]

I believe that unrestricted immigration can only produce additional problems, additional suffering and additional hardship unless some kind of limitation is imposed and continued ... there is an economic necessity to have a certain amount of immigration but a social reason for control.

(Roy Hattersley, *Hansard*, 1965)

The main purpose of immigration policy ... is a contribution to peace and harmony ... If we are to get progress in community relations, we must give assurance to the people, who were already here before the large wave of immigration, that this will be the end and that there will be no further large-scale immigration. Unless we can give that assurance, we cannot effectively set about improving community relations.

(Reginald Maudling, 1971, cited in MacDonald, 1983, pp. 16–17)

People are really rather afraid that this country might be rather swamped by people with a different culture ... the British character has done so much for democracy, for law, and done so much throughout the world, that if there is any fear that it might be swamped, people are going to react and be rather hostile to those coming in. So if you want good race relations, you've got to allay people's fears on numbers.

(Margaret Thatcher, 1978)[2]

It would not be in the interests of the ethnic minorities themselves if there were a prospect of further mass inward movement. That prospect would increase social tensions, particularly in our cities. That is why we say that firm immigration control is essential if we are to have good community relations.

(Douglas Hurd, Secretary of State at the Home Office, *Hansard*, 1987)

2.2 The historical context

Of the major migrations to Britain during the last 150 years, three are of particular demographic and political significance, especially in relation to statistics and control: Irish migration since 1840, East European Jewish migration before the First World War, and migrants from the New Commonwealth after the Second World War.[3]

Until 1844 British citizenship was only possible to an 'immigrant' by means of a private Act of Parliament. Since then, legislation has been introduced to exclude 'aliens' or 'foreign citizens' or 'immigrants' from entering the country. A range of reasons lay behind immigration legislation: the protection of the labour market or the existing social composition, the exclusion of individuals considered undesirable on political or criminal grounds, or – as in the five statements quoted above – the maintainance of 'good' 'race' or community relations, or to facilitate 'integration'.

The Naturalisation Act of 1870, for example, introduced a five-year residential qualification; the Aliens Act of 1905 controlled the flow of Jewish migrants into Britain; the British Nationality and Status of Aliens Act of 1914 introduced 'good character' criteria, while the 1920 Aliens Order provided the basis for control until 1971. From 1920, 'foreign citizens', as 'aliens' were now called, were obliged to complete landing and embarkation cards. These records formed and informed legislative change until the 1960s.

2.3 Migration statistics and measurement

Much early immigration policy was introduced on the basis of almost nonexistent statistics and, where data were available, they were often based on inadequate definitions and measurement. In 1905, before the passage of the Aliens Act of that year, Bonar Law, answering a parliamentary question seeking statistics on immigration from 1895 to 1904, replied: 'I regret I am not in a position to give this information.'[4]

Immigration statistics have invariably been produced as a by-product of exercising control, rather than used to assess whether further legislation, and of what kind, is necessary. The often heated political debates about numbers and projections that have characterized much parliamentary debate on immigration, have often had the effect of triggering further immigration flows of people fearing an increase in controls on entry in the future.

There are obstacles to the collection of reliable immigration statistics. One is scale. For example, in 1985, 37 million people entered Britain from overseas (about the same number left). Of these 37 million, only an estimated 200,000 were intending immigrants (that is, people who stated an intention of staying for twelve months or more); 8.5 million were subject to full immigration control; 6 million were EC citizens; and the other 22.5 million, mostly UK citizens, were not subject to immigration control. In 1985, over 74 million people arrived in and/or left the UK, a number greater than the population of England and Wales and 50 times the number of births and deaths in any year (see Coleman, 1987, pp. 1140–1).

2.4 The IPS and Home Office statistics

Until 1961 the only official statistics on immigrants came from passenger statistics collected by the Board of Trade. In 1961 a voluntary survey was established. Drawing on a 5 per cent sample of arrivals and departures, it formed the basis of the International Passenger Survey (IPS).[5] One limitation of the IPS is that intending immigrants form only a small fraction of the traffic flow (in 1964, for example, they comprised only 1.3 per cent of arrival interviews and about 2 per cent of departure interviews). In the IPS, information on movement from countries involved in substantial migration flows to Britain is based on only a few hundred interviews. So, for example, the figure of 26,000 estimated Australian immigrants in 1975 was based on 479 interviews, and the estimated 23,000 from all the EC countries on only 91 (OPCS, 1978; Coleman, 1987, p. 1152). In general, the IPS permits too much interpretation to be based on responses from too few people.[6]

Home Office statistics analyse acceptances for settlement by nationality. They are based on information on the landing card: name, birth-place, date of birth, nationality, occupation, sex, UK address and details of arrival or departure. No analysis of these variables by acceptances is published in the annual *Control of Immigration Statistics*. The published data deal only with arrivals: an annual statistical bulletin on immigration from the Indian sub-continent provides additional information on age of children on entry, year of marriage and year of entry of spouse (Home Office, 1985; Home Affairs Committee, 1985).

Information on acceptance for settlement by nationality can be found in the *Control of Immigration Statistics Annual Abstract of Statistics* and, occasionally, in *Social Trends*. Figures for 1990 showed that 52,400 people were accepted for settlement: a quarter of these were from the Indian sub-continent and a further 20 per cent from the rest of Asia (Home Office, 1991). This was considerably less than the 80,750 admitted in 1976.

Contemporary migration statistics tend to be asymmetrical and record the flow of incoming persons – so, for example, detailed analysis of the kinds of persons return-migrating is not available. There is no control of emigration from the UK and thus no Home Office emigration figures. IPS figures are the only source on emigration data.[7]

> Home Office statistics do not treat immigration in a demographically very useful way. They measure flows only in one direction, provide no demographic or socio-economic characteristics on those accepted for settlement ... At present they add nothing to our social or demographic picture of the immigrant population of the UK.

(Coleman, 1987, p. 1162)

2.5 The British-born minority ethnic group population

Immigrants represent a declining proportion of Britain's minority ethnic group population. Nine out of every ten minority ethnic group children aged under 5 were born in the UK. In 1984 the third PSI survey estimated that 40 per cent of Britain's black population was British born; moreover, PSI further estimated that 50 per cent of those who came to Britain as immigrants had lived in Britain for over fifteen years (Brown, 1984, p. 2).

2.6 The importance of 'white' immigration

The word 'immigrant' is often wrongly used to refer only to black people. The majority of immigrants are white – from Eire or the Old Commonwealth (Australia, New Zealand and Canada) or from other European countries. The 1981 census, for example, revealed that nearly 3.4 million people in Britain were born overseas. Of these, 1.9 million were white – 607,000 were born in Ireland, 153,000 in the Old Commonwealth and about 1.13 million in other countries including Western Europe.[8] The remainder, 1.41 million, were born in the New Commonwealth and Pakistan (NCWP). A further 100,000 white people were born in the Indian subcontinent and East Africa while their parents were on overseas service.

2.7 The importance of emigration

Britain is traditionally a net exporter of people. Between 1971 and 1983, more people left Britain than came in. Overall the net loss of population during this period was 465,000, mainly as a result of emigration to Australia, Canada, New Zealand, the USA, South Africa and the EC. In 1988 the net loss was 21,000. NCWP immigration, substantial though it has been, has helped reverse the overall pattern to give a net population gain from migration only in the years 1962, 1972 and 1983–5. Taking the minority ethnic group population alone, analysis of LFS data has revealed a net gain of around 30,000 migrants each year to the UK population: about 24,000 of these come from NCWP countries (Shaw, 1988, p. 29).

2.8 Migration from the New Commonwealth and Pakistan

Since 1962 successive governments have passed laws to control NCWP immigration. The 1981 British Nationality Act introduced a tiered system of citizenship. It gave several million existing 'patrial' citizens (i.e. those with UK-born grandparents – almost all white) the same right of abode in the UK as British citizens had. At the same time, British dependent territories citizens, British overseas citizens, British protected persons and British subjects without citizenship of any Commonwealth country had no right of abode under the Act. The majority of people in these categories are of Indian, Chinese, Afro-Caribbean or other non-European descent (Nanda, 1988, p. 270; Action Group on Immigration and Nationality and Immigrations Laws, n.d., pp. 2–3).

The 1962, 1968, 1971 and 1988 Immigration Acts considerably reduced the inflow of migrants. Total immigration from NCWP countries has declined substantially from 136,000 in 1961 and 68,000 in 1972 to 22,800 in 1988. In 1988 citizens from the NCWP accounted for 46.3 per cent of the total acceptances for settlement in the UK (see *Table 2.1* and *Figure 2.1*).

Table 2.1: acceptances for settlement in Great Britain, by nationality, 1984–8

	1984	1985	1986	1987	1988
All nationalities	50,950	55,360	46,980	45,980	49,280
	%	%	%	%	%
Foreign	47.6	46.5	50.1	48.2	47.4
Commonwealth	52.4	51.5	49.9	51.8	52.6
NCWP	48.7	48.9	47.4	45.3	46.3
Old Commonwealth	14.6	14.7	13.8	15.1	15.0

(Central Statistical Office, 1990b)

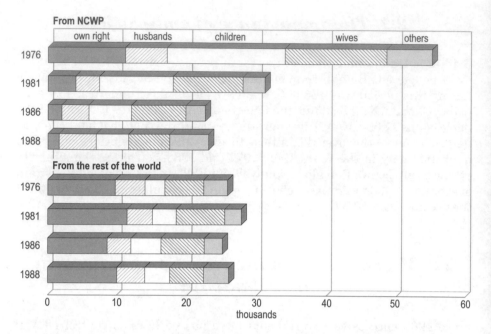

Figure 2.1: acceptances for settlement in Great Britain, by category of acceptance
(Adapted from Central Statistical Office, 1990a)

The 1971 Immigration Act imposed strict controls on the entry of males seeking work. Primary immigration (men accepted for settlement on arrival) peaked in 1972 at 18,000, fell to 6,400 in 1983, and is now confined to people with job skills in short supply. Secondary immigration (i.e. family reunification) has also been cut dramatically, from 50,000 in 1972 to around 11,500 in 1988. Nearly 54 per cent of the NCWP citizens granted settlement in 1988 were wives and children (see *Figure 2.1*).

In the Indian subcontinent, newly received applications for wives and children and other dependents fell from 24,680 in 1977 to 12,480 in 1986. In Bangladesh, demand also fell dramatically. In 1977 there were 15,200 newly received applications for entry made by wives and children and other persons. In 1986 the figure was 5,540.[9]

The 1971 Immigration Act stated that the rights of those already settled in the UK would not be adversely affected: for example, male Commonwealth citizens settled in Britain when the Act became law on 1 January 1973 had an automatic right to be joined here by their wives and children. The 1988 Immigration Act abolished this right. The third major migration phase, highlighted at the beginning of this section, is drawing to an end.[10]

2.9 Refugees and asylum seekers

In 1982 Britain granted full refugee status to 1,700 people (Gordon, 1989a, p. 5). Since 1987 the number of people seeking asylum has increased dramatically. People from Iran, Turkey, Somalia, Sri Lanka and Uganda account for most of the increase. In 1989 about 16,300 people were estimated to have applied for refugee status in the UK, three times the average for 1985–8 and ten times more than in 1979. Of these, 3,040 applications were granted. On 13 March 1991, in a written reply in the House of Commons, the Government revealed that the number of people applying to the UK for asylum nearly doubled in the previous year to 30,000 (see *Figure 2.2*).[11] It was expected to rise to 50,000 in 1991.[12] At the time the first edition of this book went to press the fate of the then Home Secretary Kenneth Baker's Asylum Bill, designed to isolate genuine asylum seekers from those the government claims are attempting to jump immigration queues, was uncertain (see Section 2.12).

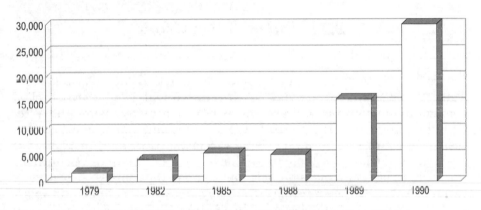

Figure 2.2: applications for refugee status in Great Britain
(Adapted from the Guardian, 3 July 1991)

2.10 Illegal immigration, deportations and detentions

A corollary of restrictive immigration controls is the increasing importance attached to measures aimed at those already in Britain. Since 1979, the number of removals of illegal immigrants, deportations and detentions has increased.

Illegal immigration estimates vary. Of those people detected each year, approximately a half are Commonwealth citizens.[13] In 1979 deportations totalled 1,275. Between 1979 and 1987, 16,460 deportation orders were made, an average of 1,800 each year (Gordon, 1989a, p. 7), and 7,300 people were removed as illegal immigrants. In 1990, 4,280 people were removed from the UK either as illegal entrants or under the deportation process, a fall of 260 from 1989 (Home Office, 1991).

The use of immigration detention has also increased. The number of detainees – people held without trial in prisons and detention centres – reached 11,000, its highest ever level, in 1986. Under the 1988 Immigration Act, people who have not lived in Britain for seven years lost their right to appeal against deportation on compassionate grounds. The rights of Members of Parliament to intervene in immigrant issues – hitherto the most effective way of questioning the decisions of immigration officials – has also been severely restricted by government order (Gordon, 1989a, p. 10).

2.11 Entry for visitors

Before 1986 visitors from the Indian subcontinent, the Caribbean, and other Third World countries arriving in Britain without visas were checked through by immigration officers. Since 1986 short-stay visitors have required a six-month visa from British embassies and high commissions in their own countries. However, visitors from the USA and Australia, for example, do not have to obtain these short-stay visas. The Joint Council for the Welfare of Immigrants (JCWI) has claimed that this is indicative of racial bias. In 1990 the refusal rate for Guyanese visitors to Britain was 1 in 87, compared, for example, with 1 in 3,600 for Norwegians. A parliamentary reply in July 1989 revealed that Home and Foreign Office entry clearance officers at the British High Commission in New Delhi had rejected 5,350 out of the 42,410 (or 1 in 8) applications for visitors' visas (the corresponding figures were 1 in 4 for Bangladesh and 1 in 6 for Pakistan). There was a backlog of 21,800 unheard appeals from disappointed travellers by the end of 1989. The number of Jamaican visitors turned back at Heathrow almost tripled between 1987 and 1989. The Jamaican foreign minister told British ministers in October 1989 that the issue had caused 'a lot of ill feeling and tension', both on the island and in the Jamaican community in Britain.[14]

2.12 Developments since 1992

Between 1981 and 1991, Britain's population grew by an average of 130,000 a year – a rise of 0.2 per cent. Of those 130,000, 21,000 were 'immigrants' (white and black). This increased the population by less than 0.04 per cent each year (*Socialist Review*, November 1993). Most 'immigrants' come from the 'white Commonwealth', Europe and the US (CSO, 1992, p. 34).

Between 1988 and 1992 the number of British citizens leaving the country to live abroad was, on average, 134,000 a year, a fall of 11 per cent compared with 1978–82. Between 1988 and 1992 there was a net average loss of 31,000 citizens during the same period compared with a net average gain of 46,000 non-British citizens (CSO, 1995, p. 23).

In 1993, 55,600 people were accepted for settlement in the UK; of these 49 per cent were from the New Commonwealth, and 51 per cent were from the rest of the world. By nationality 29 per cent of New Commonwealth people accepted for settlement in 1992 were from the Indian subcontinent, 19 per cent were from South Asia, 17 per cent from Africa and 14 per cent from the Caribbean. The numbers of wives and children from the New Commonwealth continues to decline. Between 1981 and 1993 the total number of acceptances for settlement (including husbands) from the New Commonwealth fell by 12 per cent (CSO, 1994, pp. 28–9; 1995, p. 26; OPCS, 1994a).

Figures published for the Council of Europe show that British citizens formed the largest outflow of 'economic migrants' to other European Union (EU) member states over the past 20 years (*Daily Telegraph*, 20 February 1995; Runnymede Trust, 1995c). The Council discounted claims that the rest of the world is desperate to get into Britain. The 'race' cards of 'flooding' and 'swamping' were belied by the figures (*Independent on Sunday*, 19 February 1995). Byron has predicted that up to one third of migrants of Caribbean origin will return to the islands where they were born. Her research revealed that 1 in 10 original Caribbean settlers in the UK had already returned to the Caribbean, leaving descendants to remain in this country (Byron, 1995; *Independent*, 6 January 1995).

Immigrants into the USA, Canada and Europe have put more into the public purse via taxes than they have taken out in welfare payments and services (Simon, 1993). The Institute for Public Policy Research (IPPR) found that the switch to attracting skilled migrants has brought entrepreneurs, income-generating overseas students and tourists into the UK. The IPPR urged politicians to take the lead in educating public opinion to counter racism and xenophobia and to increase awareness of the contribution migrants make to the UK and its economy (Spencer, 1994). In the summer of 1994, the Government announced new immigration rules designed to target migrant millionaires from Hong Kong and South Africa, encouraging them to buy their way into Britain and fast-tracking them through the system, in a move to attract investment (*Independent*, 25 May 1994).

A Home Office report in April 1995 exploded the myth that asylum seekers are mostly poor economic migrants seeking illegal entry. Research by the Home Office Research Unit and the University of Salford showed that only 1 in 5 asylum seekers have no educational qualifications; a third have been to university and had professional occupations. Since entry to Britain, most were unemployed and had experienced racial discrimination. Thirteen per cent said they had been physically attacked (Runnymede Trust, 1995f).

Politicians, Conservatives in particular, persist in playing the 'race' card using rhetoric which cannot be supported by official statistics and independent research. In 1993, Winston Churchill claimed that immigrants were 'flooding' British cities: a 'relentless flow' of tens of thousands of immigrants risked breaching British toleration, exacerbating 'the pressures within our society which are fostering increased racial tensions' (*Guardian*, 20 July 1993). Government Minister Peter Lloyd told BBC Radio 4's *The World Tonight*: 'we can't have the whole of Asia and Africa coming to live in London' (Edwards, 1993). In 1995 Charles Wardle, a former Home Office minister, resigned from his junior role with the Department of Trade and Industry over fears that the creation of a frontier-free Europe without effective border controls would lead to a substantial influx of non-EU immigrants into Britain, especially black Africans and migrants from Arab nations currently living in European countries (*Independent on Sunday*, 12 February 1995).

In July 1993, the new Asylum and Immigration Appeals Act became law, removing a visitor's right of appeal if refused entry. Christmas 1993 saw nearly 200 jet passengers from Jamaica detained amid scares about a Yardie influx. (A Yardie is a member of an organized crime institution with roots in Jamaican politics that has become increasingly involved in drug dealing in the 1980s–90s.) Seventy-one of the Jamaican passengers were subsequently admitted to the UK, a similar number were refused entry (*Independent*, 23 December 1993). In April 1995, in the High Court, Judge Mr Justice Tucker described the detention of one of the Jamaicans as 'not only wrong but irrational' (*Independent*, 10 April 1995). *Figure 2.3* shows the UK entry refusal rate. The rates for Jamaica and Bangladesh are far higher than most other countries; for example, one in 63 visitors from Jamaica was refused entry compared with one in 328 from Pakistan.

A Government decision in 1986 to impose a visa requirement on India, Pakistan, Bangladesh, Ghana and Nigeria had transformed the refusal patterns. Jamaican entrants who were not covered by visa regulations were increasingly refused entrance to the UK. By the early 1990s the refusal rate for Jamaica was 1 in 60 a year (in 1979 the Jamaican refusal rate was 1 in 729) (*Guardian*, 24 December 1993). Black and Asian people make up 10 per cent of all visitors to the UK, yet they form 70 per cent of all refusals (Runnymede Trust, 1993b; *Independent*, 27 December 1993).

The 1993 Asylum Act is expected to have an immediate effect with a rise in detention for asylum seekers. Official figures for the period prior to its becoming law disclosed in March 1994 that more than 9,000 asylum seekers

Passengers refused entry to UK by selected countries. The ratio represents 1 refusal for every X number of visitors admitted

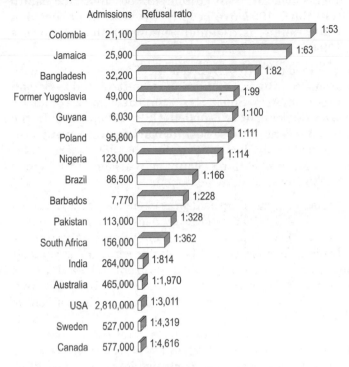

	Admissions	Refusal ratio
Colombia	21,100	1:53
Jamaica	25,900	1:63
Bangladesh	32,200	1:82
Former Yugoslavia	49,000	1:99
Guyana	6,030	1:100
Poland	95,800	1:111
Nigeria	123,000	1:114
Brazil	86,500	1:166
Barbados	7,770	1:228
Pakistan	113,000	1:328
South Africa	156,000	1:362
India	264,000	1:814
Australia	465,000	1:1,970
USA	2,810,000	1:3,011
Sweden	527,000	1:4,319
Canada	577,000	1:4,616

Figure 2.3: UK entry refusal rates, 1992
(Guardian, *24 December 1993*)

and other immigrants are incarcerated each year in British prisons and detention centres. Seven hundred (a record) were held at any one time, most being held for two weeks. Between April 1991 and January 1994, the numbers held for a month or more rose from 120 to 429. In the month following the Act the number of detentions doubled. Under the 1971 Immigration Act immigration authorities do not have to give any reason for detaining entrants (*Guardian*, 29 March 1994). There is also no time limit on the length of detention; over 18 months is not uncommon (Penal Affairs Commission, 1993; Ashford, 1993). Two 1994 studies testified to the physical and mental hardship of detention (Amnesty International, 1994; Medical Foundation for Care of Victims of Torture (MFCVT), 1994). Richard Dunstan, Amnesty's refugee officer, commented:

> We don't have a criminal justice system whereby police officers can send people to prison without telling them why or allowing them to go before a court, so why do we have such a system for refugees?

(*Independent*, 18 October 1994)

Home Office data published in the summer of 1994 revealed that over a half of refugees waited 16 months or more, and a fifth had to wait 2.5 years or more, before a decision could be reached on their cases. Many suffered from stress, anxiety and depression, and 1 in 10 complained of chronic health problems or disabilities. Since 1987 five people have died in prisons and detention centres while being held under Immigration Act powers (Runnymede Trust, 1994h).

Asylum applications declined to 22,370, from a peak of 44,840 in 1991, with 46 per cent of applications coming from Africa (a rise attributed to Somali refugees) and 23 per cent from Asia (South East Asian data were excluded); Africa accounted for over 60 per cent of refusals (CSO, 1995, p. 25). In the first half of 1994, only 4 per cent of those seeking asylum were granted it. Due to the sharp rise in asylum applications in the late 1980s there is also a backlog of 45,805 asylum applications requiring decisions to be made (Runnymede Trust, 1995b).

The impact of the 1993 Asylum Act on refusals has been dramatic, doubling the numbers of detainees. In July 1994, the Runnymede Trust revealed that refusals rose from 14 per cent of decisions to 74 per cent after the Act (remove Balkan refugees and the proportion would be 80 per cent). First quarter figures for 1994 show that 78 per cent of Tamils from Sri Lanka were refused, compared with over 95 per cent being allowed to stay before the Act. In addition, 99 per cent of Zaireans, 99 per cent of Angolans, 99 per cent of Sierra Leoneans, 78 per cent of Sudanese and 73 per cent of Turkish Kurds were refused (Runnymede Trust, 1994e). Latest data, released in June 1995, showed that in 1994 the number of people granted asylum decreased by over a half on the 1993 figure, despite applications rising eight fold since 1988. The number of refusals rose from 10,700 to 16,500 in 1994 (Runnymede Trust, 1995g).

A test case ruling which could have led to the release of hundreds of asylum seekers was overturned by the Court of Appeal in February 1995. Civil rights and immigrant groups immediately called for new legislation which would release asylum seekers on bail pending a decision. Concern intensified since the Asylum Act 1993 took away the right to appeal. Despite a High Court ruling that persons claiming political asylum could not be held in custody, the Home Secretary reversed the decision in the Court of Appeal (Home Office v Khan and Others, 3 February 1995).

Claude Moraes, the Director of the Joint Council for the Welfare of Immigrants, commenting on the 1993 Asylum Act, reflected:

> When you consider that in 1992 one in 4 Bangladeshis and Ghanaians arriving here were refused entry, but only 1 in 3,012 citizens from the USA, you can see why the nationals and UK relatives of people from black countries regard the new Act as a tool for undermining family unity, potentially barring thousands of black people from the UK.
>
> (*Guardian*, 29 December 1993)

In 1992 the Home Office made 881 deportation orders, as against 3,524 'notices of intention to deport', the previous stage in the deportation process (*Guardian*, 4 August 1993). A joint Church publication called for the Government to grant amnesty to over 1,000 families who, though they have lived here for five years, face family break-up and deportation (Churches Commission for Racial Justice, 1994). *Network First*'s programme 'Desperately Seeking Asylum' (ITV, 14 February 1995) revealed that in 1993, 2,000 asylum seekers were deported back to war zones and brutal dictatorships. JCWI figures indicate that 6,100 people were deported in 1993 compared with 2,700 in 1987 (Runnymede Trust, 1994f).

A package of new measures was hastily announced in the Commons including the injection of £37 million to speed up the processing of the backlog and further constraints on asylum applications. On the basis of an 80 per cent refusal rate it is expected that an escalation in deportations will occur from 1996/7, rising to as high as 7,000 a year (*Guardian*, 16 February 1995). Perhaps this is not surprising since it has been revealed that, as part of their staff appraisal, immigration officers are to be paid by quota of rejections (*Independent*, 13 December 1994).

On 28 July 1993, Joy Gardner, a Jamaican woman who came to Britain on a six-month visitor's visa in 1987, collapsed as she was being served with a deportation order. She died four days later without regaining consciousness. She had been restrained by standard deportation equipment – including leather belt and handcuffs, leg straps, and a mouth gag with belt. A second post mortem showed she died of suffocation. Her death was the subject of a Police Complaints Authority (PCA) inquiry. No independent public inquiry was granted. The 20 member special unit used in deportations since 1980, known in the Met as 'the Extradition Squad', was subsequently suspended. The Home Office and Metropolitan Police announced a joint deportation review (Runnymede Trust, 1993g; *Guardian*, 4 August 1993). A police investigation was delivered to the PCA in February 1994, following delays in deciding upon the cause of death. Five out of seven pathologists agreed Mrs Gardner died from oxygen starvation as a result of a gag, but two said head injuries were involved (*Independent*, 11 February 1994). The Crown Prosecution Service subsequently charged three police officers with manslaughter over Mrs Gardner's death. Each was found not guilty in June 1995. A subsequent PCA inquiry decided that no officer would face disciplinary charges. The Home Office announced the extension of the ban on gags but confirmed that body belts and leg restraints would continue to be used (*Independent*, 13 July 1995). After these decisions there were renewed calls for an independent inquiry into the role played by Home Office officials in the tragedy. Joy Gardner's death was one of several involving Home Office/police raids in the 1990s. The struggle for justice goes on (Channel 4, *Justice for Joy*, 20 June 1995).

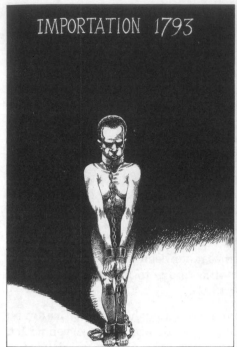

(Independent, *9 August 1993*)

Charles Wardle, then a junior Home Office minister, told the Commons that unregistered private security firms 'would continue to be used' in arresting deportees (*Guardian*, 1 December 1993). Security firms are not bound by the stringent controls imposed on police involved in extradition cases, prompting claims that the new regime may be even less regulated than at the time of Joy Gardner's death (*Guardian*, 27 April 1994). At the Police Federation National Conference in 1993 the use of stun-guns on deportees was advocated (C.H. Rolph, 'Personally speaking', *Police Review*, 10 September 1993). In 1995 the Home Office and Metropolitan Police Joint Review of Deportation Procedures revealed that, having considered the use of pepper sprays and gas guns on immigration deportees, they had decided against these (Runnymede Trust, 1995b).

The JCWI, following the production of its Charter for Immigration Detainees in May 1994, announced plans in 1995 to complain to the United Nations about the UK's 'appalling treatment of asylum seekers, migrants and refugees' (*Independent*, 20 January 1995; Liberty, 1995). Interim measures announced by the Home Office in July 1995, designed to target illegal immigrant fraud, could exacerbate the climate of fear in black and Asian communities, immigration welfare workers claimed, and amounted to nothing more than a 'snooper's charter' (*Guardian*, 19 July 1995). Home Office figures estimated there were 13,000 illegal immigrants in 1994, of which 6,500 were deported. The Home Office, however, were unable to estimate the numbers fraudulently claiming benefit (*Independent*, 19 July 1995). New immigration legislation is planned for the autumn of 1995. It is speculated that measures imposing stricter controls on asylum seekers will be proposed (*Guardian*, 13 February 1995).

British immigration and nationality law: a brief history of policy

British immigration policy has historically been characterised by two priorities: first, the need to meet the demands of Britain's labour market by providing cheap unskilled labour and, second, the need to control the entry of dependants, particularly from New Commonwealth countries. The cumulative effect of the legislation has been to help foster a climate of opinion where people of Afro-Caribbean and Asian origin are seen as unwelcome 'outsiders'.

Before 1914 all those born within the Crown's dominions were British subjects and under the common law rule of *ius soli* had the right of abode in Britain, a position sustained until 1982. Descendants were restricted to the legitimate male line to the first and second generations born outside the dominions.

The British Nationality and Status of Aliens Act 1914 imposed restrictions on descent, allowing only the first generation to acquire citizenship. Citizenship continued to be based on the *ius soli* principle.

The Aliens Order 1920 required people to demonstrate that they were able to support themselves and their families.

The British Nationality Act 1948 did not subscribe to equal access to citizenship irrespective of nationality or gender; the Act favoured Commonwealth citizens over aliens, and men over women. Registration was introduced to give citizens of independent Commonwealth countries an entitlement to citizenship based on a 12 month registration period (extended in 1973 to five years). Colonial subjects were yoked to the UK in a unified 'UK and Colonies' citizenship. While the *ius soli* principle was officially maintained, the 1948 Nationality Act was implemented in a racist way when it came to allowing Anglo-Indians and Anglo-Pakistanis living in India and Pakistan to register as 'UK and Colonies' citizens under clause 12(6) of the Act on grounds of 'close connection' with Britain –

that is, because of descent through the male line. Illegally, the maternal line was checked out to ensure that no one who had less than '75 per cent European blood' could register and migrate to the UK. Effectively, this system of 'racial classification', as one Government official called it, debarred first-generation Anglo-Indians and Anglo-Pakistanis from registering despite the paternal descent rule (Harris, 1994).

The Commonwealth Immigrants Act 1962 removed the unfettered right to enter and reside in the UK. For the first time immigration controls were introduced which ran contrary to common law – *ius soli*. This was a turning point in UK control of black migration and settlement. Commonwealth citizens were required to obtain employment vouchers, and demonstrate, as an entry prerequisite, a reasonable prospect of self-maintenance. Black immigration was the problem, not immigration itself.

The Immigration Acts of 1968 and 1971 extended the controls introduced by the 1962 Act and recommendations within the Labour Party White Paper of 1965. The 1968 Act amended the restrictive measures introduced in 1962. The 1971 Act effectively 'disembowelled' nationality by removing the right of abode from those who could not establish a 'close connection' with Britain. Right of abode was now only available to those who were called patrials – that is, those who had 'close connection' with Britain or those who were born, adopted, registered and naturalized in the UK. Women could acquire this right by marriage to a man who had the right of abode. Right of abode status was now separate from issues of nationality.

The British Nationality Act 1981 renamed those with the right of abode British citizens. Those without the right became British dependent territories citizens.

The Immigration Act 1988 tightened the rules further, imposing the 'independent of public fund' test on those dependants of people who had settled in Britain before 1973.

The Asylum and Immigration Appeals Act 1993 increased refusals and escalated detention for those seeking asylum to the UK.

Proposed immigration legislation in autumn 1995 is expected to reinforce stricter controls to try to curb illegal immigration.

Notes

1 Letter of 22 June 1948 to the Labour Prime Minister, Clement Attlee, signed by eleven Labour MPs two days after the ship, the *Empire Windrush*, had brought 500 Afro-Caribbean migrants to the UK. Cited in Carter *et al.* (1987) p. 2.

2 Margaret Thatcher, 30 January 1978, in an interview on Granada Television quoted in Gordon (1989a).

3 Immigration policy since 1945 is analysed in J. Solomos, 'The politics of immigration since 1945' in Braham *et al.* (eds) (1992) (ED356 Reader 3).

4 Parliamentary Reports, 1905, cited in Coleman (1987) p. 1145. The figures used at this time were ten-yearly census data on 'aliens' domiciled in Britain: a set of data was published in 1901.

5 The IPS provides a sample of intending immigrants and emigrants of all nationalities and all origins and destinations (except the Republic of Ireland). A migrant is a person intending to stay in the UK for up to twelve months, having been outside the country for at least twelve months: and *vice versa* for an emigrant. Data are obtained on citizenship, country of previous residence and of birth, gender, age, marital status, previous occupation and UK destination. Response rate to the IPS is about 85 per cent.

6 Analysis by occupation and age of IPS data is usually published in coarse categories and is seldom cross-tabulated. New Commonwealth and Pakistani arrivals are not cross-tabulated by age and gender together.

7 See Devis (1985) pp. 13–20. Curiously enough, in the nineteenth century the preoccupation was with the control of emigration, not immigration.

8 See 1981 census, Country of Birth, Table 1, OPCS.

9 See S. Helm, 'Immigration: fears of a flood which has shrunk to a trickle', *Independent*, 4 December 1987.

10 The next major migration phases could be white migrants from South Africa and people from Hong Kong.

11 Quoted in the *Independent*, 'Question and answer: written replies', 13 March 1991.

12 *Independent*, 28 May 1991; *Guardian*, 3 July 1991.

13 The total includes overstayers as well as persons entering the UK illegally. See Coleman (1987) p. 1156.

14 See *Independent*, 9 November 1990.

3 RACIAL VIOLENCE AND HARASSMENT

▼ ▬▬▬▬▬▬▬▬▬▬▬▬▬▬▬▬▬▬▬▬▬ ▼

As a boy sleeps, a pig's head, its eyes, ears, nostrils and mouth stuffed with lighted cigarettes, is hurled through the window of his bedroom. A family do not leave their home after seven in the evening; they stay in one large room, having barricaded their ground floor. A family are held prisoner in their own flat by a security cage bolted to their front door by white neighbours. A youth is slashed with a knife by an older white boy as he walks along a school corridor between classes. A family home is burned out and a pregnant woman and her three children killed. A ticket collector is stabbed in the eye with a metal stake and killed simply because he refused to take racial abuse from some white passengers.

These cases, all reported in the last few years, are part of the black experience of Britain in the 1980s, part of black people's reality.

(Gordon, 1990, p. v)

▲ ▬▬▬▬▬▬▬▬▬▬▬▬▬▬▬▬▬▬▬▬▬ ▲

3.1 The context of racial violence and harassment

Racial violence and harassment are not recent phenomena. In 1919, there was a series of attacks on black people in the dock areas of Britain – Cardiff, Glasgow, Liverpool, Hull, Manchester and London. In the 1940s there were attacks in Liverpool (1948), Deptford (1949) and Birmingham (1949). In the late 1950s black people became a particular target for racist white youths. The 1960s brought 'paki-bashing' and attacks by white 'skinheads'. The 1970s saw racial violence and harassment escalate, culminating in *Blood on the Streets*, a report that illustrated the scale of violence suffered by the Bangladeshi community in the Spitalfields area of Tower Hamlets (Bethnal Green and Stepney Trades Council, 1978). The report raised concern and awareness about the intensity of the problem. Evidence suggests that the situation worsened in the 1980s. The Home Affairs Committee in its 1986 report, *Racial Attacks and Harassment*, accepted as its starting point that: 'the most shameful and dispiriting aspects of race relations in Britain is the incidence of racial attacks and harassment' (Home Affairs Committee, 1986, p. 22).[1]

The Runnymede Trust estimated that between January 1970 and November 1989, 74 people died as a result of attacks which were either known to be racially motivated because of evidence at subsequent trials, or widely believed to be so within the black community.[2]

Racial violence and harassment are not solely British problems. The EC has estimated that the number of racist attacks across the twelve community states rose by between 5 and 10 per cent in the late 1980s. The EC has called for a European Charter to protect its minority ethnic group population of 14 million, claiming that they will face increasing harassment, violence and discrimination unless member countries act to curb neo-facism, anti-semitism and organized racism.[3]

3.2 Under-reporting of racial incidents

Assessing the incidence of racial harassment is difficult because incidents often go unreported. In 1989 a Home Affairs Select Committee highlighted a significant level of under-reporting of racial incidents revealed in Home Office and police evidence to the committee's inquiry.[4] The committee's chairman, Conservative MP John Wheeler, called racial harassment: 'a particularly disturbing, very horrifying crime ... [which] affects not only individual victims but minority ethnic group communities as a whole. It engenders fear and militates against the creation of a decent and civilised multi-racial society.'[5]

In England and Wales, estimates based on incidents reported to the police suggest there are 7,000 racially motivated attacks each year.[6] The EC has argued that the real figure could be ten times higher, bringing the number of attacks to 70,000 (European Parliament, 1990, p. 68). Local studies in the UK have pointed to the low level of reporting. A London Borough of Newham (1987) report argued that the real level of racial attacks was about 20 times higher than the figures given by the police. In May 1991, a survey for Victim Support, backed by the Home Office, estimated that the number of incidents recorded by the police in England and Wales – between 3,000 and 6,000 – represented between 2 per cent and 5 per cent of the actual total. This study, of 700 cases over a two-year period in Camden, Southwark and Newham, also argued that, while cases that were reported were treated sympathetically at first, often 'nothing appeared to be done to arrest or charge the perpetrator' (Victim Support, 1991). In commenting on this report, a representative of the Community Involvement and Crime Prevention Branch of the Metropolitan Police questioned the narrowness of its sample and also offered an alternative and, he claimed, broader definition of what constitutes a racial incident: 'an occurrence where racial motivation is thought by the victim, the police, or any other person to be present' (*Independent*, 18 May 1991).

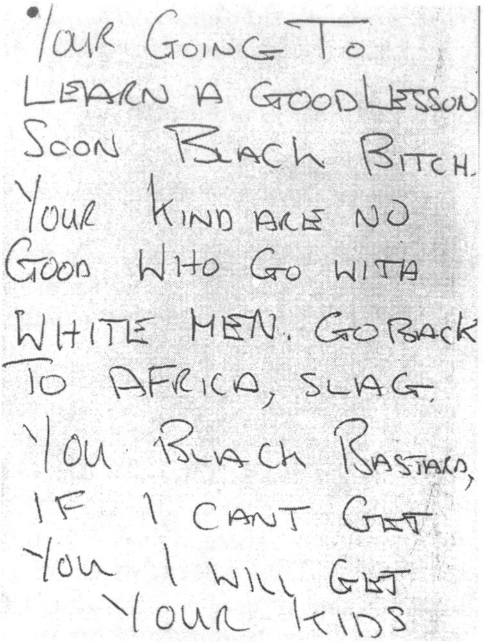

> Your Going To
> Learn a Good Lesson
> Soon Black Bitch.
> Your Kind are no
> Good who Go with
> White Men. Go Back
> To Africa, Slag.
> You Black Bastard,
> If I cant Get
> You I will Get
> Your Kids

Figure 3.1: hate mail pushed through the letterbox of a black family
(Independent, *13 February 1990*)

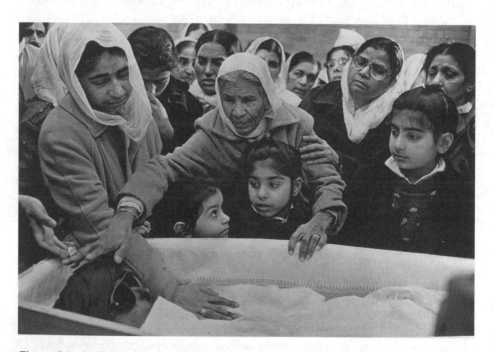

Figure 3.2: the funeral of murdered minicab driver Kuldip Sekhon. The dark glasses and turban hide multiple stab-wounds

3.3 The extent of racial incidents

The number of racially motivated incidents in England and Wales during 1988, 1989 and 1990 were 4,383, 5,044 and 6,359 respectively. The available figures for Scotland for the same years were 299, 376 and 636.

(Runnymede Trust, 1991a, p. 7)

Provincial police forces and the Metropolitan Police, in evidence to the Home Affairs Committee, have reported an increase in the number of racial incidents. In 1984, 1,515 racial incidents were reported to the Metropolitan Police. By 1988 this had risen to 2,214. In the first six months of 1989, 1,290 incidents had been reported. Serious racial assaults recorded by the Metropolitan Police in the first half of 1989 rose by 60 per cent compared with 1988 (from 120 to 190). Official figures showed increases in racial incidents in six out of eight of London's police areas (*Guardian*, 14 August 1989). In his annual report for 1989, the then Metropolitan Police Commissioner, Sir Peter Imbert, identified a 22 per cent rise in 'racial incidents' and a 25 per cent rise in racially motivated assaults. He commented:

Racial attacks and any form of harassment on racial grounds are not only against the law they are also morally repugnant. Everyone has the right to feel safe at home and on the streets, but not all people do. Far too many are afraid of becoming victims of harassment or attack … It is encouraging that more people are now willing to come forward and report these incidents but depressing that there are still those who are of such a bigoted nature that they indulge in such attacks. The clear-up rate for racial incidents in 1989 stood at just over 30% and we are determined to tackle this particular crime with increasing vigour.

(Metropolitan Police, 1990)

In June 1991, at a press conference introducing his 1990 annual report, Imbert reiterated his concern about the escalating number of reported racial incidents. In 1990 these rose by a further 8 per cent. He also reported that one officer had been disciplined in connection with racist behaviour in 1990, and one in the first half of 1991. Fewer than one in twelve complainants from minority ethnic groups had complained about an officer's racial attitudes. The force was often unable to prove complaints because of the standard of proof required at disciplinary hearings (*Independent*, 13 June 1991).

In the provinces, other research has confirmed the upward trend in racial incidents. According to a study in Leicester in 1987, many Asian families were living in a self-imposed curfew within their own homes because of the increase in attacks (Chambers Community Consultants, 1989). In Sheffield, a city council report concluded that all minorities were affected (Racial Harassment Project, 1989). Research in the first nine months of 1988 found that 25 per cent of incidents reported involved physical violence resulting in broken bones, facial injuries, loss of teeth and multiple bruising. All black people, male or female, rich or poor, were potential targets, irrespective of where they lived in the city. A quarter of the victims were under nineteen, as were the attackers. In 30 per cent of cases the attacker was actually known to the victim, either as a work colleague or a neighbour. Many Chinese people had come to see racial harassment as a condition of living in Britain: one told the research team it was 'almost as British as the weather'. Sheffield's Yemeni community complained of harassment at work, in the street, and in school.

The 1988 British Crime Survey, which covered many crimes not reported to the police, showed Asians to be disproportionately more likely to be victims of crimes such as vandalism and victimization by groups of strangers that could not be accounted for by demographic or residential factors. The survey concluded that racism contributed to Asians becoming the victims of crime far more than it did with Afro-Caribbeans (Mayhew *et al.*, 1989).

Figure 3.3: room after a racist attack

3.4 Racial incidents in people's homes

In 1987 the Commission for Racial Equality (CRE) published a report on racist incidents in people's homes (1987a). Based on a national sample of local authorities and agencies such as Community Relations Councils

(CRCs), law centres and voluntary housing aid centres, it emphasized that the scale of the problem continues to go unreported. Over a third of the 142 local authorities that had policies on racial harassment considered the problem to be increasing. Among agencies surveyed, over 80 per cent thought racial harassment was an issue in their areas. By the end of the 1980s the situation had deteriorated, particularly in London where some boroughs were reporting a significant escalation in the number of reported racial attacks. For example, Southwark reported a 56 per cent rise between 1987 and 1989 (*Independent*, 13 February 1990). Section 7.7 of this book summarizes trends in housing department responses to racial harassment and violence, especially what courses of action can be taken against racist council tenants.

3.5 Racial incidents in educational institutions

In 1988 a major national report highlighted the pervasiveness of racial incidents in schools and colleges. *Learning in Terror* concluded: 'Racial harassment is widespread and persistent – and in most areas very little is done about it'.[7] The report found that the problem increasingly affected all the education system, and encompassed the lives of pupils and students, staff and parents. They found it a feature of largely white schools in rural and suburban Britain as well as schools in the inner cities. Of the 115 educational institutions surveyed, only 47 had published or were working on guidelines to combat racial harassment.[8]

3.6 Inter-ethnic group conflict

There have been reports of some tension between young members of ethnic communities living in the Tower Hamlets area of London. For example, it was reported that despite great efforts by Bengali elders and community workers, the pressures of recession and poverty had led to clashes between young Bangladeshis and young Somalis who had arrived since the war of 1988. But the Capa Organisation, a voluntary group which monitors police activity in Tower Hamlets, has claimed that among the causes of tension between young Bengalis and Somalis are the absence of facilities for the Somali community (unlike the Bengalis they had no youth centre) and police harassment of the Asian community in general. Tim Kelsey reported the creation of small vigilante groups of young Bengalis watching out for the police (Tim Kelsey, *Independent on Sunday*, 26 May 1991).

3.7 Developments since 1992

The most shameful and dispiriting aspect of race relations in Britain is the incidence of racial attacks and harassment.

(Home Affairs Committee, 1986, p. 22)

Racial attacks will not be tolerated, and those who perpetrate them must be caught, convicted and punished.

(Home Secretary, Michael Howard, to the Conservative Party Conference, 6 October 1993)

A dramatic increase in racial violence and harassment occurred across Britain in the 1990s (BBC2, *First Sight*, 14 January 1993; BBC1, *Panorama*, 'Racial attacks', 6 December 1993; Runnymede Trust, 1992a–c; 1993a–i; 1994b–h; Virdee, 1995).[9] Between 1988 and 1993, official Home Office statistics showed that 'racial incidents' rose by over 80 per cent. *Table 3.1* gives a breakdown of data on reported 'racial incidents' for all England and Wales between 1989 and 1993/94. Care must be taken with these data since interpretation and definition of a 'racial incident' vary; also, the data deal only with reported incidents. The Metropolitan Police Force (MPF) define a 'racial incident' as 'any incident which includes an allegation of racial motivation by any person' (P. Martin, 'The colour of blood', *Independent* magazine, 12 June 1993).

Table 3.1: reported racial incidents in England and Wales, 1989–94

	1989	1990	1991	1992	1993	1993/94*
Provincial police total	2,347	3,451	4,509	4,566	5,329	5,873
Metropolitan Police total	2,697	2,908	3,373	3,227	3,889	3,889†
England and Wales (inc. London)	5,044	6,359	7,882	7,793	9,218	9,762
Scotland	376	636	678	663	726	–
Total	5,420	6,995	8,560	8,456	9,944	–

* Figures for April 1993 to January 1994.
† Police estimate.
(Socialist Review, *April 1995, p. 11; figures compiled by the Home Office*)

Racial attacks affect black and Asian groups, in all places. It is a national problem and not one confined to urban areas. In 1993, over 40 per cent of the recorded incidents were in London where police clear-up rates generally were only 20 per cent. In 1993 racial violence in the South East was at an all-time high. In London there were 3,550 incidents, over half in the East and

South East districts. More than a tenth of all recorded racial incidents in England and Wales occurred in London's East End. One in ten minority ethnic households in London (48,000 households) suffered racial harassment, a quarter had members who had been physically attacked, while 17 per cent had been threatened. Only 50 per cent of victims had reported incidents to the police (London Research Centre, 1993). In 1991, only three prosecutions were taken out for 'racially offensive conduct' (*Guardian*, 8 July 1993). The MPF clear-up rate for racial incidents was 20 per cent in 1992, although there were significant variations. Plumstead, in the East End, had the highest clear-up rate of 46 per cent (*Guardian*, 8 July 1993; Home Office, 1993, p. 3). MPF data for 1994 show that serious racist attacks in Tower Hamlets doubled, assaults trebled, and the number of reported racial incidents rose by 12 per cent.

In Scotland 678 incidents were reported (Runnymede Trust, 1993c). In West Lothian more than half of all black women experienced racist attacks (*Glasgow Herald*, 22 January 1993). Strathclyde also reported a doubling of racial incidents in 1992 (*Scotsman*, 21 January 1993).

In Derby and Leicestershire racist incidents doubled (*Searchlight*, March 1995). In Newcastle upon Tyne police reported a doubling of racial attacks during 1994, particularly targeting the South Asian communities (*Independent*, 30 May 1994). One particularly disturbing aspect of the increase in racial incidents is that people's homes are becoming more likely targets as sites for racial violence and harassment (Hesse *et al.*, 1992). In 1993, the CRE annual report stated that racially motivated attacks had risen to more than 365 each day in Britain, with at least 30 needing police action (CRE, 1994a).

These figures, however, represent an under-recording of the real level of racial incidents. The British Crime Survey (BCS) put the figure of recorded incidents at 10 per cent of the real total (Home Office, 1994a). For the BCS an incident is racially motivated if the victim perceives and describes it as such. If we assume the maximum BCS estimates to be realistic, there were 171,000 racial incidents against Asians and Afro-Caribbeans in 1991. Of these 49,000 were assaults, 78,000 were threats, 48,000 were acts of vandalism. Peter Lloyd, the Home Office minister, in evidence to the Home Affairs Select Committee investigating racial attacks and harassment, testified that the real total could be as high as 140,000 a year. The Labour Party have put the figure at between 175,000 and 200,000 incidents (Ruddock, 1994). Between 1988 and 1992 there was a marked increase in the vulnerability of South Asian people. In 1988, 36 per cent of South Asian people perceived the assaults against them to be racially motivated, whereas in 1992, the proportion was 56 per cent (for Afro-Caribbeans the figures were 34 per cent and 24 per cent, respectively) (Home Office, 1994a). Unfortunately the BCS does not break down South Asian into Pakistani and Bangladeshi groups.

In evidence to the Select Committee into Racial Attacks and Harassment the chairman of the Commission for Racial Equality, Herman Ouseley, revealed that 49 per cent of victims of racial attack were Asian, 23 per cent Afro-Caribbeans, 22 per cent white, and 7 per cent Jewish (*Independent*, 2 December 1993). These data, however, beg certain questions. Who are white people attacked by? Is it not the case that any 'attack' by a black person on a white is seen as 'racial' when the real motive may be money?

Research reveals that small shopkeepers of Asian origin have increasingly become targets for attack. In London, 32 per cent of Asian shopkeepers were racially abused in the twelve months prior to July 1993; in the Midlands the figure was 37 per cent (Hibberd and Shapland, 1993). Research has also shown links between victim and 'racial' motivation. In 1989, 36 of London's murder victims were black; in 1991, this figure had risen to 74 (*New Statesman and Society*, 8 January 1993). In 1992 there were twelve murders in England and Wales where 'race' was considered the only motive (Sivanandan, 1994; *Today*, 10 September 1993). Black people are three times more likely than whites to be murdered (*Police Review*, 18 June 1993).

The evidence across Britain is of racial incidents spreading to towns and rural areas. Paul Gordon told the 1992 conference of the Howard League of Penal Reform that: 'what little we know suggests that isolated black families are even more vulnerable to attack and abuse' (Runnymede Trust, 1992b, pp. 10–11; *Independent*, 4 September 1993). The 1990s have witnessed a growth of black and Asian networks and self-help groups in rural communities and small towns to combat racial violence and harassment. A study in Norfolk found that virtually everyone from black and Asian minority groups had experienced racial harassment, taunts, discrimination or violence (*Independent*, 8 December 1994; Norwich and Norfolk Race Equality Council, 1994).

Legislation seems ineffectual and inadequate in dealing with racial incidents. For example, only three prosecutions were served in 1991 for 'racially offensive conduct' (*Guardian*, 8 July 1993). By March 1994, only fourteen prosecutions had been served under the 'incitement to racial hatred' section of Part 3 of the 1987 Public Order Act, and of these, only seven had resulted in a conviction (*Hansard*, 1994c).

What can be done under existing legislation? The 1976 Race Relations Act has a civil not a criminal focus and is relatively impotent (except in a few racial harassment cases). There are several Acts which can be utilized to resolve cases where racial violence or incitement is featured in the offence: the 1986 (and 1987) Public Order Acts; the 1988 Malicious Communications Act; Section 222 of the Local Government Act (which gives local authorities the power to intervene and prosecute to protect inhabitants of their area);

Section 5 of the 1936 Public Order Act; Sections 20 (on grievous bodily harm), 42 (common assault) and 47 (actual bodily harm) of the 1861 Offences Against Persons Act; the 1971 Criminal Damage Act; the 1953 Prevention of Crime Act, and the 1968 Firearms Act.

Using housing legislation remains problematic. Children under 18 are not normally tenants (except under special licence) so they cannot be prosecuted. Very often the perpetrators of racial violence and harassment on council tenants, for example, are children under 18 (BCS figures show that 58.5 per cent of racially motivated incidents in London in 1991–93 were committed by persons under 20, where an estimate of age of offender was given; 30 per cent were under 15). There is still a reluctance amongst many local housing authorities to take action against racist tenants. Either the harassment or violence persists, or the victim moves. The eviction of housing tenants for racial violence and harassment is still a relatively rare event. The housing section analyses evidence on local authority housing response to racial violence and harassment.

In March 1994 the Racial Hatred and Violence Bill 1994, which had called for extra penalties where racial motivation could be established and which recommended a new criminal offence of 'racial harassment', was talked out at its second reading (*Hansard*, 1994b). A month later an amendment to the Criminal Justice Bill 1993 by the Labour Party and supported by the Home Affairs Committee, that up to five new offences of racially motivated assault be created, was defeated (*Hansard*, 1994d). In June 1994, Home Secretary Michael Howard announced new powers enabling the courts to impose up to six months' imprisonment for proven cases of racial harassment (*Independent*, 12 June 1994). In November 1994, Lord Taylor, the Lord Chief Justice, in the Court of Appeal (Regina v Ribbans), ruled that although the law does not have a specific offence of racial violence, a proven racial motive in any crime of violence will be regarded by the court as adding to its seriousness, thus justifying an increased sentence (*Guardian*, 28 November 1994). The Home Secretary, addressing the Runnymede Trust National Conference on 'The Future of Multi-Ethnic Britain', the first to speak in public on 'race' law since Roy Jenkins in 1976, argued that progress towards good race relations would not be achieved by more legislation, and that the existing criminal law was sufficient (*Guardian*, 24 September 1994). By spring 1995, all attempts at introducing legislation which criminalized racial violence as a separate offence had failed. The late 1990s may see the debate renewed in the light of European discussions on expanding international racial discrimination legislation. The outcome of the private prosecution brought by the Lawrence family for the murder of their son Stephen, the first of its kind in history, and the reverberations of the conviction of an Asian, Badrul Miah, for the murder of Richard Everitt, will also be monitored for implications for the efficacy of contemporary legislation.

AND YOU GET ANNOYED ABOUT JUNK MAIL.

Imagine going to your door and finding, there, on the mat, not bills, or a paper, or junk mail, but pieces of dog excrement. As you stare, shocked, a heavy boot kicks the door. Hateful voices outside scream obscenities, telling you to get out, threatening your family. Why are they persecuting you? When will they stop?

The attacks have been happening ever since you were moved to this estate.

It seems a Saturday night doesn't go by without a window or two being smashed.

Usually after closing time at the pubs.

Two or three times a month they shove something disgusting through your letterbox.

It's not always dog excrement.

Sometimes you find a filthy brown rat squealing on your doormat. You shoo it out of the house before your children see.

Once, you came from the kitchen to find a firework screaming around the hallway. What if the kids had been playing here? Or if something had caught fire?

Recently you heard of a man in Bristol who came home to find his house blazing.

Someone had poured petrol through the letterbox and put a match to it. His wife and three young children had died in the fire.

Who would do such a thing?

You may find it difficult to imagine being harassed in your own home like this.

But for thousands of ethnic minorities

Figure 3.4: advertisement about racial harassment from the Commission for Racial Equality
(Independent, *3 October 1994*)

it's an almost everyday occurrence in life.

Shaida, a young Asian woman living in London's East End, gives a typical account.

"For years these people put shit through my letterbox, spat on me, kicked my child's pushchair and screamed at our visitors."

You might think that racist attacks are carried out by a small, right-wing minority.

The truth is even more frightening.

Shaida continues, "They were normal people, you know, other mothers. So nice to each other. Animals to us."

In fact, it has been estimated that most cases of racial harassment are perpetrated by 'normal' people, not fascist groups.

And it's happening right now on housing estates and quiet streets all over Britain.

The police recognise the problem but lack the specific powers to fight it.

Unbelievably, racial harassment is not considered an offence in its own right.

At present the maximum sentence is only a fine of £1,000. (These days you can get a harsher fine for a traffic violation).

Councils have a duty to protect their tenants, but they too claim to lack power.

Instead of punishing the tenants who are causing trouble, it's often easier to rehouse the victims in another area.

Unfortunately, this makes the victims suffer twice over and gives the perpetrators exactly what they wanted in the first place.

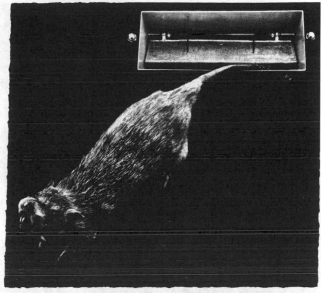

It is clear to see that this is quite wrong.

At the Commission for Racial Equality we believe much more could be done.

Since we were set up by the 1976 Race Relations Act we've been working to end all racial harassment and discrimination.

In our experience we've found that the best way to deal with harassment is by a method called the multi-agency approach.

This is when several bodies combine their resources to deal with the problem.

For example, the case of Mr and Mrs Majid, who complained about continued incidents of late night harassment.

The police alerted a victim support group and liaised with the council to find the culprits. A man was prosecuted and promptly evicted from the housing estate.

If this approach was taken all over the country, harassment could be reduced.

There are other ways Local Authorities can help, from providing reinforced letterboxes, and closed circuit TV, to improving the design of housing estates to make them safer.

Victims and witnesses can help too, by reporting every incident. Everywhere (It doesn't just happen on council estates)

Even if the police can do nothing they must at least take note of every racial incident and report it to the Home Office.

If the government is aware of the scale of the problem they may be encouraged to change the law so that racial harassment becomes a specific criminal offence.

We believe it's every person's right to live free of hatred and persecution.

Not just a few people's privilege.

It's something to consider the next time you get up in the morning and go to your letterbox. And discover nothing more threatening than bills, circulars and junk mail.

COMMISSION FOR RACIAL EQUALITY
CRE Communications Section, Elliot House, 10-12 Allington Street, London SW1E 5EH.

Figure 3.5: the funeral of Stephen Lawrence
(Independent/*John Voos;* Independent, *9 August 1993*)

Notes

1 Evidence for the mounting scale of racial harassment was presented in CRE (1981); Home Office (1981); GLC (1984); Runnymede Trust (1986).

2 See Gordon (1990) pp. 8 and 43. This should not be taken as the maximum total. Other attacks may well have gone unreported.

3 See European Parliament (1990) p. 68; BBC Radio 4, *Special Assignment*, 'Racism in Europe', 11 July 1990; *Guardian*, 15 October 1990; and MEP Mr G. Ford's letter to the *Guardian*, 17 October 1990. The Institute of Race Relations (IRR) is undertaking a research project in the mid-1990s on the rise of racism throughout Europe. IRR publish a digest on developments. For an excellent compilation of racism in European countries refer to the IRR *European Race Audit*, which is published bi-monthly. The address of the IRR is given on p.268.

4 Home Affairs Select Committee (1989). Police forces in England and Wales have been required to collect statistics on racial incidents since 1986, and in Scotland since 1987.

5 At the press conference to launch the report and quoted in the *Independent*, 21 December 1989.

6 In June 1991, Peter Lloyd, Parliamentary Under Secretary of State at the Home Office, was reported as telling the House of Commons that 6,459 racially motivated attacks were reported to the police in England and Wales in 1990/1 (*Independent*, 9 June 1991). See also Mayhew *et al.* (1989) and Gordon (1989b).

7 A. Hayes, CRE Chief Executive in his foreword to CRE (1988a) p. 5. The report was based on a national LEA monitoring exercise in 1987 in England, Scotland and Wales. See also Gordon (1990) pp. 14–15 for a list of media reports on racial violence and harassment in schools and on young people on their way to and from school, or outside school.

8 For a fuller discussion of racial incidents in schools see Troyna and Hatcher (1992) (Open University course ED356 Reader 1).

9 The Runnymede Trust's *Multi-Ethnic Britain: facts and trends* (Runnymede Trust, 1994a) contains a useful summary of early 1990s' trends.

4 'RACE', INEQUALITY AND POVERTY

▼ ▬▬▬▬▬▬▬▬▬▬▬▬▬▬▬▬▬▬▬▬▬ ▼

Blackness and poverty are more correlated than they were some years ago. In spite of government concern with racial disadvantage, and the undoubted limited success of positive action and equal opportunities in helping to create a black middle class, the condition of the black poor is deteriorating.

(Amin and Leech, cited in Oppenheim, 1990, p. 79).[1]

Officially, poverty does not exist in Britain. The government does not define a 'poverty line'. It argues that an objective definition is impossible, that any attempt to count the poor is doomed because it will depend on the subjective judgements of experts about what it is to be poor.

(Frayman, 1991a, p. 2)

▲ ▬▬▬▬▬▬▬▬▬▬▬▬▬▬▬▬▬▬▬▬▬ ▲

4.1 Poverty and inequality: the general context

In the autumn of 1990 the Child Poverty Action Group (CPAG) estimated that ten and a half million people – 18.5 per cent of Britain's population, including three million children – were living in poverty.[2] The scale of the problem was confirmed by the Market and Opinion Research Institute (MORI) survey for the 1991 television series *Breadline Britain 1990s* (see *Figure 4.1*).

In December 1990 research conducted for the United Nations International Children's Emergency Fund (UNICEF) and the National Children's Bureau by Professor Jonathan Bradshaw of York University reinforced CPAG findings. Between 1979 and 1987 the number of children whose families earned less than half of the average income increased from 1,620,000 to 3,090,000 – a rise from 12 per cent to 26 per cent of all children.[3]

In 1990 the CPAG concluded that Britain had begun to witness a reversal of a long-term trend: the share of income of the poorer sections of UK society shrank in the 1980s (Oppenheim, 1990, pp. 24–44).[4] According to figures released by the Department of Social Security (DSS) in July 1990, income inequality widened between 1979 and 1988, becoming greater than at any time since the Second World War (Oppenheim, 1990, p. 35; Atkinson, 1990). *Figures 4.2* and *4.3*, analysing DSS figures, confirm the *Breadline Britain* survey findings: more children were living in poorer families and the incomes of the poorest increased the least (DSS, 1990).[5]

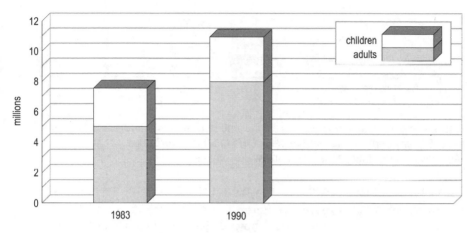

Figure 4.1: numbers in poverty in Great Britain
(Adapted from Frayman, 1991a, p. 9)

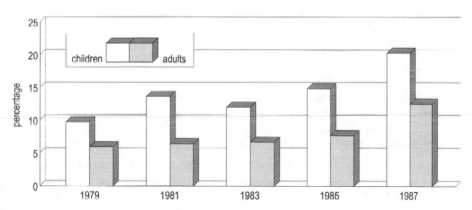

Figure 4.2: percentage of children and adults in Great Britain living in households where income is less than half the national average
(Adapted from the Independent on Sunday, 29 July 1990)

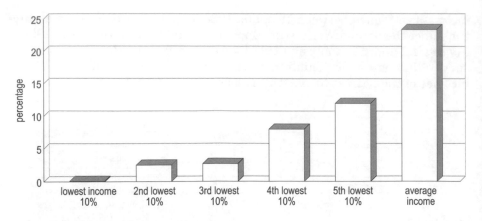

Figure 4.3: percentage increase in real income in Great Britain (discounting inflation), 1978–87, for people in the bottom half of the income distribution
(*Adapted from the* Independent on Sunday, *29 July 1990*)

Other research confirmed the relative impoverishment of the poor:

- In March 1991 research by Peter Townsend, Professor of Social Policy at Bristol University, showed that the incomes of the poorest 20 per cent of the population fell by just under 5 per cent between 1979 and 1989 while the income of the richest percentile increased by 40 per cent (Townsend, 1991).[6]

- In April 1991 the EC found that between 1980 and 1985 the increase in the number of people living in poverty – from 8.2 million to 10.3 million – was greater in the UK than in any other EC country. One in five of all EC residents defined by the EC as poor lives in the UK (*Independent*, 17 May 1991; *Guardian*, 8 April 1991).

- In May 1991 a House of Commons committee estimated that between 1979 and 1988 the number of people with incomes below half the national average grew by 3.7 million to 9.1 million (Social Security Committee, 1991).

- In October 1991 the CPAG reported that 11.8 million people lived in poverty, more than double the figure in 1978 (*Guardian*, 23 October 1991; CPAG, 1991).

Figures 4.4 and *4.5* show the risk of poverty by economic and family status in 1987. Of all single parents – whether in or out of work – nearly half were living in poverty. Children at greatest risk lived in families where there was unemployment (nearly 8 children out of every 10 in unemployed families lived in poverty) or where there was a single parent (6 children in every 10 in single-parent families lived in poverty). In 1987, 1.1 million children living in poverty were found in lone-parent families – 45 per cent of *all* children in poverty. Seventy per cent of children in lone-parent families were living in poverty compared with 13 per cent in two-parent families (Oppenheim, 1990, pp. 29–33).

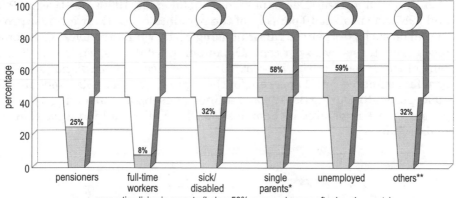

Figure 4.4: risk of poverty in Great Britain, by economic status, 1987
(Adapted from Oppenheim, 1990, p. 30)

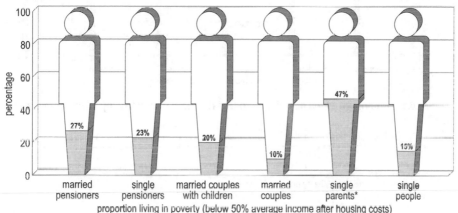

Figure 4.5: risk of poverty in Great Britain, by family status, 1987
(Adapted from Oppenheim, 1990, p. 30)

Figure 4.6 shows the groups most at risk from poverty. The television series *Breadline Britain in the 1990s* found that the two groups most at risk were the unemployed and single parents (Frayman, 1991a, p. 10). *Figures 4.7* and *4.8*, based on data from the Family Expenditure Survey and other government statistics, show the extent to which the skilled members of British society have gained relatively more than the poor during the 1980s.[7]

In September 1990 the government's New Earnings Survey showed that the gap between high- and low-paid employees was wider than at any time since records began in 1886 (Department of Employment, 1990a). Between 1979 and 1987, the poorest 10 per cent of the population saw their incomes grow in real terms by 0.1 per cent after housing costs, whilst the average income rose in real terms by 23 per cent (Oppenheim, 1990, p. 44). In 1987, 70 per cent of the income of the poorest 10 per cent came from social security benefits compared with 17 per cent for the population as a whole (Oppenheim, 1990, pp. 34–6). During the 1980s, 1 million households – involving 3 million people – were registered as homeless, while another million were refused registration.[8]

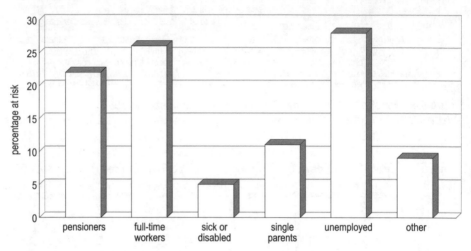

Figure 4.6: percentage of the population in Great Britain in poverty, by vulnerable group, 1987
(Adapted from Oppenheim, 1990, p. 30)

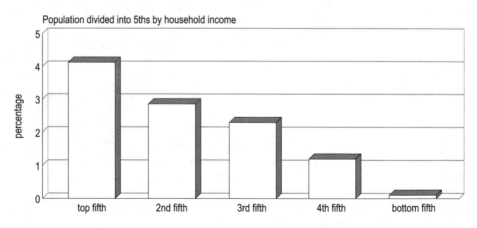

Figure 4.7: real income growth per year in Great Britain, 1977–90

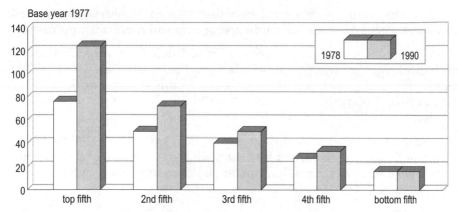

Figure 4.8: real personal disposable income in Great Britain in £millions: population divided into fifths by household income

Child benefit contributes 11 per cent to the incomes of the poorest 10 per cent. It was frozen between 1987 and 1991. During the 1980s, CPAG estimated that while tax allowances had increased in real terms by 25 per cent, the value of child benefit dropped by 8 per cent.[9] The unfreezing of child benefit in the March budget of 1991 did little to recover this real loss of benefit.

In July 1991 the DSS revealed that, in 1990, 27,000 people were refused loans from the Social Fund, the government's safety net for the poor, because they were too poor to repay the loan.[10]

4.2 'Race', poverty and the labour market

Very little empirical work exists *specifically* about 'race' and poverty.[11] The DSS's *Households Below Average Income* and *Low Income Families*, the official data sources for estimating poverty levels in Britain, include no breakdown by 'race' in relation to several indicators which, as our general analysis suggests, are key factors in any measure of poverty.

Between 1987 and 1989 the Labour Force Surveys (LFS) figures showed that the male unemployment rate for minority ethnic groups was 14 per cent, compared with 9 per cent for white people. Thirteen per cent of women in minority ethnic groups were unemployed, compared with 8 per cent of white women (see also Section 10.6) (DoE, 1991).

The young are especially affected. During the same period, 25 per cent of Afro-Caribbean, 16 per cent of Indian and 27 per cent of Pakistani or

Bangladeshi young people aged between 16 and 24 were unemployed, compared with 12 per cent of white people (Oppenheim, 1990, pp.79–80).

When in employment, black people tend to be located in low-pay industries, often involving shift work or intermittent, cyclical work (DoE, 1990b). Black people still tend to work in the manufacturing and manual work for which they were first recruited in the 1950s and 1960s, their job status shaped by immigration policy and vulnerable to recession.[12]

In 1982 the third Policy Studies Institute (PSI) survey revealed that West Indian and Asian men earned less than white men: PSI found that white women earned more than Asian women, but less than West Indian women (Brown, 1984, p. 214).

Table 4.1: weekly earned income for each household member in the 1982 PSI survey: studied groups compared by household type

	Extended households	Lone parents	Others with children	Adults without children
White	£46	£20	£37	£59
West Indian	£37	£24	£32	£51
Asian	£27	£21	£27	£50

(Brown, 1984, p. 231)

Table 4.1 compares the weekly earned income for each household member in the PSI survey in relation to dependency ratios. In extended households and in nuclear families the earned income per person is lower among West Indians than among whites, but is particularly low among Asians.

In 1988, 53 per cent of men from minority ethnic groups were employed in the distribution, hotels and catering sectors where wages are low, compared with 36 per cent of white men (DoE, 1990b). LFS data showed that in the same year 55 per cent of men from minority ethnic groups worked in industries where 30 per cent or more of the workforce earned below £130 per week, compared with 33 per cent of white men.[13] Residential location and segregation also predisposes black people towards unemployment and low pay. At the time of the third PSI survey, 70 per cent of Asians and 81 per cent of Afro-Caribbeans lived in the former metropolitan county areas, mostly in inner city locations, compared with only 31 per cent of white people (Brown, 1984, pp. 54–67). The industrial retreat from the city heartlands during the recession of the early 1980s had a disproportionate effect on opportunities for black people.

4.3 Are black people more at risk?

No government statistics provide breakdowns of benefit claimants by ethnic origin. The third PSI survey found that 34 per cent of white households claimed child benefit compared with 60 per cent of West Indian and 75 per cent of Asian households. Asian extended households were far more reliant on child benefit than white and West Indian households (Brown, 1984, p. 242).

Black people are less likely than white people to claim benefits to which they are entitled. The data are therefore likely to underestimate the number of black people eligible for benefits (see Section 5 on health and Section 6 on social services and welfare benefits).

> Fear of creating problems, concern that any fuss might affect residence, the lack of translated information, and no recognition by the DSS of any responsibility to provide interpreters, have all created a climate in which black citizens are less likely to assert their rights, doubting their entitlement to benefits.
>
> (Oppenheim, 1990, p. 89)

Official data sources fail also to measure the extent to which immigration policy has forced some black people *outside* the welfare net. The 1971 Immigration Act, for example, introduced a rule allowing wives and children of Commonwealth citizens into the UK only if a sponsor could support and accommodate them without recourse to 'public funds'. 'Public funds' – clearly defined in 1985 for the first time – referred to housing benefit, family income supplement (now family credit), supplementary benefit (now income support), and housing under Part III of the Housing Act 1985. Some black people have thus suffered hardship in the struggle to settle in the UK without help from the state. The extension of means-tested benefits under 1988 social security legislation further exacerbated the situation (for example, questions on the date of arrival in the UK have been added to the income support claimant form).

Table 4.2 illustrates how residence conditions can impact on 'race' and poverty by limiting welfare options (Oppenheim, 1990, pp. 84; 89–90). For example, in order to claim child benefit, the claimant must have been in the UK for six months.

Oppenheim's survey also reveals that:

- the age profile of black people is younger than that of whites, making black people more susceptible to freezes in child benefits and cuts in income support;
- Afro-Caribbean families are over three times more likely than white families to be lone-parent families. Lone-parent families are particularly vulnerable to poverty, low pay for women and expensive child-care provision tending to keep lone parents on benefit (Oppenheim, 1990, p. 86).

Child benefit
Present in UK for 6 months

Severe disablement allowance
Residence in the UK for 10 out of the previous 20 years

Invalid care allowance, attendance allowance
Residence in the UK for 26 weeks in the previous 52 weeks

Mobility allowance
Residence in the UK for 52 weeks in the previous 18 months

Non-contributory widows benefit and category C retirement pension
Resident for 10 years in the period 5 July 1948 to 1 November 1970 or date of claim

Category D retirement pension
Resident in the UK for 10 years in the previous 20 years

Note: In addition to a residence test, people generally have to have been in Britain for a period of 6 months before claiming.
(Oppenheim, 1990, p. 90)

Extended families are also more vulnerable. PSI found that 17 per cent of West Indian people and 22 per cent of Asian people lived in households with more than three adults, compared with 6 per cent of white people (Brown, 1984, p. 45; see also Section 1 on demographic trends).

Changes in taxation can also have a disproportionate effect on black households, especially large ones. For example, at the time of the introduction of the Community Charge, 75 per cent of families with three adults or more were estimated by the government to lose out compared to only 25 per cent who gained.[14]

Oppenheim concludes:

> Every indicator of poverty shows that black people and other ethnic minority groups are more at risk of high unemployment, low pay, shift work and poor social security rights. Their poverty is caused by immigration policies which have often excluded people from abroad from access to welfare, employment patterns which have marginalised black people and other ethnic groups into low paid manual work, direct and indirect discrimination in social security and the broader experience of racism in society as a whole.

> (Oppenheim, 1990, p. 91)

4.4 Developments since 1992

A range of Government reports and data have confirmed a growth in UK poverty in the 1990s (see Chapter 5 of all the *Social Trends 22–25* from 1992 to 1995). Independent research has also begun to demonstrate more fully the relationship between poverty and 'race' – emphasizing the disproportionate disadvantages falling on minority ethnic groups in UK society. Carey Oppenheim, updating her seminal book on poverty in Britain, *Poverty: the facts*, concludes:

> every indicator of poverty shows that black people and other ethnic minority groups are more at risk of high unemployment, low pay, poor conditions at work and diminished social security rights.

(Oppenheim, 1993, p. 130)

In 1992 the Low Pay Unit estimated that over a third of the population lived in poverty (Low Pay Unit, 1992; *Independent*, 31 March 1992) and that the gap between the highest and lowest paid was greater than in 1909 when Winston Churchill called poverty 'a serious national evil' (*Independent*, 16 February 1993).

In 1992 the Runnymede Trust and the CPAG examined the relationship between 'race' and poverty, and showed how black people could fall into an 'underclass', experiencing the lowest incomes and worst poverty in what the authors called 'vicious circles of cause and effect' (Amin and Oppenheim, 1992; Runnymede Trust, 1992c, p. 5). 'Race' and poverty were, they concluded, 'intimately connected with unemployment, low pay, industrial structure and racism' (Amin and Oppenheim, 1992, p. 20).

The June 1993 Government report on Households Below Average Income (HBAV) showed that the poorest 10 per cent of British people suffered real falls in their income between 1979 and 1992 (DSS, 1993a). While average household income rose by 36 per cent during this period, the bottom 10 per cent saw incomes fall by between 1 per cent and 14 per cent (*Independent on Sunday*, 4 July 1993).

In August 1993, the Government admitted that since the General Election of April 1992, numbers living in poverty had risen sharply (*Guardian*, 27 August 1993). According to Government data, 2.5 million people became dependent on income support between 1990 and 1992. In 1993, 10 million people were income support dependent (*Guardian*, 20 July 1993; *Independent*, 27 August 1993).

OECD research revealed that a quarter of Europe's poor lived in Britain in 1993 (over 12 million out of Europe's 50 million living in poverty). In 1993, the UK remained the only country in Europe without legal pay protection for its poorest workers (Channel 4, *Cutting Edge*, 15 February 1993).

In September 1993, Jane Miller, reader in social policy at the University of Bath, reported that a quarter of Britons lived in poverty. Four million children were poor compared with 1.4 million in 1979. Numbers of people with incomes below the level of supplementary benefit rose by nearly a fifth between 1979 and 1992. Miller emphasized the extent to which Afro-Caribbean groups were especially vulnerable because of their disproportionate distribution in lone-parent families (*Independent*, 1 September 1993). Amin and Oppenheim have observed: 'it may well be that Afro-Caribbean lone parents who are likely to be poorer in general and more likely to be single will find themselves at the very bottom of an already poor pile' (Amin and Oppenheim, 1992, p. 97).

Government statistics in 1993 revealed a sharp rise in the numbers of people claiming income support (the main benefit for persons aged 18 and over). Ten per cent of Britons – 5.6 million people – claimed income support, a rise from 4.1 million in 1989. One in three UK households received at least one means-tested benefit in 1995, while more than one in four were dependent on means-tested benefits as the major source of their income (*Independent*, 9 August 1995).

Nearly a half of those claiming income support were unemployed, a sixth were lone parents, while 1.5 million children lived with parents on income support. The data were not analysed by ethnicity, but the CPAG and the Runnymede Trust maintain black and Asian groups to be over-represented among support claimants (DSS, 1993b).

HBAV data in 1994 revealed the full extent to which children were living in poverty, rising from 3.9 million to 4.1 million since 1990/91 (DSS, 1994; Runnymede Trust, 1995c). Government figures showed that one in three children in London received a school meal in 1994 – a rise of 60 per cent on the 1991 data (*Observer*, 2 January 1994; *Independent*, 1 February 1994). In 1995, HBAV data revealed that the income of the bottom of 10 per cent of the population had fallen by 17 per cent since 1979 (DSS, 1995).[15]

Barnardos' research pointed to the worrying evidence of deteriorating social conditions among children and people at home at a time when income difference in Britain widened on an 'unprecedented scale'. The number of children under 4 receiving serious injuries doubled, child protection registers quadrupled, while among older children, the suicide rate increased by 70 per cent, in the ten years 1984–94 (Barnardos, 1994; *Independent*, 17 July 1994). Paul Goggings of the Church Action on Poverty commented:

> Poverty has increased remorselessly, reaching utterly scandalous levels. Yet we still have no indication of regret or remorse from the Government, nor any signs of a plan to reconstruct those who are systematically cut adrift from mainstream society.

> (*Independent*, 15 July 1994)

In 1994, the Institute for Fiscal Studies and the Joseph Rowntree Foundation reported that the poorest 10 per cent of the British population were no better off than in 1967. The authors found that among this 10 per cent was a 'new poor', many of whom were recession-hit owner-occupiers (Goodman and Webb, 1994; *Independent*, 3 June 1994; *Guardian*, 5 March 1994). Swansea University research showed that between 1979 and 1991, the poorest sixth of the population saw their income fall in absolute terms. These reports testified to the vulnerability of minority ethnic groups, especially highlighting the plight of the long-term unemployed minority employees who were falling into poverty in increasing numbers (Department of Economics, Swansea University, 1994).

In May 1994, the Department of the Environment published its *Index of Local Conditions*: an analysis based on 1991 census data. The report produced league tables of local authority districts of England which show the most deprived enumeration districts (ED) in the country. The Government used six indicators including poor housing and overcrowding, at ED level, to produce tabulations showing multiple deprivation. The Runnymede Trust's report on multi-ethnic Britain (Runnymede Trust, 1994a) used Department of Environment analysis of the 40 most deprived districts to demonstrate the degree, extent and intensity of deprivation in areas with relatively high black and Asian populations (Runnymede Trust, 1994a, p. 35).

Modood's policy statement for the Institute for Public Policy Report (IPPR) emphasizes, however, just how close too are the levels of multiple deprivation experienced by white groups, and reaffirms the necessity for wide-ranging needs and class-based programmes to reduce levels of multiple deprivation in such districts:

> Colour is a factor in the total analysis of social disadvantage and inability to achieve full citizenship, but it is a weak indicator of need over and beyond the elimination of discrimination, for while some non-white groups may have more members in need of assistance, others may have less, and the needs in question will not always be based on race but will sometimes be identical to those of white people ... some aspects of racial disadvantage can only be tackled within wide-ranging needs-based or class-based programmes.

> (Modood, 1994, p. 16)

In February 1995, the Joseph Rowntree Foundation (JRF) published a detailed report on British poverty which highlighted the significant levels of poverty experienced by minority ethnic groups. The report's inquiry team included both the leader of the CBI and the General Secretary of the TUC. The report did not just testify to the increasing extent of the poverty divide, the widest since 1945, but to the escalating growth of the gap especially in the past decade. Inequality was, the report concluded, widening further in the UK than in almost any other comparable country to the point where the bottom 20 to 30 per cent have failed to benefit from the rising prosperity of the years of Conservative hegemony.

The report recommended that substantial investments be made to re-integrate excluded minorities into work and society. These included new benefit strategies which would rise faster than inflation when living standards were generally increasing; without such measures 'millions of people have no stake in future prosperity' (*Independent*, 10 February 1995; Joseph Rowntree Foundation, 1995). There was, the JRF concluded, no sign that a trickle-down effect had occurred. Inequalities had sharply increased since 1979 (Joseph Rowntree Foundation, 1995; *Independent*, 10 February 1995).

The JRF research crucially examined the relationship between 'race' and poverty (see *Figure 4.9*). The information is only available for 1990, before the 1990s' recession.

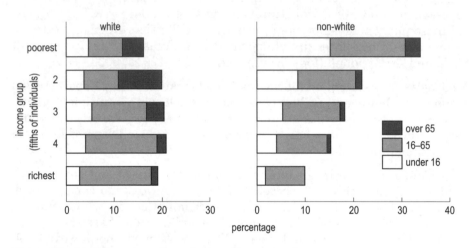

The non-white population has a much higher probability of low incomes than the white population

Figure 4.9: ethnic group and age, by income group
(Runnymede Trust, 1995c; adapted from: Joseph Rowntree Foundation, 1995; Independent, *10 February 1995)*

'We are particularly concerned', the JRF inquiry states, 'at what is happening to the non-white population'. In 1990, only 18 per cent of the 'white' population was in the poorest fifth of the population compared with one in three of the 'non-white' population. The JRF reported 'alarming' disparities between ethnic groups in terms of young people without qualifications, where people of Pakistani and Bangladeshi origins were most disadvantaged, and pointed to disproportionate levels of unemployment for particular minority groups (impacting worst of all on people of Pakistani origin). The report highlighted the plight of minority group women, for whom the poverty gap was felt to be even greater: 66 per cent of white women were in work in 1988–90, but only 48 per cent of all minority ethnic women, and 16 per cent of those of Pakistani origin.

Another JRF report documented further the extent to which Afro-Caribbean single-parent families were susceptible to poverty (Utting, 1995). Utting demonstrated how the proportion of income paid in tax and national insurance by couples with two children had increased, while housing policy had further helped to create 'ghettos' of poor and vulnerable children. Utting called for changes in taxation, housing, employment and benefit policies to assist this 'new underclass' (*Independent on Sunday*, 26 February 1995; Utting, 1995). Gordon and Forrest's work on 1991 census data exploring spatial dimensions of inequality showed that there were very few black and minority ethnic group people living in Britain's richest districts, whereas what the poorest districts had in common were the extremely high levels of black and minority ethnic group residents (Gordon and Forrest, 1995).

The Government's decision to abolish Wages Councils in 1993 has had detrimental effects on the extent of poverty, especially on areas traditionally associated with minority ethnic group employment. A 1994 survey of 48 Citizens Advice Bureaux (CAB) in London showed that pay for many of those in work, especially minority ethnic group 'twilight' workers, had fallen by £1 an hour during a four-month period in the year. The CAB report showed how, since the abolition of Wages Councils in 1993, arbitrary very low pay awards in local areas and severe cuts in pay (rather than rises) had occurred (Citizens Advice Bureaux, 1994). The Wages Councils enforced minimum rates of pay for 2.5 million workers but CAB research, and that by the Low Pay Network (LPN), has shown how, for hundreds of thousands of already low-paid jobs, pay has been depressed. Standards of pay for those in employment have fallen sharply since the Conservatives came to power in 1979, from just under half the national average in 1979 to one third in 1994 (*Guardian*, 1 June 1994).

Research by the LPN found that one third of jobs formerly covered by Wages Councils were paying less than the rates the Councils would have set (Low Pay Network, 1994). Moreover, the LPN found that 27,000 jobs had been lost in the hotel and catering sector since Wages Council abolition. This is a key sector for minority ethnic group employment, where they are nearly twice as likely to be employed (Abercrombie *et al.*, 1994). The LPN survey covered 5,918 jobs advertised in 128 Job Centres around the country. The extent of underpayment was highest in the North, the North West, Yorkshire and Humberside, and lowest in East Anglia and the South East (Low Pay Network, 1994; *Independent*, 30 August 1994).

PSI research revealed the extent to which unemployment and poverty in Britain's deprived urban areas deteriorated between 1984 and 1994. The study of 36 inner city areas showed a higher mortality rate for areas of multiple deprivation (*Independent*, 21 November 1994).

The widening gap between rich and poor has gathered political momentum (and controversy) in the 1990s. In his Christmas message of 1994, the Archbishop of Canterbury, Dr George Carey, referred to 'deep pits of darkness, hundreds of thousands officially classified as homeless, the yawning gap between the poorest sections of society and the rest of us' (*Guardian*, 27 December 1994). In February 1995 a leaked report by Whitehall civil servants blamed the Government for creating 'islands of poverty' in Britain. Sir Robin Butler, the Cabinet Secretary, was widely quoted as admitting to the rise in UK poverty: 'it was clearly not arguable that the number of poor people was increasing, even if it was not certain that in absolute terms the poor were getting poorer' (*Sunday Telegraph*, 12 February 1995; *Today*, 13 February 1995; *Independent*, 13 February 1995).

The following month, Prime Minister John Major announced that he would not be attending a United Nations summit that would oblige the Government to draw up an anti-poverty strategy for 1996, the International Year of Poverty Eradication (*Independent*, 13 February 1995). Peter Townsend, a renowned expert on British poverty, raised doubts about the Government's commitment to tackle the extent and scale of British poverty (*Independent*, 10 March 1995; *Guardian*, 10 March 1995). Townsend accused the Government of 'abdicating its responsibility to the poor'. He concluded:

> Conditions among the poorest people in Britain are desperate and getting worse. We have to recognise humbly that we have to put right the problems in our own backyard if we are to acquire any authority to tell the Third World how they should behave in Government.
>
> (Peter Townsend, quoted in the *Independent*, 10 March 1995)

In 1995, Save the Children Fund disclosed that an unprecedented 10 per cent of its work world-wide was now confined to the UK where it was using its expertise to fight increasing levels of poverty (*Independent*, 13 March 1995). Later that spring, Teesside announced the first full-scale attempt by a local authority to introduce free school breakfasts to counteract poverty and poor health (*Guardian*, 31 March 1994).

Notes

1   Readers should note that this section is particularly related to the sections on demographic trends, immigration, health, welfare and the labour market.

2   What is poverty? In their 1990 analysis, CPAG used the two most commonly accepted definitions: (a) people on 50 per cent of average income, (b) people with incomes at supplementary benefit level. In addition, CPAG took account of people living just above each of these poverty lines. CPAG

described anyone living on between 100 and 140 per cent of supplementary benefit or between 50 and 60 per cent of average income as living on 'the margins of poverty' (Oppenheim, 1990, p. 18). The 10.5 million figure relates to (a) above – the official EC poverty line – and was arrived at after deducting for housing costs (see Atkinson, 1990). See also Frayman (1991a) where the definition of poverty was based on people lacking 'life necessities' (e.g. domestic heating, essential clothing, two meals a day, savings, etc.) For a fuller analysis of CPAG's findings see Frayman (1991b).

3   See Bradshaw (1990). The television series *Breadline Britain*, transmitted in 1991 by London Weekend Television, revealed that 11 million people in Britain were living in poverty. The series' previous survey, in 1983, showed 3.5 million to be living in poverty.

Note that the statistics referred to here are snapshots – they do not show the length of time people are living in poverty. The people living on or below supplementary benefit or 50 per cent of average income in 1987 may be different people from those living on those levels in 1979.

4   We are greatly indebted to Carey Oppenheim's invaluable work which has framed much of this analysis.

5   Reproduced in *Independent on Sunday*, 19 July 1990.

6   This was the first publication of a unit established because of concern about the use of statistics by government. See also Statistical Monitoring Unit (1991).

7   Figures 4.7 and 4.8 are drawn from P. Ormerod and E. Salama, 'The rise of the British underclass', *Independent*, 19 June 1990.

8   See Malcolm Dean, 'The poor state of Major's nation', *Guardian*, 5 December 1990.

9   See DSS (1990) table G1 and annex 1 table G1. See also *Independent*, 29 October 1988.

10   See *Independent*, 18 July 1991.

11   DSS (1990; 1988). A wealth of official statistical sources on poverty were lost during the 1980s. For example, the Royal Commission on Income and Wealth and the Supplementary Benefit Commission, which regularly published information, were abolished.

12   See Brown (1984) pp. 185–227. The *New Earnings Survey*, Department of Employment, does not provide breakdowns by 'race' or ethnic origin. Much of what we know about 'race' and income is reliant on independent research. See, for example, West Midlands Low Pay Unit (1988).

13   See Oppenheim (1990) p. 81. The figures combine data from the New Earnings Survey, 1988 (DoE, 1989) with the LFS.

14   Department of Employment press release, 15 February 1988, Table 10.

15   HBAV data still do not record ethnic background. From 1995/96 more minority ethnic group data will be available on 'race' and poverty when the Department of Social Security publishes its annual Family Resources Survey.

5 'RACE' AND HEALTH

It is clear that the ... services of Britain have been slow to accommodate to the changing needs of an increasing multi-ethnic and multicultural society. Many of the 'problems' and needs identified 10 or 20 years ago are still key issues awaiting resolution ... there is still a long way to go before the 'caring institutions' can be said to care equally for all irrespective of racial or ethnic origins – and in the meanwhile all the pressure that can be brought to bear is required.

(Johnson, 1987, p. 133)

5.1 'Race' and health data

The general problem of data availability is particularly acute in the area of inequality in health and the health service:

> Another important dimension to inequality in contemporary Britain is race. Immigrants to this country from the so-called New Commonwealth, whose ethnic identity is clearly visible in the colour of their skin, are known to experience greater difficulties finding work and adequate housing ... Given these disabilities it is to be expected that they might also record rather higher than average rates of mortality and morbidity. This hypothesis is difficult to test from official statistics, since 'race' has rarely been assessed in official censuses and surveys.
>
> (Townsend and Davidson, 1982, p. 58)

5.2 'Race', morbidity and mortality

Section 4 traced the links between 'race' and poverty, particularly in childhood. The 1990 Child Poverty Action Group (CPAG) survey also revealed the significant relationship which exists between material deprivation and ill health (Oppenheim, 1990, pp. 58-61). Research into poor health and premature death has long pointed to the deleterious effect that adverse socio-economic conditions have on the health of children of all ages: more recently evidence of differential health related to 'race' has emerged (see, for example, Townsend and Davidson, 1982, p. 58; Whitehead, 1987). In 1990 a study of 593 children admitted to an East London hospital – mostly suffering from respiratory tract infections and gastroenteritis – found that minority ethnic group children were disproportionately represented: 48 per cent came from families whose head of household was Asian, African or Caribbean, though these groups accounted for only 18 per cent of the population in Hackney and 11 per cent in Tower Hamlets. The authors concluded that good health was more likely to be facilitated by improving housing conditions and ameliorating poverty than by improving hospital and medical services (Carter et al., 1990). The British Medical Journal, reappraising the Black Report ten years on, reaffirmed the strong relationships that exist between health and class divisions in British society: it concluded that the evidence from studies of differential mortality 'reiterates the fact that British society is stratified to a fine grain from top to bottom' (Davy Smith et al., 1990).

Office of Population Censuses and Surveys (OPCS) figures examining infant mortality by mother's country of birth from 1982 to 1985 show that while mortality for immigrant mothers from India, Bangladesh and East Africa corresponds to the indigenous-born population, the infant mortality rate for children born to mothers from Pakistan and the Caribbean is considerably higher (see Figure 5.1).

All immigrant groups showed excess perinatal and neonatal mortality over the indigenous population, but after the first month of life mortality was only raised for Caribbeans and Pakistanis. Caribbeans and Pakistanis were thus the only immigrant groups to reveal excess mortality throughout infancy (Britton, 1989, pp. 21–2). Looking at infant mortality trends from 1975 to 1984, the Radical Statistics Race Group (RSRG) study observed that:

- rates have been consistently higher for mothers born in the New Commonwealth and Pakistan (NCWP) than for those born in the UK;

- rates were falling faster for mothers born in the UK than for mothers born in the NCWP;

- mothers born in India and Bangladesh revealed a considerable recent reduction in rates.

From this they concluded that there are 'considerable disparities in health experience between white and black populations as a whole at and around childbirth' (Bhat et al., 1988, pp. 180–1).

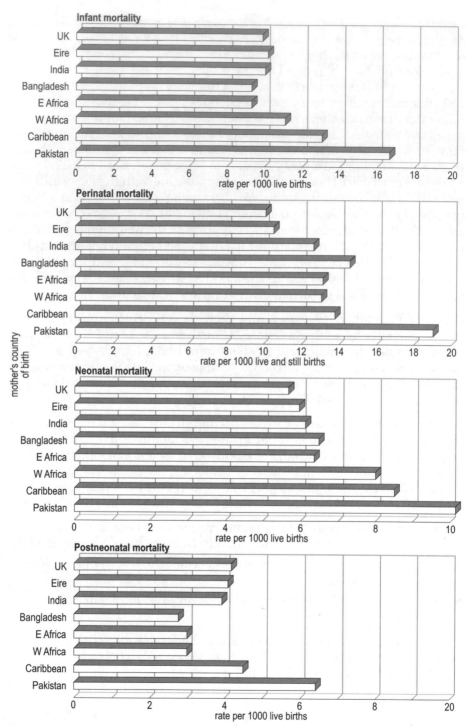

Figure 5.1: infant, perinatal, neonatal and postneonatal mortality rates, by mother's country of birth, 1982–5, England and Wales
(Adapted from Britton, 1989, p. 21)

Britton's study for the OPCS in 1989 concluded:

> Throughout infancy Asian infants, and Pakistanis in particular, showed raised mortality from *congenital anomalies*. This was combined with higher levels of mortality from *perinatal conditions* in the perinatal period. On the other hand *sudden infant deaths* and deaths from *respiratory diseases* occurred at a lower rate for most Asian infants. For West African and Caribbean infants congenital anomalies were not the major causes of death; instead they experienced relatively high mortality throughout infancy from perinatal conditions. The Caribbeans had a rate of sudden infant death roughly similar to the level for the UK group.
>
> (Britton, 1989, p. 22)

Research has highlighted other differences surrounding childbirth. For example, maternal mortality rates are relatively higher among those women born in Africa, the Caribbean and the Indian subcontinent. Department of Health and Social Security (DHSS) findings published in 1982 into maternal deaths in England and Wales for the periods 1970–2, 1973–5, and 1976–8 show maternal death rates from obstetric causes to be 0.32 per 1,000 live births for women born in NCWP compared with 0.11 for other women.[1]

5.3 Ill-health specific to minority ethnic groups

Sickle cell disease (mainly affecting Afro-Caribbeans) and rickets (mostly affecting Asians) are the two conditions differentially affecting the black British population which have received most attention.[2] Other work has pointed to:

- birthweight differentials between the white and black populations;
- anaemias other than sickle cell;
- tuberculosis, now of rising concern among the homeless (see Section 7.6);
- health problems caused by the long-acting contraceptive Depo-provera, disproportionately prescribed to black women;
- the low take-up of antenatal and postnatal care services by black people (see Community Relations Commission, 1977; Torkington, 1983; Darbyshire, 1983).

5.4 Mental health: admissions, diagnosis and treatment

The relationship between 'race' and mental health is an issue of increasing concern to black people and to some psychiatrists in Britain.

In 1989 an article in *Psychiatry Bulletin* argued that the question of 'race' was not simply another discrete demographic factor that could be understood within a medical theory of cause and effect, but one that touched on and reawakened doubts about psychiatry's function and role within society (Frances *et al.*, 1989, p. 482).

The reasons for this anxiety have a long history.[3] Measures used to indicate the psychiatric state of Britain's black population are problematic. Statistical evidence is disparate. National Health Service (NHS) and official statistics, such as the Hospital In-Patient Mental Health Inquiry, do not give data on ethnic origin. Moreover, many of the early independent research studies tended to rely on country of birth as a measure of ethnicity, and thus were unable to identify British-born black people.[4] This early evidence suggested, once age and gender factors had been taken into account, that admission rates for Afro-Caribbean-born males and females were significantly higher than for the British-born population, and that admission rates for Indian, African and Pakistani women may also be greater than for other women (Dean *et al.*, 1981; Hitch, 1981).

Once admitted to hospital, black people appear to experience different diagnoses from whites. Cochrane found that Afro-Caribbeans were far more likely to be diagnosed as schizophrenic, the rate per 100,000 being 290 compared to 87 for those born in England and Wales (Cochrane, 1977). Dean *et al.* (1981) argued that, once age differences had been taken into account, Indian males were three times more likely to be diagnosed as schizophrenic, and Afro-Caribbean males and females five times more likely to be so diagnosed than UK-born first admissions.

Further research by Littlewood and Lipsedge (1988), in a six-year study in inner London, showed that people born in Britain to Afro-Caribbean parents were three times as likely to be admitted to hospital as diagnosed schizophrenics as other black people, and 12 times more likely than white Britons. In a 1989 BBC *Horizon* documentary, Glynn Harrison, a Nottingham psychiatrist, reported that the rate of diagnosed schizophrenia was 16 times higher for British-born blacks aged 16–19 than for British-born whites in the same age cohort.[5] Two reviews of the evidence collected in the 1960s and 1970s concluded that mental illness among minority ethnic groups revealed more diagnosed psychosis, but an under-representation of psychoneuroses and non-psychotic disorders (Ineichen, 1980; Rack, 1982).

Ineichen's research in four inner-city wards in Bristol illustrated how black people, especially Afro-Caribbeans, were more likely to come to hospital on a compulsory admission (Ineichen *et al.*, 1984, pp. 600–11; Ineichen, 1986). Looking at Bradford first-time admissions, Hitch and Clegg (1980) found that across all admissions, people born in the New Commonwealth were up to four times more likely than white patients to reach hospital on the basis of police or social worker referral.

Rwgellera's research in London reported that significantly fewer black patients were referred by a General Practitioner than 'English' ones (Rwgellera, 1977, pp. 317–29; 1980, pp. 428–32). Pinto (1970), looking at admissions under the 1959 Mental Health Act, argued that black patients were twice as likely as white patients to be admitted under Section 136, and twice as likely as whites to have been admitted to hospital from prison – a finding substantiated by the research of Littlewood and Lipsedge (1982). In a three-year study of police referrals under Section 136 of the Mental Health (Amendment) Act 1983, MIND reported a disproportionate number of Afro-Caribbeans among all police referrals, and criticized the police for displaying 'inherent racism'.[6] Lipsedge argued that a black person diagnosed as mentally ill and arrested by the police was far more likely than a white counterpart to be imprisoned rather than admitted to hospital.[7] A study in Birmingham estimated that young people born in Britain to West Indian parents were 25 times more likely to be placed by courts into psychiatric care than their white counterparts. The researchers also claimed that British-born black women were 13 times more likely to be diagnosed as schizophrenic than white women.[8]

Research into psychiatric treatment suggests black people tend to receive harsher forms of medication than equivalent white groups (Littlewood and Cross, 1980, pp. 194–201; Bolton, 1984, pp. 77–84). During the mid-1980s, Rosemarie Cope found that Afro-Caribbeans are more likely to receive treatment in secure facilities (Cope, 1989, pp. 343–5). Moreover, black patients are more likely to receive electro-convulsive therapy (ECT) treatments than whites. Littlewood and Cross's research in an East London hospital found that the majority of patients given ECT were diagnosed as depressives, but that 39 per cent of black patients receiving ECT had *not* been diagnosed as depressed, compared with only 16 per cent of white patients receiving ECT. The administration of anti-depressant drugs to black women in particular (especially Afro Caribbeans) has also been a recurring feature in mental health research and 'race' (Littlewood and Cross, 1980, pp. 194–201; Bryan *et al.*, 1985).

5.5 Racial inequalities in the NHS: doctors, nurses and ancillary staff

During the 1980s research pointed to racial inequalities in NHS employment patterns, from consultant doctors to ancillary workers. Yasmin Alibhai revealed that in 1988 there were then only two Caribbean psychiatrists working in British mental hospitals (Alibhai, 1988, pp. 2–3). In 1980 a Policy Studies Institute (PSI) survey of 2,000 doctors found that 45 per cent of UK-born doctors were consultants, compared with only 9 per cent of Asian-born doctors (Smith, 1980). In 1985 DHSS figures showed that while overseas-born doctors formed 28 per cent of all hospital doctors, they were confined to the lower professional ranks. Where they had reached a higher job status, they were confined to the less popular branches of the profession (DHSS, 1986). In 1987, in a study which extended PSI analysis to British-born black doctors and overseas-born doctors trained in Britain, the Commission for Racial Equality (CRE) reported that racial inequalities among NHS doctors still confined minority ethnic group doctors to less popular and low status jobs, for example, in geriatrics and psychiatry. Doctors from minority ethnic groups suffered from poor training, lower promotion prospects and low pay. The research also showed that among doctors born overseas, nearly a third had to make more than ten applications before getting a job. The CRE study also reported that half of 'non-white' doctors and 40 per cent of their white colleagues believed there was racial discrimination in the NHS (CRE, 1987b). The then chair of the CRE, Sir Peter Newsam, observed:

> The commission is particularly concerned about the similar trend which seems to be developing among wholly British trained ethnic minority doctors. The research gives no ground for believing that this group will escape the discrimination that overseas doctors have experienced.

> (*Guardian*, 29 January 1987)

Discrimination also extended to selection for medical education. In February 1988 the CRE's formal investigation into St George's Hospital Medical School found that the school had directly discriminated on racial grounds, contrary to the Race Relations Act 1976, through the operation of its admissions computer program and in its candidate selection process (CRE, 1988c).[9]

Nurses are the largest category of NHS employees. A study of overseas nurses in Britain in 1971 showed that one in ten NHS hospital nurses were 'immigrant' and that 'immigrants' formed 20 per cent of pupil nurses, 15 per cent of midwives, and 14 per cent of student nurses. 'Immigrants' were, however, under-represented in senior nursing career grades (Thomas and Williams, 1972).[10] Minority ethnic group nurses, like doctors, are more likely to be found in particular specialities, such as geriatrics and mental health and other less popular career grades, for which lower academic standards have been set. Hicks' (1982) study for the *Nursing Times* found that overseas recruits were pressured into State Enrolled Nurse (SEN) rather than the higher status State Registered Nurse (SRN) training, and that black nurses encountered promotion difficulties.

Black people are also concentrated in NHS ancillary jobs, for example, in domestic, catering and cleaning and maintenance services. Doyal *et al.*'s (1980) study of migrant workers in a London hospital found that 78 per cent of its ancillary and maintenance staff were born overseas. In 1983 the CRE commented:

> the hospital service is as vulnerable to unlawful racial discrimination as other employing groups and specific cases of discrimination have taken place. Nevertheless, employing authorities do not seem to realise that racial discrimination can still take place in organisations which employ substantial numbers of ethnic minority staff.

(CRE, 1983b, pp. 14–15)

Despite progress since then, the report of the Equal Opportunities Task Force 1986–90, published in March 1991, pointed to 'glaring' racial inequalities in the NHS and called on the NHS to implement equal opportunity policies. The task force found that while most health authorities had set up equal opportunity policies, relatively few had translated their policies into a timetabled programme for action, or had allocated responsibilities or sufficient resources. Most had failed to produce data about the ethnic composition of their workforce or monitored the outcome of selection decisions, especially in regard to promotion procedures and outcomes. Few health authorities complied with the recommendations of the CRE code of practice, while equal opportunities had not yet become part of the formal and routine duties of health service managers. The report concluded that action was needed immediately even to maintain the limited progress made during the 1980s, but that the new market-style NHS, effective from April 1991, could not alone be relied upon as the means of achieving racial equality in the NHS.[11]

5.6 Developments since 1992

In 1991, in the first issue of the King's Fund Centre's bulletin, *Share*, Safder Mohammed observed that the NHS response to minority needs:

> has in all but a few cases been either to neglect or to marginalise the needs of their black populations. Such has been the state of neglect … that black people are seen as a problem … responses of the health

service to data have been characterised by a stereotyped view of black people and their health needs. The need for fundamental change is as pressing as it has ever been.

(Mohammed, 1991, p. 1)

Official statistics on health are published several years after the event. Most of the data currently available still refer to the late 1980s and early 1990s, and data on 'race' remain relatively scarce, despite the beginnings of ethnic minority group monitoring and evaluation. It is important to emphasize that the data fail to reflect the full impact of the 1990s' recession on the physical and mental health of minority ethnic group communities.

Baroness Cumberlege, Parliamentary Under Secretary for Health (Lords) with special responsibility for minority ethnic groups, told the House of Commons in 1992: 'We are finding that people with ethnic minority backgrounds do not get the full benefit of NHS services', and this applies at all levels: access and employment, treatment and outcome (*Independent*, 29 December 1992). A CPAG report of 1992 concluded that the Government response to minority health did not:

serve the needs of minority groups well. Instead certain groups will be overlooked; they will remain in the residual percentage while resources are aimed at the majority for which the target is easier to attain. Targets must be set which are directly relevant to minority groups and a strategy drawn up which meets their needs.

(Amin and Oppenheim, 1992)

Nurse training fails minority ethnic groups by providing curricula which rarely address the issues of 'race' (*Nursing Times*, 7 April 1993). The CRE reported that nurses' pay was being held back by 'race' bias and announced an investigation into doctors' career prospects (*The Times*, 17 June 1992). Medical school recruitment data disadvantage minorities. Black people are five times less likely to be accepted for a place than white (*Observer*, 11 April 1993; Runnymede Trust, 1993e). Two further surveys published in 1995 confirmed this worrying trend. Both excluded overseas students from their analyses. The first revealed that, controlling for entry qualifications, white students were five times more likely to gain a medical school place than black and Asian applicants. The study contained a league table of discrimination in the 29 medical schools studied. The second found that having a European surname is an even stronger predictor of gaining a place than a candidate's ethnic origin (Esmail *et al.*, 1995; MacManus *et al.*, 1995; *Guardian*, 24 February 1995; *Independent*, 24 February 1995).

Research has highlighted differential experiences and treatment in the NHS. Asian NHS patients in Bristol told researchers that the NHS made them feel 'like trespassers in someone else's land' (Fenton, 1989). Torkington's research revealed that black people received inferior treatment under the

Mental Health Act (Torkington, 1991), and highlighted poor health provision for minority ethnic elderly people. It emphasized the lack of translation and interpreting services; the low priority for screening for diabetes, health promotion and prevention among minority ethnic group communities; the ignorance among health professionals concerning ethnic diet and naming systems; the relatively low proportions of minority ethnic employees among senior NHS management; and the treatment of black people under the Mental Health Act.

Research has identified stressful and racist NHS working environments for black workers (Grandison, 1992; PSI, 1995); an over-representation of black patients in psychiatric hospitals; and treatment which takes place in cultures which nurture racism (CARF, 1992). There is evidence too that minorities face disadvantage and discrimination in their access to pharmaceutical care (Runnymede Trust, 1994h).

Allegations that the health needs of minorities are being ignored characterized the conclusions to a survey of 157 health districts and fourteen regional health authorities conducted by the Ethnicity Research Centre at Leicester University. The research revealed that the number of ethnic minorities on health boards was falling and there was a particularly sharp decline in members of Afro-Caribbean origin. None of the health authority chairs were of minority ethnic origin, and only two of the 141 members were of ethnic minority origin (1.4 per cent). At district level, of the 157 authorities who responded, only one reported an Asian chair. Thirty-seven (or 2.6 per cent) of the 1,405 members were of minority ethnic origin. The researchers attributed the decline in representation to recent NHS reforms (*Weekly Journal*, 23 September 1993). In April 1993, only seven out of 103 General Medical Council members were 'black' despite black people making up 25 per cent of doctors in Britain's medical profession (*Observer*, 11 April 1993).

Research by the Runnymede Trust reveals that in 1993 of 534 chairs of health authorities and trusts, four (under 1 per cent) were from black and Asian backgrounds (and three were male). Of 1,486 non-executive members, 45 (3 per cent) were from black and Asian backgrounds (Runnymede Trust, 1994a, p. 22).

In 1992, the Government's Chief Medical Officer, Dr Kenneth Calman, launched an action plan designed to meet the health needs of minority ethnic communities. He criticized the Government's repeated failure to introduce ethnic monitoring. Calman's research identified a 36 per cent extra risk of heart disease for men born in the Indian subcontinent and a 46 per cent extra risk for women; a 76 per cent greater risk of suffering a stroke for Caribbean-born men and a 110 per cent greater risk for Caribbean-born women, compared with rates for England and Wales as a whole. He also found that Asian groups had five times the rate of diabetes (Asians under 40 are three times more likely to suffer from coronary disease than the national average) (HMSO, 1992a; *Guardian*, 29 September 1992). De Bono's research for the

British Heart Foundation in Leicester found that Asian patients with heart disease wait longer for treatment after the onset of symptoms than white patients, mainly because of delays in GP referment. Asian men and women who have settled in the UK are up to 40 per cent more likely to die from heart disease than the national average (de Bono *et al.*, 1993).

Research by London and Bradford Universities suggests that the stress resulting from low incomes and poor housing, diet, diabetes and insulin resistance are crucial causal factors in Asian heart disease (*Independent*, 5 January 1994). Research in Leicester on the care of Asian heart patients has demonstrated that Asian patients received inferior coronary care treatment to that received by Europeans. Asian patients were less likely to receive early admission to a coronary unit, and more likely to be admitted late in serious condition. Communication difficulties were partly responsible but GP ignorance of the vulnerability of Asians to diabetes was considered of vital importance (Lear *et al.*, 1994; *Independent*, 5 April 1994).

Communication between the NHS and minority ethnic groups is an issue of concern, especially for those minority group people who have only a limited knowledge of English. Research in 1995 revealed that health advice on smoking, diet and weight is not reaching minority groups. The King's Fund found that the children of women of Pakistani origin are nearly twice as likely to be stillborn or die in the first week of life than those of whites (*Independent*, 23 January 1995).

Analysis of long-term illness (based on findings of the 1991 census) revealed that long-term illness rates are lowest for Chinese men and women, and highest for Bangladeshi men and Pakistani women, with whites occupying a median position (OPCS, 1994b).

From April 1993, ethnic monitoring of all in-patients and day-patients at last began in the NHS. In May 1993 the Royal College of Nursing launched a campaign to persuade more minority ethnic groups to enter the profession at a time when nursing numbers were being cut dramatically (*Weekly Journal*, 8 April 1993). In June 1993, the Government announced an action programme to improve mental health services for minority ethnic groups (*Guardian*, 8 June 1993). The action programme included ensuring that black and Asian employees are fairly represented at all staff levels.

In summer 1993, the Department of Health established an Ethnic Health Unit to meet minority group needs and to provide information to minority communities. In the autumn, Health Secretary Virginia Bottomley declared the issue of equality of treatment for minority groups to be 'the issue of the decade'. Her programme specified that all NHS employers must be able to prove within five years that there is 'equitable representation' among sister grade nurses (*Guardian*, 9 September 1993; *Independent*, 5 January 1994). Such targets, however, have to be considered in the context of resources available: the Department of Health had only allocated £500,000 towards their introduction.

In May 1994, in a considerable U-turn on past neglect, the Government made the very important decision to establish an inter-departmental working group to examine health inequalities in the UK, and address the health needs of minority ethnic groups. For many years the Government had steadfastly refused to recognize links between poverty and ill-health. The announcement came a week after the *British Medical Journal* reported that death rates were rising among people in the 15–44 age group for the first time since the 1930s (*Independent*, 4 May 1994).

People from the Caribbean experience six times the rate of schizophrenia (MIND, 1993). They are more likely to receive inferior mental health care regimes according to a documentary in the series *People First* on Channel 4, in June 1994. The National Schizophrenia Fellowship called for an extra £500 million a year of Government funding to be directed at the mentally ill. Mental health provision has continued to be plagued by resource constraint, while community care support has been subjected to consistent criticism by voluntary and public bodies. There are still over 100 mental health establishments in the UK, with 28,000 beds, with community care places available for a further 90,000 patients a year. The Institute of Psychiatry described the general situation in UK mental health care as 'in crisis' in 1994 (R. Waterhouse, 'Does the community care?', *Independent*, 19 August 1994). The Department of Health revealed that the number of children experiencing serious mental ill-health and admitted to psychiatric hospitals increased by almost 25 per cent from 7,000 in 1986 to a record 8,800 in 1991 (*Independent*, 23 May 1994). In 1995, the Mental Health Foundation (MHF) estimated that a £540 million Government investment in mental health provision was needed. The MHF claimed that 300,000 people, including substantial numbers of minority ethnic group people, were seriously mentally ill but lacked adequate community care (*Independent*, 17 March 1995).

In 1995, the Health Education Authority (HEA) revealed the importance of cultural barriers in exacerbating health disadvantage for minority groups (*Independent on Sunday*, 22 January 1995; *Independent*, 23 January 1995; HEA, 1995). The HEA survey confirmed the findings of a Department of Health study in 1993, which had shown how black minorities were especially vulnerable to mental ill-health and Asian minorities to specific illness, particularly coronary disease and diabetes. The HEA survey, of 3,500 adults in England, confirmed that minorities did not receive health advice because of language and cultural factors and that this had significant implications for their health care, particularly for pre- and post-natal care, the welfare of the elderly, and for preventative medicine. The HEA revealed that black and Asian minorities were more likely than whites to suffer from cervical cancer, and that they were far less likely to make the link between weight and health. The survey was conducted in the context of a greater incidence of disease among black and Asian minorities. The death rate among South Asians was reported to be 40 per cent higher and Afro-Caribbeans were twice as likely to suffer strokes as the general population (*Independent*, 23 January 1995).[12]

Notes

1   'Report on confidential enquiries into maternal deaths in England and Wales', Reports on Health and Social Subjects, DHSS, 1982, quoted in Bhat *et al.* (1988) p. 179.

2   See Tuck (1982); Anionwu *et al.* (1981) p. 283; Goel *et al.* (1976) p. 1141. It is important to note that progress has been made in relation to treatment. For example, in Scotland, particularly the Glasgow area, the incidence of rickets was substantially reduced by the health authorities providing calcium to all Asian parents.

3   For an excellent review of 'race' and mental health see Bhat *et al.* (1988) pp. 194–22. Much of the evidence presented here is taken from their research review. On the shortcomings of official health statistics see Doyal (1979) p. 243.

4   It is important to recognize that what is at issue in much of the data specific to Section 5 is the supposed 'neutrality' of clinical diagnosis. There is evidence which shows that clinical diagnosis in psychiatry is culturally specific. See, for example, Kubie (1971). Research has extended this analysis to linking the relationships between racism and diagnosis, particularly of schizophrenics. See, for example, Cochrane (1977); Carpenter and Brockington (1980); Dean *et al.* (1981); Hitch (1981).

5   BBC 1 *Horizon*, 'Black schizophrenia', transmitted on 13 March 1989. The figures quoted in Harrison's research for Afro-Caribbeans may be distorted by misdiagnosis and double counting, by the small numer of cases studied by Harrison, by poor statistics on the numbers of British blacks, and by relative under-counting of white schizophrenics.

6   See Rogers and Faulkner (1987). There is also disturbing evidence of the mentally ill increasingly being imprisoned. The year ending 31 March 1990 saw a 38 per cent increase in the number of inmates referred to psychiatrists, from 12,285 to 16,937. No ethnically classified data are available on this population.

7   See 'Racism "may be the cause of mental illness in blacks"', *Independent*, 25 January 1990.

8   See 'Mental health study raps "racist" police', *Observer*, 1 January 1987.

9   The St George's Report illustrates the way in which 'liberal' institutions that appear to have a good track record on admissions and training with regards to minority ethnic groups can themselves operate systems which are discriminatory.

10 We have not documented gender differences here, though these are very marked in the NHS.

11 'The work of the Equal Opportunities Task Force 1986–1990: a final report', March 1991, King Edward's Hospital Fund for London, 14 Palace Court, London.

12 *The Ethnic Health Bibliography* (Karmi and McKeigue, 1993), a useful UK guide to contemporary health issues and 'race' research, is available from the North East and North West Thames Regional Health Authority, 40 Eastbourne Terrace, London.

6 'RACE', SOCIAL SERVICES AND WELFARE BENEFITS

▼ ▼

In 1985, an HMSO report summarised the findings of nine DHSS funded studies in a report entitled 'Social Work Decisions in Child Care'. These studies explored the various aspects of the care career process ... It is pertinent to point out that not one of these nine studies focused on the 'race' dimension. This is perhaps also a reflection of the 'colour blind' approach which continues to exist in the personal social services.

(Barn, 1990, p. 229)

▲ ▲

6.1 Social services departments and equal opportunity policies

In 1989 a Commission for Racial Equality (CRE) survey showed that, while limited progress had been made in social services provision, few social services departments appeared to be taking race equality issues any more seriously than they did in 1979. Even among those departments which had committed themselves to promoting equality of opportunity, policy implementation was still embryonic. The CRE concluded that most social service departments were not meeting their duties under Section 71 of the Race Relations Act 1976 – the section requiring local authorities to take steps to tackle racial discrimination and promote equality of opportunity (CRE, 1989a).

The survey of 116 of the 208 social services departments of England, Scotland and Wales (the majority serving the needs of significant minority ethnic group communities) found that only a third of departments had a written equal opportunities policy. Only 10 out of the 70 responding departments had introduced comprehensive ethnic monitoring, 18 had introduced some form of ethnic record-keeping, while in 8 cases such record-keeping applied only to specific control areas such as residential care.

Section 11 funding had been used primarily to appoint bilingual staff as interpreters and translators.[1] The survey revealed that over half of the departments had translated information about service provision into minority ethnic group languages, while 70 per cent used an interpreting service. A third of departments had appointed specialist 'race' advisers.

Some departments had adapted existing services to meet specific needs of minority ethnic groups: 39 had prioritized children in care; 23 had focused on campaigns for finding minority ethnic group foster/adoptive parents; and 17 had issued guidelines on the needs of children in care. However, only 25 per cent of the departments replied that they had written policies on minority ethnic group fostering and adoption. In establishing these priority areas, only 41 per cent of the responding departments indicated that they had consulted minority ethnic groups.

The CRE recommended that departments review their policies in consultation with minority ethnic groups, and introduce a systematic approach to the provision and delivery of services through an effective equal opportunities strategy. Such a strategy would include the recruitment of more minority ethnic group foster and adoptive families to ensure that same-'race' placements are possible in practice.

Alternative practices, such as transracial adoption and minority ethnic group placements, have provoked considerable criticism among minority communities:

> As the proportion of children in care who were black rose, itself indicating the tremendous socio-economic pressures upon the black family and the stigmatising attitudes of many white dominated welfare agencies, the black community came to believe that it was a net donor of its most precious assets to white families. The self-respect and sense of self-determination of the community has been threatened by a situation whereby most of its children in care were growing up either in white families or in white-controlled residential settings.

(Brent Social Services, 1985, pp. 6–7)

6.2   A paradox in client experience?

Evidence suggests that black and minority ethnic groups are under-represented as clients receiving the preventive and supportive elements of social services provision, but over-represented in those aspects of social services activity which involve social control functions and/or institutionalization (Roys, 1988, pp. 209–10). In Birmingham, for example, Duncan found that while Asian communities make up 30 per cent of the population, they comprise only 8 per cent of referrals to social services in an average month (Duncan, 1986, pp. 18–19).[2] A study of the minority ethnic group elderly in Handsworth found that relatively few black elderly people were coming to the notice of social services, while it was a myth to suppose that they were supported by a wide variety of community organizations and the extended family (West Midlands County Council, 1986, p. 48).

6.3 Referrals to care: the evidence

The CRE has persistently reported the disproportionately large number of minority ethnic group children taken into care during the 1980s (see, for example, CRE, 1990a, p. 67). In their 1983 evidence to the House of Commons Social Services Select Committee Inquiry into Children in Care, the CRE revealed the findings of a local study in a northern city which showed strikingly different rates between groups for children in care: 20.16 per 1,000 for white children, 24.32 per 1,000 for Afro-Caribbean children, but 142.24 per 1,000 for children of mixed parentage (CRE, 1983a, p. 4). In another local authority, Arnold found that 54 per cent of its children in care were black, although black children comprised only 47 per cent of the child population, and black people as a whole only 19 per cent of the population of the authority (Arnold, 1982, p. 99).

Barn's case study for *New Community* cited several research studies showing the disproportionate distributions of black children in care, findings which could not be fully explained by demographic factors (Barn, 1990, p. 230). Adams's (1981) study in Lambeth showed that 54 per cent of children in care were black and Wilkinson's (1982) study in Tower Hamlets showed that over 50 per cent of the children in their care were black. Barn's own research into the London Borough of 'Wenford' revealed that black children comprised 52 per cent of the borough's children in care though only 40 per cent of the population.[3] Over half of these children in care were Afro-Caribbean. This over representation of black children in the care of Wenford's Social Services Department occurred in the five years preceding 1987. In contrast to other studies, Barn found that the differences applied when controlling for other factors such as age and gender of the children (Barn, 1990, pp. 237–40).

Barn examined the admission process of child care, comparing the 'care episode' of 294 black and 270 white children. The proportion of black children from single-parent families was 83 per cent, significantly higher than the 64 per cent of white children. Almost all the black children were born in Britain.

Of most interest here were conclusions about reasons for referral. More black children were referred because of family relationships and marital difficulties, financial reasons and material problems, and because of their mother's mental health (see *Table 6.1*); conversely, more white children were referred because of child (delinquent) behaviour and child (sexual) abuse.

Table 6.1: reasons for referrals being made to take children into care, by 'race', in percentages

Reason	Black	White	All
Family relationships	24	21	22
Financial/material circumstances	15	12	13
Parental neglect/inadequacy	21	33	27
Failure to thrive/medical health	1	6	3
Mother's mental health	11	5	8
Mother's ill-health	5	6	5
Homelessness/housing	11	11	11
Suspected child abuse	15	18	16
Child's behaviour	15	26	20
Total	(294)	(270)	(564)

The total refers to overall numbers in care. Actual percentages do not add up to 100 because of the multiplicity of reasons that could be recorded.
(Barn, 1990, p. 234)

Barn found significant differences when she examined the reasons why agencies referred black and white children. The differences are similar to those observed in Section 5.4 in relation to mental hospital referrals. For example, of the black delinquency referrals, 77 per cent came from the police compared with 35 per cent of the white delinquency referrals. In both groups the majority referred by the police were boys.

Barn discovered that children were admitted into care from situations where preventive strategies could have been attempted. Here again she found interesting differences between black and white children: lower proportions of white children were admitted for housing and financial reasons, and, where the reason for referral was mother's mental illness, greater proportions of black children were admitted into care than were actually initially referred. Barn found that black children entered care far more quickly than white children – on average nine months from referral for black children compared with over fifteen for white children. Black boys entered care at twice the rate of white boys. Comparing 'in care' age groups, Barn found that while black children of all age groups were over-represented in care, most of the 'in care' cohort were under the age of five when they entered into care. Barn's study also demonstrated the important role racial stereotypes play in pathologizing black families. It also showed the way in which black children's concerns have been omitted from the literature. Barn explained differences in the referral and admission patterns of black and white children in terms of social workers' perceptions of individual cases set against a context of the disadvantaged position of black families in the areas of housing and employment and the greater likelihood of such families needing social services help (Barn, 1990, pp. 229–45).

6.4 Social services staffing and training

> The recruitment of black social workers often makes only a marginal impact because their effectiveness is curtailed by being co-opted into existing power structures. In winning the battle for individual advancement they lose the war against racism.
>
> (Jervis, 1986, p. 8)

In 1981 concern over the scarcity of qualified black social workers led to the ethnic monitoring of applicants for professional social work courses. In his 1988 review of social services provision for the Radical Statistics and Race Group (RSRG) Report, Roys revealed that preliminary monitoring showed a small rise in successful applicants from minority ethnic groups, from 7.9 per cent in 1981 to 11.8 per cent in 1984 (Bhat *et al.*, 1988, p. 226).

The Central Council for Education and Training in Social Work (CCETSW) has also addressed the curriculum of accredited social work courses. Their document *Teaching Social Work for a Multi-Racial Society* highlighted the inadequacy of much of this provision in relation to 'race' (CCETSW, 1983, pp. 15–20). In 1983, they concluded that the particular needs of the black population are frequently seen as marginal 'and so fail to reach many students, who may well complete their professional education with scarcely any teaching on multi-racial social work' (CCETSW, 1983, p. 22).

6.5 Barriers to benefits

6.5.1 Immigration policy

Caught up in a cycle of poverty (see Section 4), minority ethnic groups have been disadvantaged by immigration legislation in their eligibility for state benefits. Under the 1971 Immigration Act, increasing numbers of people have only been allowed entry into the UK on condition that they have 'no recourse to public funds' (Child Poverty Action Group, 1987, pp. 64–5). Under the 1988 Immigration Act, male Commonwealth citizens already settled in Britain when the 1971 Immigration Act came into force on 1 January 1973, must now prove they can maintain and accommodate their relatives arriving in the UK without having to resort to public funds (Gordon, 1989a, p. 4).

6.5.2 Discrimination in social security

Black and minority ethnic groups have also been disadvantaged by social security legislation. Under the 1980 Social Security Act, specific classes of immigrants were excluded by law from receiving benefits.[4] Under the 1986 Social Security Act, the introduction of a lower rate of benefit for single, childless people aged under 25 years on income support particularly affected those groups susceptible to relatively high rates of youth unemployment, and low parental income (see Sections 4 and 10.6). And the operation of the social fund and the greater emphasis on means-tested benefits potentially increases the risk of differential outcomes for minority ethnic groups through direct or indirect discriminatory practices by welfare staff, or decisions made on mistaken assumptions (CPAG, 1987, p. 67).

People from certain minority ethnic groups, whose first language is not English, often lose benefits because welfare offices cater badly for poor English speakers, according to a 1991 report published by the National Association of Citizens' Advice Bureaux (NACAB). The NACAB report revealed that such claimants can go for months without payment because forms are printed in English only (NACAB, 1991).

Section 4 traced the links between 'race' and poverty. It illustrated how people from minority ethnic groups were more likely to be both in low paid work and more frequently unemployed, especially younger age groups (see also Section 10.6). Such patterns affect their entitlement to all contributory benefits, such as retirement pensions. First-generation migrants may have entered pension schemes later in their working lives, and so do not have enough contributions to qualify for full pension rights (Oppenheim, 1990, pp. 88–91). Brown's (1984) study found that white people were six times more likely than black people to claim retirement or widow's pensions, while higher proportions of Asian and Caribbean people claimed unemployment benefits and family income supplements (see *Table 6.2*).

Table 6.2: support from state benefits, by household type

Percentage of UK households in receipt of:	White	Caribbean	Asian
Child benefit	34	60	75
Unemployment benefit	7	17	16
Family income supplement	1	5	2
Supplementary benefit/Pension	14	20	11
Retirement/Widow's pension	35	6	6

(Brown, 1984, p. 242)

6.6 Developments since 1992

One recurring problem during the 1980s was the reluctance of many local authorities to record the ethnic origin of claimants and children in care, despite pressure from the CRE, and from the social work profession.

In 1992, the Department of Health announced a change in policy. Local authorities were told to record the ethnic origin, following 1991 census definitions, of children in care, but to add a special category for those of mixed-race parentage. Studies had showed disproportionately higher levels of black and Asian children in care, especially those of mixed-race origin. The Department of Health circular observed: 'children whose parents have different ethnic origins need to be identified and considered separately, because patterns of placement and long-term care have been shown to be markedly different from other groups' (MIND, 1993; *Guardian*, 1 July 1992).

Access to benefits continues to be a source of discrimination against minority ethnic groups. The National Association of Citizens Advice Bureaux has identified several barriers to minority ethnic group claimants (NACAB, 1991). These included communication and language barriers, delays in benefit payments, under-claiming of benefits and wrongful refusal of benefits. NACAB recommended the recruitment of translators and interpreters to the welfare benefit system. NACAB research also highlighted restrictions on benefit eligibility for people coming from abroad which further marginalized black and Asian people (Cohen *et al.*, 1992).

Craig's analysis of minority group access to Social Fund payments found that 'racist practice' was an important factor in defining minority group outcomes (Craig, 1989). Asian families often do without benefits altogether, or only claim for the most urgent of children's needs.

The Runnymede Trust in 1994 reported that research into the issues confronting black and Asian children in the care system remained relatively rare, but that analysis of their psychological needs is almost non-existent (Runnymede Trust, 1994g). Coleman's research into children in care living in Southwark where there are large populations of black children, including significant proportions of mixed-race backgrounds, revealed that damaging labels like 'half-breed' and 'mongrel' in relation to mixed-race children compounds their emotional, behavioural, cognitive and play difficulties (Coleman, 1994). She identified four areas where children were most affected. Developmental delay in learning in the first four years of life; social and behavioural difficulties including low self-esteem, apathetic and aggressive behaviour, depression; cognitive difficulties including a fear of failure and poor attention span; and poor organizational and play skills reflected in withdrawal and co-operative play. Coleman regretted the very low numbers of Afro-Caribbean social workers employed by Southwark Social Services. Her work also pays testimony to the vital importance of informal adoption among African-Caribbean kinship networks.

Further research by Barn on children in care included analysis of mixed-race children placed with black and mixed-race families. She found that stereotypically weak family structures were used as labels to justify lack of support service provision for African-Caribbean communities (Barn, 1993). Barn found that black families were much more likely than whites to maintain contact with their children throughout the care and rehabilitation process. Her research suggested that those children placed transracially with white parents were likely to lose contact with the natural parents. She concluded that black and white child carers experience different outcomes, with black children placed at a disadvantage (Barn, 1993; Johnson, 1994).

The National Audit Office (NAO) survey of Family Credit recipients confirmed NACAB's findings. The NAO survey revealed significantly lower take-up amongst minority ethnic group families for 'passported' benefits such as free dental care, eye tests and prescriptions. Only 60 per cent of minority ethnic group credit claimants received help with free prescriptions and 44 per cent help with dental care compared with 74 per cent and 62 per cent of white people (NAO, 1991).

The new system of social security offers no rights to income support for 16–17-year-olds, and a lower rate of income support for single childless people under 25. This system indirectly discriminates against minority ethnic groups according to the CPAG (Amin and Oppenheim, 1992).

The introduction of the Child Support Agency (CSA) in April 1994 has had important implications for black and Asian people. Over half of African–Caribbean, a third of African, and increasing numbers of Asian families are headed by single mothers. Black men have been particularly targeted by the Agency. The CSA machinery is recognized as being oppressive to black people since many parents – widowed, single or divorced – have been forced into identifying absent parents. In many cases black women have stopped claiming income support rather than be forced back into relationships which were violent (Runnymede Trust, 1994h).

Encouragingly, the gap in social work education has been expanded enormously, especially in the 1990s. The CCETSW decided over a decade ago to require all social work courses throughout the UK to prepare students to be competent in addressing 'race' and racism, as a condition for social work qualification. In 1989, CCETSW formal visits to its courses on law, child care and anti-racism in social work revealed uneven coverage of 'race' issues, and echoed the statement made by the Association of Directors of Social Services in 1978, that the development of social services for a multi-racial society was 'ad hoc, patchy and superficial' (Patel, 1994). An improved and sustained approach was subsequently announced by the CCETSW. This included the launch of the Anti-Racist Social Work Education Series which set the context for change by prioritizing 'race', racism, anti-racism and black struggles through a specific focus on social work and black students' views in Britain (CCETSW, 1991a).

A whole range of new curricula – well over fifty publications – with an anti-racist focus, was produced by 1994 covering mental health, learning difficulties, probation and teaching practice. Validating courses included a study of 'race' issues throughout the CCETSW curriculum, ensuring that the analysis of racism was a key part of the Diploma in Social Work established in 1989. Through these historic breakthroughs, the CCETSW became one of the first UK professional organizations to make anti-racism a criterion for validation. Its keystone was *Paper 30*, which outlined the rules for the Diploma in Social Work (CCETSW, 1991b). At the launch of the Diploma, the Health Minister Virginia Bottomley gave the paper her fullest support, going so far as to hail the innovation as 'a major achievement of which we can be justly proud' (CCETSW, 1991c).

However, conflicts in the social work profession have emerged over 'race' awareness training. In August 1993, the British Association of Social Workers (BASW) reaffirmed the importance of 'race' training for the 1990s, despite a sustained attack designed to jettison *Paper 30* (Johnson, 1994).

In 1993, the BASW declared that the Diploma in Social Work should teach that 'the CCETSW believes that racism is endemic in the values, attitudes, and structures of British society, including those of social services and social work education'. In 1993, no more than 15 hours' teaching within a two-year Diploma was devoted to race awareness training, and there were calls for more rather than less information on 'race', 'culture' and 'ethnicity' (*Guardian*, 24 August 1993; Y. Alibhai-Brown, 'Social workers need race training, not hysteria', *Independent*, 11 August 1993). However, in 1993 the Chair of the CCETSW, Jeffrey Greenwood, observed that political correctness was 'nonsense' and that it should be 'rooted out' (*Independent*, 19 November 1993).

In April 1994, the Government announced a planned 'highway code' for social workers and a new national core curriculum for all social work training courses, effectively a U-turn on previous policy statements. Virginia Bottomley told the Conservative Party local government conference: 'Political correctness' is the target, 'gone will be the notorious Paper 30 which tells us that racism is endemic in the values, attitudes and structures of British society' (Runnymede Trust, 1994c). The Government announced its intention to abolish the Black Perspectives Committee, the profession's training committee dealing with black issues (*Community Care*, 4 March 1994; Novak, 1994). The BASW response reaffirmed that the real issue was to make sure that services are appropriate to a multi-racial community (*Guardian*, 21 February 1994).

Naina Patel, the head of the CCETSW's race programme, in a paper presented to a conference on the future of multi-racial Britain, concluded that:

> the defence against unfounded assertions of 'political correctness' undoubtedly influences strategies in the struggle against racism. Furthermore, our experience raises important issues such as the varying abilities of individuals or organisations to manage antiracist change – and, indeed, the need to understand the sources of this variance.

(Patel, 1994, p. 47)

Notes

1   Section 11 funding refers to the section of the Local Government Act 1966 that empowers the Home Secretary to make payments to local authorities 'who in his opinion are required to make special provision in the exercise of any of their functions in consequence of the presence within the areas of substantial numbers of immigrants from the Commonwealth where language or custom differ from those of the community.' See Dorn and Hibbert (1987).

2   We need to be careful about conclusions we draw from this study. Duncan is not saying that Asian referrals *should* constitute 30 per cent of the population.

3   'Wenford' was a fictitious name used to refer to one of London's most economically deprived areas with one of the highest unemployment rates where people in work earned, on average, the lowest income in London. According to the 1981 census, 28 per cent of its residents were of New Commonwealth (NCWP) origin. Barn's 1987 case study encompassed all the components of 'care' – from voluntary care, interim care orders, through to full care orders and wardships (Barn, 1990, pp. 238–9).

4   For a fuller discussion see CPAG (1987) pp. 64–7.

7 'RACE' AND HOUSING

▼ ▬▬▬▬▬▬▬▬▬▬▬▬▬▬▬▬▬▬▬▬▬▬▬ ▼

One of the greatest obstacles to progress in the elimination of racial discrimination is getting white-run housing institutions to acknowledge that racism and racial disadvantage exist. Despite all the evidence, many housing managers, officers and councillors will categorically deny that racial discrimination could exist within their own organisation.

(Phillips, 1989, p. 141)

▲ ▬▬▬▬▬▬▬▬▬▬▬▬▬▬▬▬▬▬▬▬▬▬▬ ▲

7.1 The context: policy, 'race' and housing status

There were significant shifts in state housing policy and tenurial provision in the 1980s (for example, the sale of council houses). There was also a dramatic reduction in government spending on housing. In February 1991, Norman Lamont, the Chancellor of the Exchequer, told Nicholas Ridley (Conservative MP, Cirencester and Tewkesbury) that government spending on housing had fallen by more than one half in real terms since 1979 (*Independent*, 13 February 1991).

In the 1990s Britain's minority ethnic groups live in better housing conditions than they did in the 1950s. Nevertheless, major disparities in housing outcomes still remain, and housing quality remains a problem for many. During the late 1980s and early 1990s, a series of Commission for Racial Equality (CRE) formal reports and investigations across a range of tenures further pointed to the overt and covert processes, practices and procedures, including institutional racism, which help create and sustain differences in minority ethnic group housing outcomes.[1]

This section will focus on some of the more recent evidence for differential housing outcomes for minority ethnic groups within each tenure, explore evidence linking 'race' with homelessness, and report further evidence on racial harassment, particularly as it relates to council tenant eviction (see also Section 3.4).

In 1987, reviewing research into minority ethnic group housing outcomes, Phillips concluded that while the statistics showed an absolute improvement in minority ethnic group housing standards, they also revealed 'a pattern of entrenched housing inequality' (1987, p. 108). For those minority ethnic group households who had acquired decent accommodation, Phillips noted that: 'the fight has been hard won. Success in terms of housing outcome cannot always be equated with equality of treatment. The price of good housing has often been high in both financial and emotional terms' (ibid., p. 108). Phillips summarized the differential nature of minority ethnic group housing outcomes by 1987 as follows:

> West Indians and Asians are more likely to live in pre-1945 dwellings (60 per cent and 74 per cent respectively) than the white population (50 per cent). They are also twice as likely to live in the terraced property so commonly associated with inner city residence. Overcrowding remains a particular problem amongst Asians (35 per cent live in overcrowded conditions compared to 3 per cent of whites) and, in recent years, homelessness has increased greatly ... Black people may now have a bath and W.C., but they are also likely to be the casualties of other inequalities in housing provision.

> In the 1980s then, the NCWP minorities still live in significantly worse quality housing and in poorer, less popular areas than the white British population. This holds both across and within tenures. Indeed, the high level of owner occupation amongst Asians (72 per cent as against 59 per cent of the general population) provides no guarantee of good housing ... the prevailing trend in many cities over the last two decades has been one of growing residential segregation between NCWP minorities and whites, with the former becoming increasingly over-represented in the poorest areas. This is particularly true of the Asian population, whose potential for residential mixing has been reduced by their relative absence from council housing. As analyses of local authority data have shown, however, segregation within the public sector itself is all too prevalent and inequality prevails ... Within this sector, movement away from the inner city cannot necessarily be equated with access to decent housing.

> (Phillips, 1987, p. 108)

Table 7.1 focuses on intra-ethnic differences in tenure, comparing the years 1981 and 1988. In 1988, West Indian households were nearly four times as likely to rent accommodation from a local authority than households where there was an Indian head, and nearly twice as likely as those from white ethnic groups. Between 1981 and 1988 the proportion of all minority ethnic groups buying a property with a mortgage increased, but increased most for Pakistani/Bangladeshi minorities.

Table 7.1: tenure, by ethnic group of head of household in England, 1981 and 1988, in percentages

| | Owner occupied | | | | Rented | | | |
| | owned occupied | | with mortgage | | local authority | | private | |
	1981	1988	1981	1988	1981	1988	1981	1988
White	25	26	32	40	29	23	13	11
Other ethnic groups of which:	18	15	35	44	28	25	18	16
Indian	26	25	49	55	13	11	11	9
Pakistani/ Bangladeshi	32	20	39	54	18	15	11	11
West Indian	8	7	28	35	47	43	17	15
Other or mixed	15	9	26	39	28	26	31	25
Not stated	22	29	27	33	32	18	19	21
All ethnic groups	25	26	32	40	29	23	13	12

(Adapted from Central Statistical Office, 1991, p. 146)

7.2 Local authority housing

Between 1976 and 1989 house building completions by local authorities (and new towns) fell from 124,512 to 13,555, with the numbers of dwellings with three or more bedrooms falling from 42 per cent of the housebuilding completions in 1976 to only 22 per cent in 1989 (Central Statistical Office, 1991, p. 137, paras 8.4 and 8.5). The changing distribution of dwelling size is linked to the changing structure of households, but, as Section 1 reveals, recent provision does not closely correspond to the needs of minority ethnic group households, such as large families. Moreover, during the 1980s almost one and a half million local authority and new town dwellings were sold to occupiers, much of it stock of good quality in locations popular with white applicants for rented accommodation.[2]

Evidence of local authority housing disadvantage for minority ethnic groups is reviewed by Ginsburg (1992).[3] In 1989 formal investigations by the CRE, conducted in a variety of towns and cities in the UK, showed that disadvantages often accrued despite the existence of equal opportunities policies. For example, an Edinburgh study found that unlawful discrimination did occur and that a disproportionate number of black tenants were allocated in the unpopular area of Wester Hailes, where 82 per cent of black tenants, as opposed to 50 per cent elsewhere, had experienced racial harassment (MacEwan and Verity, 1989). In the London Borough of Southwark, the CRE found the borough indirectly discriminated against minority ethnic group tenants when it gave new properties from a major improvement programme mainly to white tenants (CRE, 1990d).

A 1988 CRE report into the London Borough of Tower Hamlets showed how Bangladeshis were more likely to be allocated the worst housing; how Bangladeshis ended up in the borough's poorest temporary bed and breakfast accommodation; how Bangladeshis waited longer than whites to be allocated housing; how emergency housing for those made homeless by fire or vandalism was made available more quickly for whites; and how the council discriminated against Bangladeshi families when they applied for housing. The report found that of three estates examined in the borough, the two with the lowest housing standards housed five times the number of Asian tenants as would be expected given their proportion in the borough's population (CRE, 1988b).

7.3 Owner occupation

Differential outcomes to minority ethnic groups in the owner-occupied sector has been the subject of much detailed research (Ginsburg, 1992; CRE, 1985b; Smith, 1989). Evidence in the late 1980s particularly focused on discriminatory practices of estate agencies in the housing market (Sarre *et al.*, 1989, ch. 7). Two CRE investigations, one into an estate agency in Clapham and Wandsworth, the other into an Oldham agency, resulted in the issuing of non-discrimination notices, and further highlighted the ways in which estate agencies contravene the 1976 Race Relations Act (CRE, 1984c; 1990e). The Oldham investigation revealed how one agency:

- discriminated against vendors of properties in areas of Asian population;
- segregated purchasers on racial grounds;
- accepted discriminatory instructions from vendors;
- discriminated against Asian clients in the provision of mortgage facilities.

On the positive side, the estate agency business has begun to 'put its own house in order' by developing equal opportunities policies. For example, another CRE report documents the responses of two estate agencies following advice that their branches might possibly be engaged in practices contravening the Race Relations Act 1976 (CRE, 1990c). One is among the ten largest firms of estate agents in the UK with 800 branches and 6,000 employees in 1990; the other is a smaller company operating in the Greater Manchester area. Both set up equal opportunities policies and implemented them within a short space of time. Their progress is being monitored. Following the publication of the CRE code of practice in the owner-occupied housing sector, such initiatives to combat institutional racism may be expected to occur elsewhere among housing gatekeepers (CRE, 1991b).

7.4 Housing associations

Partly in response to cuts in council housing, minority ethnic groups have increasingly looked to improve their housing situation in the voluntary sector. The Federation of Black Housing Organisations (FBHO) have broadened housing access for minority ethnic groups during the 1980s by developing links with housing associations and monitoring outcomes in the voluntary sector (Phillips, R., 1986). However, despite the establishment of equal opportunity policies as an integral part of housing association activity, as well as Housing Corporation grants to newly registered black groups, and the allocation of £100,000 a year to encourage black participation in housing associations, progress to reduce discriminatory effects remains slow. Of 2,600 housing organizations registered with the Housing Corporation in 1986, only twelve were controlled by black people, and only six owned their own property. Studies in Bradford and Rochdale have shown the potential role housing associations could play in bridging the gap in low income housing provision for minority ethnic group families (Brimacombe, 1991). Existing research suggests, however, that housing associations inherit many of the features of local authorities in the way in which they treat minority ethnic group applicants and tenants. Research undertaken into four Scottish housing associations in the late 1980s, and published in 1989, showed that black people were disproportionately found in below-standard housing in areas where locally-based housing associations had been operating for twenty years (Dalton and Daghlian, 1989).

A CRE investigation in Liverpool found that under housing allocations made by the city council white people were twice as likely as black people to get a house, four times more likely to get a new house, twice as likely to get a centrally heated home, and four times more likely to get their own garden (CRE, 1989b). The investigation followed a CRE study of Liverpool City Council in 1984. This found that black households received lower quality council housing than white households. The council had established an equal opportunities policy in 1981, employed a community relations officer in the housing department since 1982, and developed what the CRE called a 'radical' policy on racial harassment since 1983. The 1984 report had recommended that the council introduce minority ethnic group monitoring and training, improve information provision, broaden systematic in-service training, employ specialist staff and increase the proportion of black staff in the housing department (CRE, 1984b).

In looking at housing association nominations, the 1989 Liverpool report found evidence which mirrored that discovered for Liverpool's council housing in 1984. Two thousand housing association case histories were studied during 1987 and 1988. Black housing association nominees consistently received poorer properties than white nominees across all quality measures. The CRE could not explain the differential outcomes in terms of area preferences, economic circumstances, or household size. A non-discrimination notice was issued against Liverpool City Council. Another study, by the FBHO in the mid-1980s, found that, of 1,289 sheltered accommodation places for the elderly provided by Liverpool City Council and housing associations, only two were occupied by Asian or Afro-Caribbean households (FBHO, 1986).

7.5 Private rented housing

Racism in the private rented sector has a long history.[4] While signs stating 'no blacks, no Irish, no dogs' may have disappeared since the introduction of 'race' relations legislation, evidence at the beginning of the 1990s continues to show that racial bias persists in the rented sector, albeit at more subtle levels. The CRE report *Sorry, It's Gone* showed that one in five accommodation agencies in thirteen different locations discriminated against minority ethnic group applicants (CRE, 1990f). In Ealing almost half of the agencies were found to discriminate, and in Bristol a third. The report showed how agents would deny minority ethnic group applicants access to private rented property, while readily referring white people of identical status and means. The report also showed that one in twenty private landlords and landladies discriminated. The 'good news', CRE concluded, was the relative absence of discriminatory practices by owners of guest houses and small hotels. However, while the old days of blatant racial discrimination had largely disappeared, the CRE maintained that the level of racial discrimination nevertheless remained 'worryingly high':

> what we found was not discrimination at second hand, where agencies were following discriminatory instructions from landlords and landladies, but rather discriminatory decisions taken by agency staff themselves, directly, through a mixture of ignorance, racial stereotyping or plain racial bigotry.

> (CRE, 1990f, p. 5)

In a press release launching the report, the chair of the CRE, Michael Day, described the findings of the investigation as 'shameful, but not surprising'. He called for government legislation to ensure that all accommodation agencies are licensed with a code of conduct and their performance is monitored.[5] Commenting on the report, the London Housing Unit said that racism in the private rented housing sector helped to ensure that three times more black people than white were likely to become homeless.[6] There remains, also, the problem of the poor quality of much private rented accommodation. For example, a study into Kensington and Chelsea, the London borough with the highest private rented sector, found that its 214,000 minority ethnic groups – mainly Filipino, Moroccan and Latin American migrant workers – lived in the worst private rented housing in the country.[7]

7.6 'Race' and homelessness

Ethnic minorities are represented among the homeless at a disproportionately high level, and suffer racial discrimination as well as all the other problems associated with homelessness.

(CRE, 1988b, p. 7)

The rise in homelessness throughout the 1980s reflects changes in housing policy. Greve and Currie (1990) estimated that, in 1989, 356,000 households, or 686,000 people, could be defined as homeless.[8] The risk of becoming homeless is considerably higher for people on low income, single parents and members of minority ethnic groups (Oppenheim, 1990, p. 53). In 1988 research in London showed that minority ethnic group households are up to four times as likely to become homeless as white households (National Association of Citizens Advice Bureaux (NACAB), 1988; Sexty, 1990, pp. 45–6) The CRE investigation (1988b) found that the majority of the 1300 homeless in Tower Hamlets were Bangladeshi. The number of Bangladeshis on the homeless lists was also swollen by the borough's policy on divided families and immigration. A father who wanted to bring his wife and children to join him in England from Bangladesh could not be actively considered for housing until they arrived, making them automatically homeless on arrival (CRE, 1988b).

The young, especially those who are single, are particularly vulnerable to homelessness. A survey of 24 London boroughs in 1989 revealed the extent of an escalating problem. In Brent and Southwark a disproportionate number of the single homeless were young black people. In Newham, black homeless single people made up 56 per cent of referrals to hostels, 40 per cent of the referrals being under 18. The survey revealed that an increasing proportion of the single homeless were women, especially young Asians (Single Homeless in London and London Housing Unit, 1989).[9]

The negative impact of homelessness on education and life chances has been well documented. For example, a survey by HMIs found that homeless children tended not to be enrolled at school, were frequently absent, performed relatively poorly in class, and suffered from low self-esteem and expectations.[10]

7.7 Racial harassment and 'racist' tenants

Sections 3.4 and 3.5 looked at racial harassment in the home and at school. One of the problems confronting housing departments such as Tower Hamlets, where the Bangladeshi population alone rose from 12,000 to 40,000 between 1982 and 1987, is what kind of policy to adopt to ameliorate homelessness, or reduce the concentration of Bangladeshis in particular areas. Here the issue of 'racist' council tenants has to be confronted. The CRE report on the borough highlighted the level of racial harassment and abuse and the frequency of racist attacks on Bangladeshis living in the worst accommodation and on those rehoused in 'white areas'.[11]

Recording the prolonged torment of an East London Asian family who were the victims of racial harassment, John Pilger examined the testimony of a teenage girl through her diary entries on racial attacks on her family home. The girl, Nasreen, wrote to Mrs Thatcher during 1983:

> *Dear Margaret Thatcher,*
>
> *I am sorry to say you don't understand our matter … you don't care if we get beaten up, do you? My mother has asthma and she had to stay to 11am watching through the window because me and my brother and sister has to go to school. I can't stay home to look after my mother because I got exams to worry about. We have no money to repair our house since the kids in the street have damaged it.*
> *We are asking for your help, not your money, Mrs Thatcher.*
>
> *Yours sincerely,*
>
> *Nasreen*

(John Pilger, 'Nasreen, voice of outrage from a house under seige', *Independent,* 2 February 1987)

A reply came not from the then Prime Minister, but from Mr C. D. Inge at the Home Office. Mr Inge urged the family to keep reporting every incident to the police 'even if the police are unable to take any action'. He then apologized for not being 'able to give you a more helpful reply' (*Independent,* 2 February 1987).

Until the mid-1980s the response of most councils to allegations of racial harassment or attack on white estates has been to treat them as private disputes between neighbours. In the worse cases, black tenants are transferred back to other areas for their own safety – often back to overcrowded estates with high concentrations of minority ethnic group tenants. In 1984 Newham became the first local authority to evict a white family for persistent and violent harassment of their Asian neighbours.[12] By the end of 1987, six cases had been brought against white tenants, all in London, but only three had been successful. Councils began to include the perpetration of racial harassment as a specific ground for eviction in tenancy agreements. By 1988 over half of the London boroughs had introduced such clauses in their agreements. However, problems with legal interpretation and definitions of racial harassment have resulted in few councils taking action, further raising the levels of disillusionment in minority ethnic group communities.

Figure 7.1: Tower Hamlets' tenants demand to bo transferred to safer housing

7.8 Developments since 1992

In 1994, the National Housing Forum estimated that £70 billion would bc needed to ensure that all UK dwellings conformed to the standards then employed by building societies for mortgage purposes. Housing renewal investment in England fell from £1.5 billion in 1983, to less than £0.5 billion in 1992. In 1994–5 there was a 23 per cent cut in Government housing funding. Since 1991 disinvestment in housing has been felt across the housing sectors, but especially among housing associations (over £40 million since 1991) (National Housing Forum, 1994; *Independent*, 5 June 1994).

In 1992, the Government reported that over 1.3 million dwellings in England were unfit to live in (over 90 per cent of them were in the owner-occupied sector), where four out of five Indian households lived (*Independ-*

ent, 1 August 1992). *Social Trends 24* illustrated further the tenurial differences between minority ethnic groups, showing the increased reliance on owner occupation in Indian communities and on local authority housing among Afro-Caribbean communities (CSO, 1994). Evidence from the 1991 census revealed that owner occupation was highest in the Indian (81 per cent) and Pakistani (77 per cent) communities (Pearce and White, 1994) (see *Table 7.2*).

Table 7.2: tenure, by ethnic group of head of household in Great Britain, 1990–2[1], in percentages

Ethnic group	Owner-occupied	Rented
Indian	80	20
Pakistani/Bangladeshi	66	34
Black Caribbean	46	54
Other	50	50
All ethnic minority groups	60	40
White	67	33
All ethnic groups[2]	66	34

[1] Combined data for 1990, 1991 and 1992.

[2] Includes those who gave no answer to the ethnic group question.

(CSO, 1994, p. 118)

Figure 7.2 shows the extent to which Pakistani and Bangladeshi households experience the worst housing conditions (i.e. the 10 per cent of dwellings with the highest urgent repair costs and costs to make the dwelling fit for habitation).

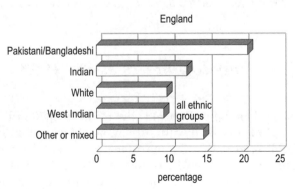

Figure 7.2: households in worst housing, by ethnic group of head of household, 1991
(CSO, 1994, p. 112)

Overcrowding particularly affected minority ethnic groups (Amin and Oppenheim, 1992; CSO, 1994; 1995). The average number of people per room was much higher for minority ethnic groups than for white people. More than half of all white households enjoyed the space of two or more rooms per person. One in seven Pakistani and Bangladeshi households had two or more rooms per person compared with one in two white households. One per cent of white households had the use of less than one room per person compared with 10 per cent for all minority ethnic groups and 33 per cent of Pakistani and Bangladeshi households (CSO, 1994; 1995). The reasons for this overcrowding are related to the stage reached in the migration/settlement cycle, household income and differential opportunities in the owner-occupied sector (Amin and Oppenheim, 1992; Oppenheim, 1993).

Households headed by a Pakistani or a Bangladeshi were also far more likely to experience overcrowded conditions than other groups. Pakistani and Bangladeshi households were also found to have experienced a large increase in overcrowding between 1981 and 1991 (CSO, 1994).

The London Research Centre (LRC) demonstrated that black and Asian children were twice as likely to suffer from overcrowded housing conditions. Overcrowding affected 150,000 children living in London local authority and housing association dwellings, an increase of 30,000 since 1986–7. The CRE commented:

> We knew they [minority ethnic groups] were over-represented
> among the homeless and overcrowded and this survey reinforces this
> ... Children and ethnic minorities will take increasing strain.

> (*Independent*, 21 September 1992)

Since 1980, London has sold off, through the 'right to buy' policies, a third of its three-bedroom and 40 per cent of its four-bedroom dwellings (London Research Centre, 1992; 1993).

In 1994, the LRC revealed that one in four of London households fell below acceptable standards. London also faced a shortfall of 100,000 affordable family dwellings by 1998 unless building programmes increased four-fold. LRC found that 831,000 households lacked basic amenities in the capital. The research report identified a 'disturbing incidence' of multiple deprivation, in particular affecting minority ethnic groups (London Research Centre, 1994).

A Federation of Black Housing Associations (FBHA) report in 1993 revealed that thousands of ethnic minority elders were living 'wretched and lonely lives' and that their housing needs were neglected in British society (FBHA, 1993).

The number of black housing associations managing their own developments fell sharply in the 1990s, and could fall further following a Housing

Corporation review, and Government cutbacks (*Housing Association Weekly*, April 1993). There is some evidence that black housing associations are becoming more independently viable. In 1992, only four could function without Government subsidy. By 1996 this figure is expected to have risen to 40 (*Independent*, 14 April 1994).

Government planning beyond 1994 includes policies designed to transfer hundreds of thousands of council dwellings, including inner-city high-rise blocks, into private ownership through housing associations. In a 'silent revolution in public housing', 31 Conservative councils had already transferred more than 140,000 council dwellings into private ownership through housing associations (*Independent*, 2 August 1994).

The CRE analysis of racial equality and housing associations in England and Scotland revealed that most of the 40 English associations had introduced racial equality policies, including ethnic monitoring and anti-racial harassment initiatives (CRE, 1993a). In Scotland few associations produced policy innovation, or raised staff levels among minority ethnic groups. Kandish Chandran, chief executive of Luton Black Housing Association, commented:

> for over 25 years access to quality housing has been denied to ethnic minorities. The Commission for Racial Equality reports show nothing changes. Discriminatory practices against black people occur in all sectors.

(*Independent*, 14 April 1994).

In 1993 the National Federation of Housing Associations (NFHA) published *Using Race Equality Targets*, which kept members informed of progress elsewhere and showed how targets could be realized through allocation procedures to transform words into action (NFHA, 1993a). The NFHA demonstrated how housing design that can accommodate diversity, especially linking the design of the house to family structures and religious practices, is crucial in meeting the housing needs of minority ethnic groups. An essential design feature is a letterbox which prevents damage from fire or attack (NFHA, 1993b).

More than 600,000 people were officially homeless in 1993 – double the figure in 1984 (Department of the Environment, 1994b; *Independent*, 12 April 1994). By the end of 1994, Government figures showed a slight fall, but Shelter estimates that the real figures identify a continuing increase during the 1990s (*Guardian*, 27 December 1994). The official figures declined because many single homeless people did not register with councils since they no longer qualified to be housed. In 1994 Shelter's case load grew to a record 64,000 people. Shelter concluded: 'It was a year when the Government made cuts in housing at every opportunity and thousands of people were left living in accommodation or sleeping rough in Britain's streets' (Shelter, 1994; *Guardian*, 27 December 1994).

Shelter researches reveal that over 150,000 young people become homeless each year. Black people spend longer in temporary accommodation waiting for rehousing. Over 30 per cent of people living in temporary accommodation are from minority ethnic groups, most are black, and most affected are the young (16–24-year-olds) (Skellington, 1993). Shelter estimates that black households are nearly seven times less likely to be permanently rehoused than white households (*Socialist Review*, January 1994, p. 7). A study for Barnardos by Staffordshire University found that of more than 14,000 people under 25 in urgent need of housing in Birmingham, over one third were from black or Asian communities, although only one fifth of the city's population were black or Asian (Runnymede Trust, 1994b; *Housing Association Weekly*, 12 November 1993). At a national conference on homelessness in 1993, lack of benefits and institutional racism were blamed for the rise in homelessness among minority ethnic groups, especially those aged 16 and 17 (*Community Care*, 22 October 1993).

Tower Hamlets received a non-discrimination notice from the CRE following a formal investigation of its homeless policies. A study by the Tower Hamlets Homeless Families Campaign (1993) showed that the housing department, severely constrained by Government refusal to respond with greater investment, had resorted to a policy which failed to consider homelessness a priority, but offered private renting at high rents with limited security, often outside the borough. In Tower Hamlets over 75 per cent of black and Asian families were homeless (Docklands Forum, 1993).

In 1994, the Department of Environment issued a Green Paper heralding new housing policies which would affect homeless people. The paper proposed the removal of the responsibility of authorities to provide permanent homes for the homeless. In future, permanent housing would only be allocated to persons on the waiting list. Given the over-representation of black and young black people among the homeless, these proposals, if implemented, will have a disproportionate negative impact on minority ethnic groups ('Housing and urban policy', *New Community*, **20** (3), pp. 520–5, 1994). The Government's decision to make squatting an illegal offence has also added to the homeless problem. CHAR, the Campaign for the Homeless, has estimated that three-quarters of squatters occupy local authority dwellings which otherwise would be empty (CHAR, 1992).

The Tower Hamlets experience illustrated how a council could allocate dwellings to Asian families on estates noted for racial harassment. A Local Government ombudsman report severely criticized the failure of the borough to respond adequately to racial incidents on its Teviot Estate. Racial incidents were neither recorded nor monitored. Moreover, no action was taken against the perpetrators. The victims, mainly of South Asian origin, were neither given priority to leave the estate, nor offered suitable accommodation elsewhere. In 1992, the Law Centre recorded 228 racial incidents on the Teviot Estate – the biggest recorded in the country – including 47 assaults, eleven cases of racist graffiti and seven involving people being threatened with weapons or dogs. Home Office research showed that the level of attacks on Teviot was three times higher than in other estates and was more dangerous. The Borough Homeless Persons Unit allowed appeals for the first time on the grounds of racial harassment; eight families had appealed before the appeals system was abolished. One family reported suffering nearly 30 racist incidents, including several assaults, and had been racially abused 'too many times to count' (Observer, 24 March 1993; Donnellan, 1993).

Research by the LRC into other boroughs confirms the extent to which racial harassment is endemic, and how vulnerable Afro-Caribbean people are to homelessness (Housing Association Weekly, 3 September 1993). More recent disclosures about housing policies in Westminster and Wandsworth, where housing which could have been allocated to the homeless was transformed for political reasons into housing for sale, tend to support the view that some inner-London boroughs are not fulfilling their responsibilities to the homeless (Independent, 2 March 1995).

In 1995, the Single Homeless in London organization (SHIL) showed that the number of emergency direct access hostel beds for the homeless in London fell by 60 per cent between 1985 and 1995, from 4,943 to 1,820. They also disclosed that 90 per cent of this decline occurred within the 13 inner London boroughs, while 22 boroughs had no direct access provision (SHIL, 1995; Independent, 31 January 1995). At Christmas 1994, the Homeless Network six-monthly audit revealed a 7 per cent increase in people sleeping rough in London, while Shelter Nightline reported it could not find emergency beds for a third of people who called the service. One of the reasons for this problem is that the Government's £86 million 'rough sleepers' initiative, launched in 1993, was designed to focus in 1994–5 on permanent accommodation needs.

Pressure is continuing from housing charities for the Government to extend its rough sleepers initiative beyond 1996. In March 1995, the Government allowed local authorities to house homeless families in private rented accommodation with leases of a year or less. This may go some way to ease the homeless crisis, since councils had hitherto only begun to scratch the surface of the private rented sector. Now they can house the homeless while retaining their own dwellings for waiting list applicants (Independent, 10 March 1995).

Local authorities are still reluctant to evict racist tenants or their families. A white family was evicted for harassing a Pakistani family in Birmingham in 1992 – the first eviction of its kind in the city (Guardian, 28 July 1992). In March 1993, Leicester City Council also took its first action against racist tenants (Independent, 19 March 1993). One problem is that the ways in which local authorities respond to and investigate racist incidents vary so much around the country. Since 1993 there have been further isolated cases of eviction for racist tenants but still the perpetrators remain relatively unpenalized while the victims remain trapped in fear, or are moved to other council dwellings (Hemans, 1993). In March 1995, the Association of Metropolitan Authorities, in a meeting with the Lord Chancellor, demanded a legal reform package which would allow court proceedings against racist tenants to be speeded up, witnesses to be guaranteed anonymity, the rules on hearsay evidence relaxed, and criminal prosecutions brought on tenants who break civil injunctions on racial harassment (*Independent on Sunday*, 26 March 1995).

In autumn 1993, a CRE formal report into housing allocation policies of Oldham Council found that the Council had contravened the 1976 Race Relations Act. Oldham's Bangladeshi community was particularly affected by discriminatory practices (CRE, 1993b). This was the first time an investigation had been conducted into racial discrimination through segregation policies. Oldham's policies were found to disadvantage South Asian applicants by allocating inferior accommodation to Bangladeshis. The CRE did not impose a non-discrimination notice on assurance that Oldham would produce a two-year action plan ('Housing and urban policy', *New Community*, **20**, ibid.).

Between 1992 and December 1993 (only), local authorities were allowed to invest in full any receipts realized from the sales of assets, including dwellings under the 'right to buy' scheme. Since the Local Government and Housing Act of 1989, they had only been permitted to invest a quarter of 'right to buy' income (HMSO, 1992b; 'Housing review', *New Community*, **19** (3), pp. 539–45, 1993). The amount released for local authorities varied but this temporary relaxation, for example, enabled Leeds City Council to spend some of the £31.8 million raised through its 'right to buy' scheme. Money was subsequently invested in the construction of new housing and schools, benefiting minority ethnic areas (*Independent*, 19 July 1994). By 1995, however, the situation had reverted to the previous policy with little income from sale of assets available for much needed investment.

Changes in urban regeneration policy have further eroded the reform potential of local authorities to improve housing opportunities. In 1993, the creation of a single regeneration budget (SRB) – which also included Home Office Section 11 and other programmes targeted at ethnic minority provision – cut the total amount of resources available to authorities. This followed the failure of the City Challenge initiative to advance the housing opportunities of minority ethnic communities. Section 11 funding faced an estimated 42 per cent cut in real terms. Cuts in the Standard Spending Assessment (SSA) were expected to constrain local authority budgets and disadvantage authorities with substantial minority ethnic communities because less weighting would be given to the presence of minorities ('Housing and urban policy', *New Community*, **20**, ibid.). The new SSA calculations show that the top ten losing local authorities all housed substantial ethnic minority populations (Wandsworth, Birmingham, Lambeth, Hackney, Brent, Hammersmith, Kensington, Haringey, Ealing and Newham).

Local authority housing departments for the first time have been given the power to inform on persons suspected of being illegal immigrants under new guidelines issued by the Department of the Environment. The new policy, which permits housing officials to investigate a homeless person's immigration status, could, according to Judith Beale of the Department of the Environment, 'have an adverse effect on race relations' (Runnymede Trust, 1993e). Hitherto this was a power only granted to Home Office officials. A CRE spokesperson explained: 'The danger is that, without guidance, over-stressed and under-trained housing officers will form a view on the basis of whether people are "foreign looking" – and that will usually mean black or brown.' The CRE believe the move may introduce unlawful practices into housing departments, and be harmful to race relations (*Independent*, 25 September 1993).

Notes

1   The research evidence on 'institutional racism and racism in housing' is substantial, and there is a developing literature on policy implementation in the area of equal opportunities. For a fuller discussion of institutional racism in housing and a review of some of the evidence that emerged in the 1970s and 1980s see Ginsburg (1992) (Open University course ED356 Reader 3). For a useful discussion of the particular housing needs and experiences of minority ethnic group women – usually ignored in research – see Sexty (1990) ch. 3. For more details of evidence for racism in housing see CRE (1988a; 1989b; 1990b); MacEwan and Verity (1989); Dalton and Daghlian (1989). For information on equal opportunities policies in relation to housing see Phillips (1989) p. 142; CRE (1989c; 1990c; 1991b).

2   See Forrest *et al.* (1990, p. 212) and 'Lending to council house tenants', Nationwide Anglia Building Society, May 1990. No breakdowns were available on house sales and ethnic background at the time of publication.

3   See also Henderson and Karn (1984); CRE (1984b); Phillips, D. (1986); Sarre *et al.* (1989) ch. 5.

4   For a useful review of landlord discrimination see Smith and Hill (1991).

5   CRE Press Release, 13 September 1990.

6   *Independent*, 14 September 1990.

7   Grant (1989). The 1987 London Earnings Survey showed that the borough had the lowest pay in London but that council rents were the highest.

8   Official statistics relate to a flow of households rehoused during a year, not to the number of households without a home at any one time.

9   See also *Roof*, January/February 1989, p. 10; Sexty (1990) p. 47.

10   *Independent*, 6 August 1990.

11   *Independent*, 2 September 1988.

12   See Phillips, R. (1986) p. 13. For a fascinating discussion of council tenants' experiences of and attitudes to racism see *Tenants Tackle Racism*, Dame Colet House/Limehouse Fields Tenants Association and Tower Hamlets Tenants Federation (1986).

8 'RACE' AND THE CRIMINAL JUSTICE SYSTEM

8.1 Inequalities in judicial provision

8.1.1 The judiciary

At a meeting with barristers and solicitors in London on 6 November 1990 the Lord Chancellor, Lord Mackay of Clashern, was reported as saying:

> The bench in 10 or 20 years time should look very different in terms of racial and sexual composition from that of today ... Nothing would be worse for the reputation of the judiciary in this country than for me to lower standards for appointment to the judiciary simply to ensure a different racial or sexual mix ... It is worth stressing that it is not a function of the judiciary to be representative of the population as a whole.

> (*Independent*, 7 November 1990)

A month later in the House of Commons, Sir Patrick Mayhew, the Attorney General, replying to a question from Mr Brian Sedgemore MP about the ethnic composition of the judiciary, said:

> Candidates for judicial appointment are considered on their merits regardless of sex or ethnic origin. The Lord Chancellor has, however, repeatedly made clear his wish to appoint more women and members of ethnic minorities to judicial office ... At the moment, there are relatively few women and ethnic minority candidates in the legal profession in the appropriate age groups with the right experience ... It is impossible, however, to predict the composition of the pool of suitably qualified candidates for judicial office, or the number of appointments needed, 10 years ahead, and it would therefore be inappropriate to set targets.

> (*Hansard*, 1990, p. 113)

Figures produced by the Law Society in March 1991 revealed a huge disparity in the proportions of men, women and members of minority ethnic groups on the bench, and the pool of potential candidates from which that bench is selected (see *Table 8.1*).

Table 8.1: the make-up of the judiciary in England and Wales

Judges	Total	Women	%	Minority ethnic groups	%
House of Lords	10	0	0%	0	0%
Court of Appeal	27	2	7.41%	0	0%
High Court	83	2	1.66%	0	0%
Circuit judges	429	19	4.4%	1	0.2%
Recorders (part-time)	744	42	5.7%	3	0.4%
Assistant recorders (part-time)	443	27	6.0%	2	0.4%
The candidates					
Practising barristers	5,994	1,246	21.0%	376	6.0%
Practising solicitors	54,734	12,683	23.2%	709*	1.3%

* 16,622 respondents to the Law Society survey declined to specify their ethnic group
(Based on Lord Chancellor's Department 1991; Law Society 1989–90; Bar Council 1989–90)

Of a total of 1,736 full- and part-time judicial posts, 92 were held by women and only 6 by people from minority ethnic groups. The Law Society is concerned that the current appointment system may be illegal under the 1976 Race Relations Act because of its dependence on 'word of mouth' selection which may indirectly discriminate against minority group candidates (*Independent*, 27 February and 8 March 1991).

8.1.2 Jury composition

In the early 1990s, the Lord Chancellor's Department examined the make-up of juries to assess the justification for fears that minority ethnic group defendants are being placed at a disadvantage in criminal trials because the juries do not reflect the ethnic composition of British society. The essence of the jury system is random selection, but in recent years this system has consistently failed to achieve jury panels that reflect ethnic composition. Black solicitors claim that the abolition in January 1989 of the defence's right to challenge jurors pre-emptorily has exacerbated the problem.

In a major study, Baldwin and McConville (1979) examined the jury composition in 720 trials in Birmingham and London. They identified 'immense' under-representation on juries of people from black Commonwealth countries. Only 28 out of 3,912 jurors selected for 326 Birmingham juries (0.7 per cent) were of West Indian or Asian origin.[1] In the 1990s the problem remains. In July 1990 the CRE's Chief Executive commented:

People from ethnic minority communities appear to be under-represented among jurors ... and heavily over-represented among defendants. This imbalance is bound to undermine the confidence of these communities in the criminal justice system as a whole. There are difficulties in achieving ethnically mixed juries, but they are not insuperable ... We believe the restoration of preemptory challenge would probably assist the objective ... [but it] would need to be underpinned ... by a right for all defendants to a racially mixed jury, together with a clear declaration that all criminal justice agencies had a statutory duty to operate on a non-discriminatory basis.

(Peter Saunders, 'Ethnic balance among juries', *Independent*, 2 July 1990)

8.1.3 The magistracy

Magistrates are responsible for 98 per cent of criminal charges dealt with by the courts of England and Wales. The lay magistracy is supposed to reflect the community which it serves, but there are still relatively few black magistrates (see *Table 8.2*).

Table 8.2: black people employed in the criminal justice system

Probation service	1.9%
Police	0.9%
Solicitors	1.3%
Magistrates	1.9%
Prison staff	0.6%

Note: uses National Association of Probation Officers data
(McDermott, 1990, p. 215)

In 1970 there were only 15 black magistrates in England and Wales. By 1979 this figure had risen to 115: by 1986 it had trebled to 325 of whom 86 were women.[2] By 1 January 1988 the number stood at 455 – 1.9 per cent of the 23,730 active magistrates in England and Wales. Despite the rise since 1970, minority ethnic groups are still under-represented among the magistracy. This is the case especially for black women – female magistrates accounted for only 1.15 per cent of the total. During the 1980s, however, the proportion of black magistrates appointed rose gradually. In 1980, 1.8 per cent of magistracy appointments were to black people: by 1986 the proportion had risen to 4.6 per cent. In the late 1980s, the proportion of black appointments to the magistracy in the age range 35–54 was *higher* than their distribution in the population as a whole.[3] In April 1991 Richard Grobler, an official in the Lord Chancellor's Department, claimed that 6 per cent of appointments to the magistracy were to black people (more than their representation in the population of England and Wales). Grobler told the *Independent*, 'We do try and target particular groups – for instance by advertising in the *Caribbean Times* – to improve the balance of the benches.'[4]

8.1.4 Solicitors and barristers

There were relatively few minority ethnic group solicitors in 1988 – only 618 out of 48,494, or 1.28 per cent (see *Table 8.2*). They are located disproportionately in small practices: 22 per cent operate on their own compared with 9 per cent of all solicitors, and more than 80 per cent work in firms with fewer than four solicitors compared with 56 per cent in total.[5]

According to research conducted at Brunel University, significant barriers to entry into the legal profession operate against minority ethnic group law students seeking to become solicitors.[6] It found that, on average, minority ethnic group candidates made almost twice as many applications to solicitors' firms for articles as their white counterparts and they received proportionately fewer interview offers. After interview, 12 per cent of minority ethnic group students received more offers than rejections compared with 44 per cent of white students. The former were also found to have a poor chance of finding a job with a commercial law firm, where the salaries are higher than in other areas of legal practice.

Firms were found to operate a policy based not on 'race', but on what they saw as 'excellence'. They may, for example, require applicants to have an Oxbridge degree or a 'prestigious' educational background. Minority ethnic group candidates were found to be disproportionately disadvantaged by such criteria. The study concluded that solicitors' firms needed to reappraise their selection criteria and procedures radically. It also recommended that universities and polytechnics place less emphasis on A-level grades as the entry qualification for law degree courses and extend part-time and day-release study for such courses. In 1991, another study examining the implications of the Law Society-controlled College of Law clearing house system for allocating places on solicitors' finals courses found that the two entry criteria used – whether students have been offered articles (professional training) by law firms and the class of degree they are likely to obtain – may potentially prevent black law graduates studying at polytechnics from entering finals courses.

Minority ethnic group barristers fare better than solicitors: but they make up no more than 5 per cent of the profession. However, more than 75 per cent of minority ethnic group barristers work in only 19 sets of chambers. In 1990 the majority of chambers contained no black barristers. In May 1991 the Bar Council, the profession's governing body, approved guidelines which instructed chambers of barristers that at least 5 per cent of their members and pupils should come from minority ethnic groups. It also asked clerks, the

Crown Prosecution Service, government departments, local authorities and large companies to ensure that at least 5 per cent of the work sent to chambers be directed to black and Asian barristers. The Bar Council also announced their intention to monitor the programme, appoint an equal opportunities officer, and produce a directory of black barristers.[7] The first black woman Queens Counsel was appointed on 28 March 1991.[8] In October 1991 the Bar Council adopted a race relations policy to encourage more people from minority ethnic groups into the profession.[9]

8.1.5 Probation officers

Black people are also under-represented in the probation service. In 1985, 127 out of 6,800 probation officers – less than 2 per cent – were black. The British Council of Churches (BCC) report which disclosed these figures remarked with regret that this was one area that showed little increase in black representation, 'partly due to black officers leaving in disgust or despair' (British Council of Churches, 1990, p. 3). A 1988 National Association of Probation Officers (NAPO) report revealed that only 1.9 per cent of probation officers were from minority ethnic groups (see *Table 8.2*).

8.2 Differential outcomes: arrests, remands, prisoners and prisons

In August 1989 Stephen Shaw, director of the Prison Reform Trust (PRT), claimed that if white people were jailed at the same rate as black people the total prison population of the UK would be 300,000. It is under 50,000. The PRT calculated that the black imprisonment rate for England and Wales was then 775 per 100,000 of the population compared to 98.2 per 100,000 for the population as a whole. The PRT figures indicate that black people could be eight times more likely than white people to end up in prison. Shaw concluded:

> Black people are more likely than their white counterparts to be stopped by the police. If stopped, they are more likely to be arrested. If arrested, more likely to be charged. If charged, more likely to be remanded in custody, and if convicted, more likely to receive a sentence of imprisonment.
>
> (Quoted in T. Kirby, 'Black jail figures would shame South Africa', *Independent*, 7 August 1989)

An investigation by the National Association for the Care and Resettlement of Offenders (NACRO) in 1990 showed black people to be more vulnerable at most stages of the criminal justice system than white people. They were more likely to be stopped and searched by police, to be prosecuted and to receive a prison sentence than their white counterparts. They were also more likely to be charged immediately and less likely to be cautioned.[10] A Home Office spokesperson commented, 'while it may be hard to prove discrimination in any one particular case, the figures would tend to show there is some kind of subtle discrimination' (*Independent*, 14 January 1991).

In 1986 it was estimated that 63 per cent of black youths had experienced some adversarial contact with the police, compared with 35 per cent of white people of the same age. The Forum for the Advancement of Training and Education for the Black Unemployed (FATEBU) reported that, given the trends of the late 1980s, one in ten black males are likely to be imprisoned by their twenty-first birthday (Burns, 1990, p. 7).

According to a NAPO report, black people made up 20 per cent of the remand population of England and Wales and 38 per cent of the remand population in London in 1987–8 (compared with 4.4 per cent of the general population). Afro-Caribbean defendants on remand were twice as likely to be acquitted as their white counterparts. The assistant general secretary of NAPO commented, 'The evidence strongly suggests that the system is discriminatory.' NAPO also revealed that in 23 prisons more than one-quarter of the inmates were black. Their data (see *Table 8.2*) showed that at that time the professional groups involved in the remand process had poor records of recruiting black staff (Fletcher, 1988, pp. 8–11).

In 1991 black people comprised 15 per cent of the prison population of England and Wales: 66 per cent of black people under sentence were of West Indian, Guyanese or African origin. While offence categories varied between the groups, certain offences stood out in the 1991 figures. For example, whereas only 5.6 per cent of whites were under sentence for drug offences, the figure for West Indians/Guyanese/Africans was 22.5 per cent, and for Indians/Pakistanis/Bangladeshis 31.3 per cent.[11]

Black women are more likely to be in prison than black men: 24 per cent of women imprisoned or remanded in custody before trial in 1989 were from minority ethnic groups (NACRO, 1991).[12] A NACRO study in 1987 revealed that women were more than twice as likely to be sent to prison as they were in 1977. On 30 June 1987, 26 per cent of women in custody whose records were known had no previous convictions, compared with 8 per cent of men. Overall, sentenced black prisoners had fewer previous convictions than white prisoners punished for the same type of offence. This study also showed that black people were significantly less likely to have been granted bail (NACRO, 1988).[13] Commenting on the report, NACRO's director said:

> These figures do not show that black people are more prone to crime than white people, but they do suggest that black people who offend are more likely to go to prison ... Some useful first steps have been taken by

the prison service, the police, the probation service, and the legal profession: but a comprehensive strategy is essential if we are to ensure that the administration of justice is fair, and seen to be fair in our multi-racial society.

(Vivien Stern, Director of NACRO, quoted in the *Independent*, 14 June 1988)

In a three-year study of five Midland prisons, McDermott (1990) argued that perceived racism is an instrinsic part of the prison service.[14] When all prisoners in her survey were asked to evaluate whether or not they thought staff were racist in their attitudes, nearly three out of five blacks, almost half the Asians and a third of whites thought the prison staff were racist. But the racism applies also to 'the cons'. One of McDermott's prisoners explained the subtleties behind some staff and prisoner interactions:

> There's a lot of racism here, open and unopen. You can break it up into the screws and the cons. The cons are racist between themselves. They'll say nigger this and nigger that, but it doesn't really go further because a lot of the black guys are physically a lot bigger. Now the screws do it openly, but they do it in such a way that it's unopen; like it's supposed to be a joke. But what can you say or do about it? You can't complain to the Governor because his officers can't lie ... You can't cross them because you know you'll come out the worst. They have the power.

(McDermott, 1990, p. 221)

In July 1991 the Institute of Race Relations (IRR) recommended that the government establish a Royal Commission to investigate deaths in custody. The call for a Standing Commission on Deaths in Custody followed extensive research into 75 black people who have died in police, prison and hospital care between 1970 and 1990. Only one of the 75 cases resulted in a prosecution of the police and in only one case did the family of the deceased receive compensation. The 75 deaths included many people who were diagnosed as mentally ill; others were refugees claiming asylum. The IRR report concluded that consideration of the unequal treatment of black people at all stages of the criminal justice system should form the basis of a Royal Commission (IRR, 1991).

In spite of efforts to recruit minority ethnic group members on to important public boards and committees associated with the prison system, representation on these bodies has not caught up with black representation in the prison population. For example, in 1987 NACRO reported that of the 67 Parole Board members only 7.5 per cent were from minority ethnic groups; of the Local Review Committee, only 5.7 per cent; and of the members of the Board of Visitors, only 9 per cent (McDermott, 1990, p. 216).

8.3 Education, training and black offenders

According to FATEBU, the overwhelming majority of people known to the prison and probation services are unemployed and have had very poor previous experiences of education. In the early 1990s FATEBU, NACRO and the Prison Service's Education Branch launched a series of individually tailored schemes to allow the courts to consider community based sentences, instead of custody, especially for young black offenders (Burns, 1990, p. 8). Examining such initiatives, Burns observed:

> One of the central issues remaining is that in all parts of the criminal justice system black offenders are overwhelmingly dealt with by white staff. The system clearly needs to become more responsive to black organisations and attempt to involve black people much more in its institutions. This process should inform our education and training activities. Black educators as well as consumers have a part to play in that change.

(Burns, 1990, p. 8)

8.4 Police and policing

8.4.1 The thin blue line: black police officer recruitment

BBC1's *Nine O'Clock News*, 8 April 1991, ten years after the Brixton disturbances, reported that only 12 out of 300 officers in the Brixton force were black. A survey conducted by *Today* newspaper in the autumn of 1990 revealed that of our 51 police forces, only 1,308 police officers, 0.9 per cent, were drawn from minority ethnic groups (see *Table 8.3*).

According to this survey, the proportions for the large urban connurbations were: West Midlands 2.41 per cent; Metropolitan Police, including the City of London, 1.63 per cent; West Yorkshire 1.56 per cent (where the pool of black potential recruits in the appropriate age cohorts is over 15 per cent); Greater Manchester 1.54 per cent; and Merseyside 0.9 per cent. Bedford-shire with 2.96 per cent and Leicestershire with 2.53 per cent were the most successful forces in terms of black recruitment. Dyfed-Powys, Lincolnshire, and Norfolk, all areas with small minority ethnic group communities, had no black officers.

Table 8.3: numbers of black and Asian police officers in Britain

Force	Total strength	Minority ethnic group officers	Force	Total strength	Minority ethnic group officers
Metropolitan Police (including City of London)	24,468	463	Lancashire	3,167	18
			Leicestershire	1,743	44
			Lincolnshire	1,197	0
Avon and Somerset	3,080	20	Lothian and Borders	2,440	2
Bedfordshire	1,047	31	Merseyside	4,810	43
Cambridgeshire	1,187	20	Norfolk	1,400	0
Central Scotland	638	1	Northampton	1,141	18
Dumfries and Galloway	363	0	Northern Scotland	624	0
Dyfed, Powys	943	0	North Wales	1,327	1
Cheshire	1,865	4	Nottinghamshire	2,344	50
Cleveland	1,497	9	North Yorkshire	1,379	2
Cumbria	1,144	2	Northumbria	3,593	12
Derbyshire	1,793	23	Royal Ulster Constabulary	8,260	6
Dorset	1,281	3			
Devon and Cornwall	2,846	2	South Yorkshire	2,937	21
Durham	1,375	3	Staffordshire	2,202	17
Essex	2,902	18	Strathclyde	6,825	14
Gloucestershire	1,164	11	Suffolk	1,204	6
Greater Manchester	7,008	108	Sussex	2,960	9
			Surrey	1,659	9
Grampian	1,158	1	Tayside	1,036	3
Gwent	1,002	4	Thames Valley	3,685	47
Hertfordshire	1,658	19	Warwickshire	1,007	9
Humberside	1,989	3	West Mercia	2,023	19
Hampshire	3,173	9	West Midlands	6,859	165
Kent	2,991	20	West Yorkshire	5,279	82
			Wiltshire	1,098	9

(Today, *2 October 1990*)

Since the mid-1980s, police forces have become more engaged in recruitment drives directed at black and minority ethnic group communities, using targeting in specific localities, often linked to local minority ethnic group organizations and backed by advertisements in minority ethnic group media (Oakley, 1989). In 1989 only 27 black or Asian men and 8 women joined the Metropolitan Police.[15] In January 1990, they announced measures to increase black recruitment. The minimum height ruling for police officers (5ft 8in for men and 5ft 4in for women), which was felt to exclude recruitment of many people from Asia and the Indian subcontinent, was scrapped.[16] The Metropolitan Police also announced a television advertising campaign – for the first time in fifteen years.

8.4.2 Police career prospects

A CRE study in 1988 revealed that black officers are very poorly represented in ranks above that of police constable, and scarcely at all above sergeant. Black representation among non-uniformed police staff was also disproportionately low (Oakley, 1989). A report for the Commons Home Affairs Committee in autumn 1989 noted that there were no black or Asian officers in the ranks of chief superintendent or above.[17] At the end of 1989, the highest ranking black police officer was a Leicestershire superintendent. There is also evidence that wastage for black recruits is higher than for whites.[18] In 1989, 26 out of 35 black or Asian recruits to the Metropolitan Police left the force.[19]

8.4.3 Racism within the force

It's [racism] routine in some parts of the service. If it's routine in the force, it's almost certainly routine to some degree with some police forces to members of the public.

(John Newing, Chief Constable of Derbyshire, quoted in the *Independent,* 1 December 1990)

Two landmark industrial tribunal cases in 1990–1 highlighted the extent to which racist abuse and banter is rooted in police force culture. A Nottingham industrial tribunal found that PC Surinder Singh was unlawfully discriminated against by Nottinghamshire Constabulary in his training for the CID, and in the force's decision not to attach him permanently to the CID. The tribunal also found that two other Asian officers were discriminated against in their transfer applications to Nottinghamshire CID. In Ashford an industrial tribunal found that PC William Halliday had been unlawfully victimized by the Metropolitan Police following a racial abuse complaint. Since the Halliday case, the Metropolitan Police has installed a confidential 24-hour helpline to support officers suffering discrimination or abuse.

The Nottingham tribunal found that racist language permeated most levels of the force. A Channel 4 television dramatization revealed that such phrases as 'Come on coon, we've got work to do' and 'Nigger boy, you are getting above your station' were common parlance.[20] The Nottingham tribunal concluded:

> We consider there are no excuses – there can be no degree of acceptability. It does not matter in what context it was used. Any use displays racial prejudice. It offends minority ethnic group officers and diminishes them. There is little evidence that senior officers reprimanded anyone heard using such language.

> ('Race bias in the force', *Equal Opportunities Review*, 35, January/February 1991, pp. 6–7)

In 1989 the Gifford Report examined the extent of racism in Liverpool, particularly within its police force:

> We concluded from the evidence of many witnesses, black and white, that there is a wholly unacceptable level of racist language and racist behaviour by officers, including officers of rank, in the Merseyside Force.

> (The Gifford Report, July 1989, quoted in the *Independent*, 19 August 1989)

8.4.4 How people see the police

In 1989 a Scotland Yard inquiry revealed that 66 per cent of black people perceived the police to be racially prejudiced, compared with 41 per cent of white people.[21] Mass Observation Limited, who conducted the research, had already screened out of their analysis young blacks who showed 'very negative views of the police'. A third of whites, 39 per cent of Asians and 53 per cent of Afro-Caribbeans said they would never consider joining.

Young blacks' perceptions of the police have been the subject of considerable research. One of the most detailed studies, conducted in the mid-1980s by Gaskell and Smith (1985), found that 60 per cent of whites held the view that the police were 'good' or 'very good' compared with 30 per cent of blacks. By contrast, 41 per cent of blacks as against 16 per cent of whites felt the police to be 'bad' or 'very bad'. The authors' conclusion adds an interesting dimension to the range of factors that could explain these differences: it is not merely a question of unemployment, he argues, or of negative contacts with the police:

> We believe that another factor is involved – that blacks feel police hostility as a kind of group experience ... What almost amounts to a 'folk history' of unpleasant, perhaps frightening, experiences with the police has worked its way into the shared experiences of black

youngsters. Even without direct personal experience, young blacks evoke an unpleasant stereotype about the police, and this, of course, affects any contact they have with them ... Yet at the same time, young blacks do plainly see some good points about the police. They recognise the need for policing, but object to the way it is done.

(Gaskell and Smith, 1985, pp. 261–3)

8.4.5 Black people as victims of crime

According to the 1988 British Crime Survey, black people of Afro-Caribbean and Asian origin tend to be more at risk from many types of crime than white people. The survey found that black people were more likely to experience burglary and car theft. Afro-Caribbeans were also more likely to be assaulted, threatened, and to suffer robbery or theft from the person. Asians, on the other hand, appeared to be particularly vulnerable to vandalism and threats. A quarter of Asians felt that many crimes against them had a racial element, as against 15 per cent of Afro-Caribbeans. The study found that while black people were no less likely than white people to report crime to the police, black people expressed lower levels of satisfaction with police response. The report concluded that, although the pattern of crime against minority ethnic groups differs when factors other than 'race' are taken into account (for example, residential and social circumstances), black people were still more likely to be victims of some crimes than white people (Mayhew *et al.*, 1989).

8.5 Developments since 1992

The Runnymede Trust's submission to the Royal Commission on Criminal Justice claimed that unequal treatment occurred at all stages of the system, from initial contact with the police to imprisonment (Runnymede Trust, 1992c). As targets of crime, the risk of being a victim remains highest among the minority ethnic group population, with Asians at greater risk of vandalism and robbery/theft from the person. Black (Afro-Caribbean) people in London are three times more likely than white people to die from bullet or knife wounds, according to Metropolitan Police statistics. While murder rates for Asians reflect their presence in the population, Afro-Caribbeans are three times more likely to be murder victims (*Police Review*, 18 June 1993).

To summarize a range of research, it has been established that Afro-Caribbean people, irrespective of age or income, are more likely to be stopped and searched by police; that Afro-Caribbeans are much less likely to be cautioned, and more likely to be arrested; that Afro-Caribbeans are more likely to face more serious charges than other people for the same offence; that Afro-Caribbeans are more likely to be charged for victimless crimes (e.g. driving offences); that black and Asian people are more likely to be remanded in custody than white; that black and Asian people are far less likely to have social inquiry reports ordered; that black and Asian people are less likely to receive probation orders, and that black and Asian people have lower perceptions of the police, and less confidence than whites in the criminal justice system (The 1990 Trust, 1994). The *Diversity Directory* of spring 1995 contains a detailed summary of the differential treatment experienced by black and Asian people across the criminal justice system (*Diversity Directory*, 1995).

There remains, however, a relative dearth of information from *official* sources on minority ethnic groups and the criminal justice system. Among the dozens of tables on the criminal justice system in the *Social Trends* of the 1990s, only two analysed data by ethnicity, one to demonstrate that sentenced male adult prisoners in 1993 from black, Indian, Pakistani and Bangladeshi groups were two and half times more likely than whites to be in custody for drug offences (CSO, 1995, Table 9.24). Two Home Office studies, subsequently shelved in 1994, revealed that young black people (14 to 25 years of age) were less likely to commit crime than their white counterparts. The research also indicated that white youths were twice as likely to have used or sold drugs than black youths (Bowling *et al.*, 1994; Runnymede Trust, 1994e).

In 1995, the Runnymede Trust reported that the number of black and Asian people stopped and searched by the MPF in London was double and often treble their number as a proportion of the population (Runnymede Trust, 1995d). The figures, published in *Hansard*, revealed that nearly one in two of all stop and searches in Brent, Haringey, Hackney and Lambeth involved a black person. *Table 8.4* provides the data for London, and *Table 8.5* the picture for England and Wales. Nationally black and ethnic minorities are five times more likely to be stopped and searched than white people.

In April 1995, new laws under the Criminal Justice Act made it easier for the police to stop and search a person. Previously they had to have reasonable grounds to suspect that a prohibited article would be found, but this condition has been removed. Voluntary groups and 'race' agencies now fear a return to the days of the 'sus' laws of the 1970s and early 1980s.

Table 8.6 shows the ethnic origin of staff and practitioners in the criminal justice system. The table was constructed by the Runnymede Trust and is based on Home Office statistics produced in 1994. Unfortunately, Home Office data do not distinguish between African, Afro-Caribbean and South Asian people, and the term 'ethnic minority' here conceals many significant differences in representation. It is important to remember that the baseline is 5.5 per cent, and for those services based in London, around 20 per cent.

Table 8.4: stop and search figures in the MPF area, January–September 1994 (top 20 districts only)

Borough	Total	White	Black	Asian	Other ethnic minority	Unknown	Percentage who were black	Percentage black people in the population
Brent	4,149	1,548	1,928	373	113	187	46.47	16.51
Haringey	6,731	2,583	3,028	186	844	90	44.99	17.09
Hackney	12,493	4,574	5,503	508	1,547	361	44.05	22.00
Lambeth	13,077	5,648	5,688	242	430	1,069	43.50	21.82
Wandsworth	6,019	3,000	2,370	211	123	315	39.38	10.62
Lewisham	10,264	5,599	3,960	174	423	108	38.58	16.25
Hammersmith and Fulham	4,241	2,058	1,551	121	167	344	36.57	10.19
Southwark	16,169	8,840	5,318	246	605	1,160	32.89	17.76
Waltham Forest	4,742	2,282	1,485	603	143	229	31.32	11.28
Kensington and Chelsea	6,649	3,136	1,915	180	1,343	75	28.80	5.84
Islington	9,114	5,448	2,614	301	751	0	28.68	10.59
Newham	6,784	3,165	1,839	1,413	203	164	27.11	14.36
Ealing	5,803	2,502	1,515	1,370	129	287	26.11	7.07
Camden	6,057	3,709	1,271	352	358	367	20.98	5.51
Croydon	4,873	3,506	1,008	154	86	119	20.69	7.57
Westminster	24,212	14,114	4,942	1,103	2,772	1,281	20.41	7.71
Harrow	1,402	1,024	233	122	19	4	16.62	3.72
Tower Hamlets	7,990	3,550	1,208	2,470	249	513	15.12	7.08
Greenwich	8,359	6,386	1,089	168	210	506	13.03	5.36
Merton	3,509	2,754	439	74	93	149	12.51	5.74
Total[1]	202,562	116,076	52,530	12,478	12,394	9,084	25.93	

[1]Totals include data for *all* MFP districts.
(Adapted from Runnymede Trust, 1995d)

Table 8.5: stop and search figures in England and Wales, April 1993–April 1994

Police force area	Total	White persons	Ethnic minorities	Percentage of ethnic minority origin	Ethnic minority in the total population
Metropolitan Police	228,316	132,565	95,751	41.9	20.0
West Midlands	6,025	4,098	1,927	32.0	14.6
City of London	2,111	1,611	500	23.7	7.3
Bedfordshire	1,705	1,381	324	19.0	9.9
Thames Valley**	4,432	3,817	615	13.9	5.6
West Yorkshire	3,022	2,636	386	12.8	8.2
Leicestershire	11,801	10,387	1,414	12.0	11.1
Greater Manchester	42,510	38,376	4,134	9.7	5.9

e force area	Total	White persons	Ethnic minorities	Percentage of ethnic minority origin	Ethnic minorities in the total population*
nghamshire	1,992	1,817	175	8.8	4.0
ordshire	4,158	3,807	351	8.4	4.0
h Yorkshire	5,458	5,054	404	7.4	2.9
and Somerset**	3,939	3,657	282	7.2	2.0
bridgeshire	2,659	2,480	179	6.7	3.5
ashire	6,894	6,432	462	6.7	4.4
vickshire	3,357	3,138	219	6.5	3.4
ey	13,414	12,544	870	6.5	2.8
ordshire	1,673	1,567	106	6.3	1.8
nt	2,197	2,087	110	5.0	1.5
ex**	4,331	4,118	213	4.9	1.9
t Mercia**	7,866	7,500	366	4.7	1.4
hamptonshire	2,977	2,840	137	4.6	3.5
hire	1,605	1,534	71	4.4	1.7
olk	2,107	2,016	91	4.3	2.2
yshire	3,462	3,313	149	4.3	3.0
eyside	15,737	15,075	662	4.2	1.8
x	4,318	4,182	136	3.1	1.9
	3,653	3,550	103	2.8	2.3
berside	1,089	1,063	26	2.4	1.0
pshire**	2,568	2,515	53	2.1	1.8
eland	2,271	2,240	31	1.4	1.9
n and Cornwall**	958	947	11	1.1	0.6
h Yorkshire	2,278	2,253	25	1.1	0.7
shire	507	502	5	1.0	1.0
am	1,444	1,430	14	1.0	0.7
humbria**	8,134	8,064	70	0.9	1.5
olk	6,463	6,410	53	0.8	0.9
olnshire	2,298	2,280	18	0.8	0.8
bria	3,984	3,954	30	0.8	0.4
d–Powys**	7,757	7,720	37	0.5	0.7
n Wales**	8,804	8,792	12	0.1	1.6
et	1,640	1,640		0.0	0.9
h Wales**	–	–	–		3.0
cestershire	–	–	–		1.8
	441,914	331,392	110,522	25.0	

ed on the 1991 census.

these areas the police division and the local authority boundaries do not exactly coincide. In these instances it may isleading to compare the number of black people stopped and searched and their proportion in the population.

nymede Trust, 1995d)

Table 8.6: staff and practitioners in the criminal justice system in the 1990s, by ethnicity

Agency	Date of survey	Percentage ethnic minority
Boards of visitors	March 1994	7.0
Clerks to the Justices	March 1994	0.0
Crown Prosecution Service		
Total staff	March 1994	6.4
New entrants, 1993	January 1994	9.2
Resignations and dismissals, 1993	January 1994	8.7
Home Office		
Admin assistants	1993	19.0
Admin officers	1993	20.0
Executive officers	1993	2.0
Higher executive	1993	3.0
Grades 1–7	1993	0.7
Judiciary		
Judges and recorders	July 1994	see note 1
Lay magistrates: new appointments	July 1994	5.5
Legal profession		
QCs	March 1994	see note 2
Barristers	October 1993	see note 3
Solicitors	January 1994	2.3
Other magistrates court staff	March 1994	4.2
Parole Board	January 1994	8.0
Police service (see note 4)		
Total nationally	31 December 1993	1.5
Greater Manchester Police	31 December 1993	1.9
Metropolitan Police	31 December 1993	2.4
West Midlands Police	31 December 1993	3.4
By rank nationally		
Inspectors and above	31 December 1993	0.34
Sergeants	31 December 1993	0.57
Constables	31 December 1993	1.8
Prison service (see note 5)		
Grades 1–7	1 April 1994	0.4
Governors	1 April 1994	0.5
Principal officers	1 April 1994	0.5
Senior officers	1 April 1994	1.2
Officers	1 April 1994	2.4
Probation service	December 1992	5.3
Police Complaints Authority	April 1994	22.0
Police Authorities	April 1995	4.5

Notes to Table 8.6

1   As of 1 July 1994 there were four circuit judges (out of 510 altogether), 11 recorders (out of 866) and nine assistant recorders (out of 394) from ethnic minority backgrounds. There was no minority ethnic representation amongst the 95 high court judges, 29 Lords Justice, or 10 Lords of Appeal. (Source: monitoring report by the Judicial Appointments Division, July 1994, notified to the Runnymede Trust.)

2   As of 31 March 1994 there were ten ethnic minority QCs, of whom five were South Asian and four Afro-Caribbean. (Source: the Bar Council.) In 1993, fourteen applications to become QCs were made by minority ethnic people and one person (7 per cent) was appointed.

3   In October 1993, the Bar Council conducted a survey relating to the ethnicity of all barristers. The number of questionnaires distributed was 7,194; the number returned was 5,404, which is only 75 per cent. Of those who did reply, 6.1 per cent (330 out of 5,404) were from minority ethnic backgrounds. If, as is probable, the vast majority of non-respondents were white, then the actual proportion of minority ethnic barristers must be in the region of 4 per cent.

4   The figures for the police service by region are taken from *Hansard*, 26 April 1994, columns 95–96. The figures by rank are taken directly from the HM Inspectorate of Constabulary's own monitoring returns, as notified to the Runnymede Trust.

5   The figures for the prison service are quoted directly from the service's own returns, as notified to the Runnymede Trust.

(Runnymede Trust, 1994a, p. 31; based on Home Office, 1994b)

Hood's *Race and Sentencing* was published in 1992, and was based on research conducted at Crown Courts in Birmingham, Dudley, Wolverhampton, Coventry, Warwick and Stafford in 1989. The major findings included the following. Minority ethnic defendants accounted for 28 per cent of males sentenced at West Midlands Crown Courts, two and a half times greater than their proportions in the population; there was a far greater conviction rate for Afro-Caribbean defendants; there were marked differences in the proportions of each minority group given custodial sentences; the proportion of Afro-Caribbeans sentenced to custody was eight percentage points more than for whites; Asians were sentenced to custody less than either white or Afro-Caribbean defendants; there were wide variations in sentencing between Crown Court locations, with Afro-Caribbeans seventeen percentage points more likely than whites to be sentenced in Dudley; there was a wide variation between judge identity, minority ethnic group status of defendant and sentencing outcomes; a significantly higher proportion of Afro-Caribbean and Asian adults received a sentence of over three years (17.4 per cent and 15.1 per cent) compared with whites (10.6 per cent); average sentences were also longer, controlling for defendant plea and type of offence; Afro-Caribbean defendants were more likely than other groups to be given suspended sentences rather than probation; young Afro-Caribbean defendants appeared to be particularly disadvantaged by the judicial process; and, finally, Hood found very little variation between these outcomes and gender, with Afro-Caribbean women over-represented six-fold in relation to their population within the studied areas of jurisdiction (Hood, 1992).

Home Office figures in 1994 confirmed some of Hood's findings. Afro-Caribbean and Asian people received longer prison sentences than whites for the same offence. Afro-Caribbean men over 21 received the longest sentences. Afro-Caribbean and Asian males under 21 received an average sentence of 16 months, compared to 12 months for whites. For the over-21 group, Afro-Caribbean and Asian males received an average of 25.5 months, Asians 21 and whites 18 months (*The Times*, 12 August 1994).

NACRO revealed that black and Asian people were still 'severely under-represented' among staff in prisons, probation services, the legal profession, the judiciary and the magistracy. They also reported that 16 per cent of males in prison and 28 per cent of females were from minority ethnic groups – more than three times the expected number given their distribution in society and controlling for age cohorts (NACRO, 1992). Home Office data show that 12 per cent of the prison population of England and Wales had minority ethnic group origins; 9 per cent were Afro-Caribbean and African, 1.8 per cent South Asian and 1.2 per cent from other minority groups (Home Office, 1994b). Another Home Office study confirmed these findings. The proportion of Afro-Caribbean and African men in prison was seven times higher than that of white men, and the proportion of Afro-Caribbean women was 20 times higher than that of white women (CSO, 1994).

Table 8.7: the prison population of England and Wales in 1992, by ethnicity

	Men	Women	All
Afro-Caribbean	144.0	9.9	76.7
South Asian	24.3	0.4	12.4
White	19.4	0.5	9.6
Other/not disclosed	72.1	5.4	38.3
All	22.0	0.7	11.0

Figures are per 10,000 population.
(Runnymede Trust, 1994a; from CSO, 1994)

Further evidence of an increase in Afro-Caribbean women going to prison was released in 1995. Between February 1993 and February 1995 the number of women in Britain's prisons rose from 1,402 to 2,000, a rise which contained a disproportionate number of Afro-Caribbean women (*Independent*, 26 February 1995). Home Office figures further showed that 16.4 per cent of the males and 26.6 per cent of prisoners in UK prisons were from minority ethnic groups. Among UK men in prisons, 87.5 per cent were white, 9.6 per cent Afro-Caribbean, 1.7 per cent South Asian and 1.2 per cent Chinese or other origin; of women, 86 per cent were white, 11.8 per cent were Afro-Caribbeans, 0.8 per cent were South Asian and 1.4 per cent Chinese or other (NACRO, 1995; Runnymede Trust, 1995g; 1995h).

All prisons now employ a race relations officer and racial abuse is a specific disciplinary offence. Nevertheless the culture of prison officer racism is difficult to erase. One officer told a PRT researcher: 'Officers calling inmates "niggers, coons" – you think that's gone out of the window? Well it hasn't' (*Independent*, 27 July 1992). An inquiry into the deaths of Orville Blackwood and two other black inmates at Broadmoor Prison concluded that Broadmoor was 'loaded against black people' (Runnymede Trust, 1993h). The inquiry found a culture of 'organized racism'. Forty-seven recommendations for change were made, the majority rejected by Broadmoor management, including a monitoring programme to ensure that the 47 recommendations were implemented (*Independent*, 1 September 1993). In November 1993, at Holme House Prison, swastikas were displayed by prison officers in the reception area. (*Independent*, 16 November 1993). At Armley Prison, Leeds, where 14 per cent of the 1,087 inmates are of South Asian origin, an Asian prisoner was attacked by people in Klu Klux Klan hoods (Runnymede Trust, 1994f). In 1993, IRR researchers revealed that, every other month, a young black person dies in suspicious circumstances in the custody of our prisons, police and psychiatric hospitals (Sivanandan, 1994).

The number of racial incidents in prison is rising, from 106 in 1991 to 141 in 1993: 20 involved staff on prisoners. Black prisoners were also over-represented in a dossier of 163 alleged miscarriages of justice – 23 per cent of 'dubious jailings' involved black defendants (*Guardian*, 10 October 1992). A landmark High Court ruling in November 1994 criticized the secrecy surrounding the way the Home Secretary deals with miscarriage of justice inquiries. Of 634 miscarriage allegations involving prison cases between 1988 and 1992, only 28 were referred back to the Court of Appeal. Cuts in staff in C3, the division concerned with miscarriages during this period, exacerbated the problem. A new division, the Criminal Cases Review Authority (CCRA), is to be introduced in 1995–96, to replace C3 (*Guardian*, 29 November 1994).

Under Section 95 of the Criminal Justice Act 1992 judges were instructed for the first time on the avoidance of racist language (*Independent*, 22 October 1992). Lord Mackay, the Lord Chancellor, announced the launch of a two-year £1 million programme to train judges in racial awareness, especially in the way people should be addressed in court. 'Nigger in the woodpile' is clearly not appropriate, a reprimanded Judge Bernstein was reminded following his use of this phrase in a Liverpool court in 1994. The training includes oath taking, body language and cross-cultural communication. Hood's research on 'race' and sentencing was also used as part of the curriculum (*Guardian*, 31 January 1994; 20 April 1994).

Of 2,887 part-time judges serving Crown and County Courts in England and Wales, only 32 were of black or Asian origin. There are no black or Asian High Court or Court of Appeal judges. The Inns of Court were censured at the Bar's annual general meeting in 1994 for lacking commitment to stamp out racial discrimination in the legal profession (*Independent*, 18 July 1994).

The Council for Legal Education (CLE) revealed that black candidates were three times more likely than white to fail Bar examinations (45 per cent compared with 16 per cent) (*Independent*, 2 November 1992). A Bar Inquiry concluded that indirect racial bias was prevalent, and emphasized the role of 'old boy networks' (*Independent*, 19 September 1993). The Bar Council established a new race equality policy, monitoring procedures, and new training targets, but to little effect. The Inns of Court School of Law exams showed that while 21 per cent of applicants were from minority ethnic groups, only 10 per cent passed the exam; analysis also showed that white males had a far greater chance than black and Asian females to gain a place for solicitor training (*New Law Journal*, 25 March 1994). Results in 1995 from the Bar's vocational course showed a pass rate of 74–76 per cent for minority ethnic candidates and 90 per cent for white. In 1992 the minority ethnic pass rate was 55 per cent, and this had risen to 80 per cent in 1994 (*Independent*, 15 August 1995).

The PSI survey of 4,000 law students found that white students had a 47 per cent chance of getting a trainee position, compared with 7 per cent for black and Asian students (*Independent*, 21 April 1994; PSI, 1994a). The PSI concluded that minority ethnic students were suffering direct and indirect discrimination in the legal system. Less qualified white candidates were obtaining training contracts at the expense of better qualified black and Asian candidates.

In 1994 the Law Society wrote to 11,000 solicitor firms in England and Wales urging them not to discriminate against black students. Civil practice has fewer black and Asian practitioners than has criminal work (*Guardian*, 14 September 1994; *Independent*, 22 February 1995). The Law Society 1994 Report revealed that minority ethnic solicitors formed 4.4 per cent of the Society Roll (Runnymede Trust, 1995h). In June 1995, solicitors elected a new Law Society President committed to reversing anti-discrimination policies of the early 1990s. In the first contested election since 1954, Michael Mears defeated the Society's official candidate, Henry Hodge, and promised to attack 'political correctness' in the profession and to block the proposed appointment of an equality officer in the Society (*Independent*, 7 June 1995).

Following increasing concern about racial inequality at inquests, the Legal Aid Practitioners' Group announced the Victim Without a Voice campaign. The campaign is particularly concerned to highlight 'race' issues in an arena where many poor bereaved people find themselves unrepresented and without legal aid. The cost of extending legal aid to the inquest system would add 0.3 per cent to the total legal aid budget of £1 billion (*Independent*, 29 October 1993).

The chair of the CRE, Herman Ouseley, has estimated that at the present rate of recruitment it would take until the year 2030 before 5 per cent of the police force came from ethnic minorities (evidence to the Select Committee of the House of Commons on Racial Attacks and Harassment, 1 December

1993). MPF recruitment from ethnic minorities rose from 1.7 per cent in 1990 to 2.4 per cent in 1993 (from 483 to 650). Nationally the increase was from 1.08 per cent in 1990 to 1.53 per cent in 1993 (from 1,374 to 1,908). In 1993, a joint police/CRE booklet called for greater recruitment efforts in ethnic communities and in career development for black and Asian officers (CRE and Association of Chief Police Officers, 1993).

The Police Federation of England and Wales equal opportunities policy seeks to eradicate racist behaviour within the service (Police Federation, 1993). Home Office evidence to the Select Committee revealed that wastage rates for all officers were 4.5 per cent in 1990 and 4.2 per cent in 1991; for minority ethnic officers the figures were 5.2 per cent in 1990 and 4.1 per cent in 1991 (Home Office, 1993, p.7).

The Chief Inspector of Constabulary Home Office Review for 1993 revealed that black and Asian minority police recruitment had levelled out or was declining. It also highlighted 'unacceptable levels of prejudice and racist exchanges' within the service (HMSO, 1994b; *Guardian*, 14 July 1994). A new equal opportunities policy for the MPF is to be launched in 1995, directed at personnel practices, grievance structures and the force cultures (*Searchlight*, February 1995). Research into the bar culture of the MPF during 1994 found 'racism' and 'appalling behaviour' which often 'went unchallenged' (Kinsley Lord, 1994).

Minority ethnic group confidence in the police remains low. A survey of 1,800 people over the age of 16 showed that 76 per cent of white people felt the police do a fairly or a very good job, compared with 62 per cent of Asians and 52 per cent of Afro-Caribbeans. A quarter of all minority ethnic groups felt the police generally were doing a fairly or very poor job, compared with 15 per cent of white respondents (*Guardian*, 9 December 1992). In April 1993, a MORI poll found that 67 per cent of black people interviewed in 32 Merseyside districts were not satisfied with their policing (*Independent*, 12 April 1993; Runnymede Trust, 1993e). In the PSI report, *Changing Lives*, 85 per cent of black young people agreed that police harassed young black people more than their white contemporaries (the proportion of young whites agreeing was 50 per cent). Only a quarter of 17-year-olds in Leeds, Manchester, Merseyside, Birmingham and East and South London, agreed that judges and courts operated fair and equal practices and procedures.

The Criminal Justice Act 1995, by taking away the right to silence and introducing a new caution statement, may have eroded further police–public relations, especially with minority ethnic communities. Young black and Asian disenchantment with police and judiciary was considered 'hostile' (PSI, 1994b; *Independent*, 12 December 1994).

Despite the Police Complaints Authority (PCA) figures showing a slight fall from 1991 to 1993 (from 18,605 to 17,991), the number of complaints specifically focusing on racial discrimination rose from 67 in 1991 to 291 in

1993 (partly due to an improved monitoring system and heightened awareness of the issue). The report admitted that few complaints had resulted in
disciplinary action: no charges were brought in 1992; charges were brought
in 4 per cent of racial discrimination cases in 1993 (against a rate of 10 per
cent overall). The report claimed that complaint procedures and the failure
to discipline officers resulted in an under-reporting of racial discrimination
complaints (HMSO, 1994a; CSO, 1995). Operation Jackpot, which has
investigated corruption allegations in Stoke Newington Police Station since
1991, is considering 134 complaints against 45 officers, many involving the
planting of drugs on black young people. One officer has been jailed for 18
months, four have been suspended, eight transferred, and several removed
from the drug squad. So far, the police have paid out over £250,000 in
damages (*Guardian*, 2 February 1994). In summer 1995, the PCA revealed
that fewer than 8 per cent of 150,000 formal complaints made since 1985 had
resulted in an officer being disciplined (*Independent*, 11 May 1995).

The Metropolitan Police Commissioner, Sir Paul Condon, urged police to be
'intolerant of racially motivated attacks, intolerant of those who indulge in
racial abuse and intolerant of those who use hatred and violence as the tools
of their political expression' (*Independent*, 1 March 1993). Following this
speech, he received a 'large number' of offensive letters from 'people in
authority' (*Independent*, 5 June 1993). The Commissioner responded by
pledging his commitment to making racism 'the greatest challenge facing
the force' (*Guardian*, 4 August 1993).

Condon's claims, in July 1995, that 80 per cent of 'muggings' (street thefts
and robberies) in London were committed by young 'black' (Afro-Caribbean)
men, raised concerns among criminologists, 'race' relations experts and
social statisticians, by their crudity and bluntness (P. Toynbee, 'Mugging: is
it a black and white issue?' *Independent*, 8 July 1995; Runnymede Trust,
1995h). By singling out 'black' communities, the Commissioner was accused
of destabilizing progress made in police–community relations (*Independent*,
8 July 1995, 14 July 1995; *Guardian*, 8 July 1995; *Independent on Sunday*,
9 July 1995).

Toynbee's analysis of the resulting furore revealed a range of criticisms.
Criminologist Michael Keith commented: 'if you were to standardize for
everything else – education, unemployment, housing, life-chances – race on
its own would have virtually no significance'. The LRC revealed that in one
of the areas cited by Condon, Lambeth, 23 per cent of young men aged
between 16 and 23 were Afro-Caribbean; of these, 45 per cent were unemployed. Condon was referring to data showing an increase from 19,000 to
22,000 in reported street robberies and thefts, most of which took place in
areas of minority ethnic group concentration characterized by relatively
high levels of unemployment and poverty. Robert Reiner, of the London
School of Economics, observed: 'Race is of little importance. It is just a proxy
for class in some areas. If you put people of any nationality into the same

history as these young black people you would get the same results.' Robbery is not a black crime either, 81 per cent of people imprisoned for it are white; it is also a relatively rare crime compared to other reported crimes (2 per cent of crimes dealt with by the MPF in 1994) (Toynbee, ibid.). The *Voice* accused Condon of wrecking a decade of improving police and community relations (*Voice*, 8 July 1995; *Independent*, 12 July 1995). Condon's 'Eagle Eye' initiative revived memories of the 'Swamp 81' operation in Brixton, in 1981, which was identified by Lord Scarman as a major cause of the Brixton riots in April of that year.

In an exercise in perceived damage limitation, Condon commented in a London *Evening Standard* article: 'a large proportion of victims of mugging in London tell us that their assailants are black', he wrote. 'These young people, a very small percentage of black youths, are not becoming criminals because they are black. It would be an unacceptable slur to suggest that' (*Evening Standard*, 10 July 1995).

Condon endorsed the formation of the Black and Asian Police Association (BAPA) in the MPF. The BAPA will act as a network group, has an executive of seventeen senior black police officers, and is designed to become a national association during the late 1990s. Patrick Edwards, director of Greater London Action for Racial Equality (GLARE), the race equality think tank, welcomed the BAPA: 'the fact that black officers themselves have created this body starkly underlines the continued failure of the MPF to recruit more black officers and tackle racism within the force' (*Guardian*, 12 August 1994).

Sun Hill 'nick', in ITV's *The Bill*, registered a national first in January 1994 – the introduction of a black female detective inspector, 'Magic' Johnson. What is unusual for a high-profile television series which prides itself on authenticity is that DI Johnson is not just a first in fiction. In January 1994, *no* black police woman in Britain had made the rank of DI. For example, of 3,897 women police officers in the MPF, only 152 were from minority ethnic groups; four had reached the rank of sergeant. DI Johnson joined two other black officers at Sun Hill. Jaye Griffith who played her had a one-year contract (*The Times*, 12 February 1994). DI Johnson was transferred from Sun Hill in February 1995. The real police force still awaits its first black woman DI.

In June 1995, following police removal of an Asian woman and her child in the Manningham district of Bradford, two nights of violent disturbances followed between Asian youths and West Yorkshire Police. Manningham, the site of the *Bands of Hope* television drama of drugs and prostitution, which topped the ratings in the weeks preceding the unrest, is one of Britain's most disadvantaged areas. Unemployment in 1995 among Asian males in Bradford was over 50 per cent. At the time of writing, a PCA inquiry has been established with a brief to investigate complaints against the police, the force's policing policy, the policing of the unrest, and its causes.

The causes of the disturbances are very complex. Were they a response to insensitive policing techniques? Were they the result of a widening gap between Asian youth and elders? Were they related to the defence of an Islamic community? Was the increasing use of drugs and pornographic activity amongst Asian people and the methods adopted by the police to combat these important contributory factors? And what role did broader issues play: intense poverty, widespread unemployment and consequent alienation? Whatever the causes, there seems to be a vital need for improved dialogue between the Asian community and voluntary and statutory authorities, especially between young Asians and the police. In the weeks following the disturbances, and others in Luton, the Home Office expressed concern about vigilante groups set up by Pakistani and Bangladeshi communities in response to racist attacks. The Home Office warned that a 'demographic time-bomb' might explode, with young Asian males about to come of age (*Independent*, 21 August 1995).

Notes

1   See also P. Wynn Davies, 'Colour blindness in the jury room', *Independent*, 29 June 1990.

2   According to a survey of the ethnic composition of the magistracy conducted in 1986. Unless otherwise specified, figures in this section relate to England and Wales only.

3   See R. Rice, 'Secret world of magistrates' selection', *Independent*, 31 March 1989.

4   S. Wallach, 'The bench that anyone can sit on', *Independent*, 12 April 1991.

5   Ole Hansen, 'Women and blacks: more chances but less promotion', *Independent*, 28 April 1989. Hansen's figures were based on a Law Society survey in 1988. See also Ole Hansen, 'A multi coloured approach to business', *Independent*, 26 October 1990.

6   See King *et al.* (1990). The study was based on a survey of 1,141 students in the penultimate year of a law degree and 1,333 successful finalists in the 1986 Law Society final examination who were seeking employment. See also King and Israel (1989) pp. 107–20.

7   Ole Hansen (see note 5). See also the *Independent*, 20 May 1991, for Bar Council initiative details.

8   *Independent*, 29 March 1991.

9   *Independent*, 13 October 1991.

10   See also Landau (1981) pp. 27–46 and Landau *et al.* (1983) pp. 186–97.

11   See Central Statistical Office (1991) Table 12.25, p. 206. In 1985 black people accounted for 12.5 per cent of the prison population of England and Wales.

12 See also *Public Eye,* BBC2, 1 March 1991.

13 See also H. Mills, 'Black people "more likely to be jailed"', *Independent*, 14 January 1991, which summarizes the findings of two local studies supporting NACRO's conclusions. One was by probation officers in West Yorkshire (see Mair, 1986). The other examined disparities in 8,000 cases in Middlesex, controlling for type of offence.

14 See also Genders and Player (1990).

15 *Independent*, 12 December 1989.

16 The Metropolitan Police Assistant Commissioner, announcing the campaign, said that extensive research had revealed that up to 2 million potential recruits were barred by their height *(Independent,* 23 January 1990).

17 *Financial Times,* 2 February 1990.

18 Letter to the *Independent*, 7 May 1990, from Wyn Jones, Assistant Commissioner, Metropolitan Police.

19 *Independent*, 21 December 1989.

20 *Dispatches,* Channel 4, October 1990.

21 See K. Hyder, 'Young blacks "would not think of joining police"', *Independent*, 20 December 1988.

9 'RACE' AND EDUCATION

9.1 'Race', education and official statistics

The issue of education and 'race' is complex and our knowledge is partial. From 1973 to 1990 successive governments did not record the ethnic origin of school children or of students in further, higher or adult education. In 1973 the Department of Education and Science (DES) pupil census that recorded the 'ethnic origin' of pupils was terminated by Margaret Thatcher, then Secretary of State for Education. Since 1973 understanding of racial inequality in education has been informed by a wide range of research conducted by Select Committees, the former Inner London Education Authority (ILEA), the Commission for Racial Equality (CRE), trade unions and independent research. The 1990s has seen ethnic monitoring introduced on a much wider scale (see Part 1).[1]

9.2 'Race' and pupil achievement

Between 1966 and 1973 the DES recorded pupils' ethnicity on the basis of the 'immigrant' status of the parents. Studies of these data, notably by researchers for ILEA and for education priority areas around Britain, showed that pupils of Asian origin performed less well than whites, and Afro-Caribbeans less well than Asians. The data also revealed that, for both groups, performance improved with length of stay and schooling in Britain (DES, 1973).

Differential outcomes in the education levels of minority ethnic group pupils, especially as measured by examination achievement, have long been a source of concern. House of Commons Select Committees in 1969, 1973, 1974 and 1977 and the Committee of Inquiry into the Education of Children from ethnic minority groups under the chair of first Anthony Rampton and then Lord Swann (DES, 1985), all pointed to the lower attainment levels of minority ethnic group children, particular Afro-Caribbeans. These reports have been complemented by local studies which reflect the complexity of definitions, claims and counter-claims involved in the 'achievement debate'. It is worth keeping Troyna's advice in mind when perusing statistical evidence on pupil achievement:

the greatest danger lies in the possibility that ill-conceived and poorly formulated studies will perpetuate the notion of black educational under-achievement as a *given* rather than as a problematic that requires sensitive and systematic interrogation.

(Troyna, 1984, p. 164)

The findings of surveys conducted in 1979 and 1982 for the Rampton/Swann Committee in five local education authorities (LEAs) with a high proportion of minority ethnic group pupils show significant inter-minority ethnic group differences. All five surveys were conducted in inner-city areas where the average educational attainment for every minority ethnic group is lower than the national average.

Children and young people from different minority ethnic groups revealed differences in educational attainment: white and Asian children and young people achieve higher results, on average, than Afro-Caribbeans (see *Figure 9.1*).

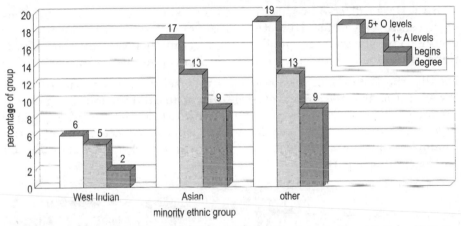

Figure 9.1: educational attainment of different ethnic groups in Great Britain, 1981–2 *(Adapted from Statham et al., 1989)*

This picture needs to be qualified in a number of ways. First, different ethnic groups are often of very different social class composition. Since educational attainment is strongly linked to social class, some of the ostensible differences in achievement between minority ethnic groups may be reflections of class differences.

Secondly, none of these ethnic categories is monolithic. The 'Asian' group, for example, is itself made up of groups of different levels of achievement. This is illustrated by data from ILEA in *Figure 9.2* which compares the examination results of fifth-year pupils of Indian, Pakistani and Bangladeshi origin or descent.

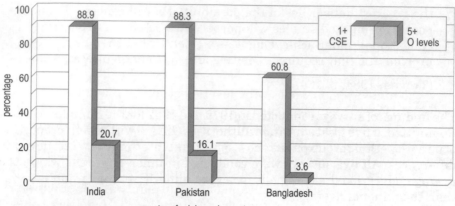

Note: '1+ CSE' means at least one CSE grade 5 or higher; '5+ O levels' means at least five O levels grade C or higher

Figure 9.2: examination results of fifth-year Asian pupils in ILEA, by country of origin or descent, 1986
(Adapted from Statham et al., 1989)

Thirdly, data collected by ILEA (which published more detailed statistics than central government or other LEAs on differences between ethnic groups) have shown Asian pupils to have distinctly higher average educational attainment than white or Afro-Caribbean pupils (ILEA, 1987).

Finally, the Rampton/Swann statistics themselves provide evidence that the educational achievements of Afro-Caribbean children and young people are increasing from year to year at a higher rate than those of other groups. *Figure 9.3* compares A-level results in 1979, when data were gathered for the Rampton Report, with those in 1982 when comparable data were collected for the Swann Report.

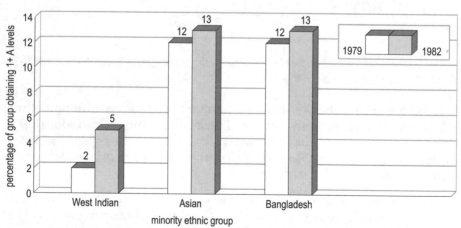

Note: There is a minor discrepancy between the 1978—9 figures for Asians as given in the Rampton Report (13%) and in the Swann Report (12%). Here we have followed Swann.

Figure 9.3: educational attainment of different minority ethnic groups in Great Britain, 1978–9 and 1981–2
(Adapted from Statham et al., 1989)

The ILEA study of minority ethnic group background and examination results was extrapolated from a pupil sample of over 17,000 in 1985 and 15,000 in 1986, providing one of the most detailed pictures so far (ILEA, 1987).[2] ILEA's findings suggest that Afro-Caribbean pupils have improved examination performance – measured in relation to CSE and O-levels – since the mid-1970s, but not to the levels reached by Asian pupils. Their findings also indicate that some Asian groups perform better in examinations than white pupils. However, ILEA emphasized that *within* the Asian category, Bangladeshi pupils scored lowest on all their measures of achievement. Moreover, the proportion of Bangladeshi pupils *not* entered for examination was higher than for all other minority ethnic groups (36 per cent in 1986), but lowest for Indian and Pakistani pupils (10 per cent for each group). The figure for white English, Scottish, Welsh and Irish (ESWI) pupils was 22 per cent.

ILEA also calculated 'performance scores' for the studied groups. In 1986 the 'performance scores' were: Bangladeshi 9.3 – the lowest group score; Caribbean 13.5; African 17.6; Pakistani 20.9; and Indian 22.0 – the highest score. The average score for Bangladeshis was significantly below the overall average of 15.2.

ILEA's data also revealed important gender differences within ethnic group performance, with girls scoring on average four points more than boys in both studied years. For example, in 1985 the average score for Bangladeshi girls, 15.1, was twice that of Bangladeshi boys, 7.6. The score for Bangladeshi girls was also four points higher than that for Caribbean boys and two points higher than ESWI boys. ILEA concluded their 1987 report by emphasizing their 'cause for concern' at the the two minority ethnic groups who performed consistently below average on most of their measures – Bangladeshi and Caribbean pupils. The ILEA report also showed that differences in expectations at intake into the secondary school were an important factor influencing outcomes. Low achievement in examination results was related to low attainment in primary school (ILEA, 1987).

A Bradford study of CSE and O-level performance in 24 secondary schools between 1983 and 1987 confirmed some of the ILEA findings, but noted a marked improvement in black (Afro-Caribbean and Asian, but mainly Asian) pupil performance compared with white. The survey found that in 1987 only 7 per cent of black pupils left school without qualifications compared with 19 per cent of white pupils. Pass grades achieved by black school-leavers were also better than those of white pupils. In 1987, 47 per cent of black pupils gained grades A to C at O-level or grade 1 at CSE compared to 39 per cent of white pupils. The Bradford researchers controlled for social class, basing their analysis on how many pupils in each studied school qualified for free meals. Using this measure they found that there was little difference among Bradford's schools in terms of black and white pupil performance.[3]

In February 1991, *The Times Educational Supplement* reported that, according to a University of London study, the introduction of the GCSE examination had failed to narrow the gap between different ethnic groups' examination results. The study analysed the results of 16,700 pupils who took their GCSEs in inner-London schools in 1988. In 1986 the School Examination and Assessment Council published criteria for the GCSE which stated that the examination should be 'as free as possible from ethnic, sex, religious, political or other forms of bias'.[4] Nuttall and Goldstein's analysis of the 1988 results showed that Indian and Pakistani pupils, who attained better results than their white classmates under the GCE system, did even better under GCSE which then gave more weight to course work in the assessment. Bangladeshi and Afro-Caribbean pupils, whose marks were below average, achieved less than ever compared to their peers. The gender gap also widened, girls gaining higher marks than boys.[5]

In the autumn of 1991 Nuttall and Goldstein released further analysis of GCSE results. The study for the Association of Metropolitan Authorities of six London boroughs' 1990 examination results looked at the examination perfomance of 5,500 pupils in relation to gender, ethnic origin and eligibility for free school meals (as a rough measure of deprivation). Pupils from India and Pakistani families fared better than those of Afro-Caribbean, English, Scottish, Welsh or Irish origin. Indian and Pakistani pupils did better in English, while those of Afro-Caribbean origin performed half a grade behind white children in mathematics.[6]

9.3 Is there a school effect?

Among the studies into pupil achievement in the 1980s, two tried to establish the effectiveness of schools. Both used statistical multi-level modelling procedures that permitted the effects of schools to be explicitly modelled in the analyses and allowed a test to be made to see whether schools were differentially effective for particular subgroups, such as minority ethnic groups. Do minority ethnic group pupils perform less well because they attend less effective schools? Do they make greater progress in some kinds of schools than in others?[7]

Smith and Tomlinson's study of eighteen comprehensive schools revealed that black pupils made more progress in some schools than in others. They concluded that 'some schools are much better than others and the ones that are good for white pupils tended to be about equally good for black pupils' (Smith and Tomlinson, 1989, p. 305).

The sample of schools used for the research was not large enough to obtain a full mix of schools with both large and small numbers and proportions of Afro-Caribbean and Asian pupils. Drew and Gray's follow-up work on Smith and Tomlinson's data has shown that more black pupils went to the less effective schools. However, they concluded that 'It did not make sense to talk of schools which were universally effective or ineffective; there was no single dimension of school effectiveness' (Drew and Gray, 1991, p. 168).

Nuttall *et al.*'s ILEA study on ethnic background and examination results and their study of GCSE findings also explored the existence or otherwise of a 'school effect' (Nuttall *et al.*, 1989, pp. 769–76). In 140 secondary schools, the attainment of Afro-Caribbean pupils could differ by as much as one 'high grade' O-level pass when the full range of school differences was considered. Amongst Pakistani pupils the differences could amount to as much as two O-level passes. On the results of their study, Nuttall and Goldstein recommended that each set of examination results should carry the warning, 'These results should not be used to compare schools nor to predict their future performance.'[8]

These studies provide some support for the view that schools make some difference. But to what extent do minority ethnic group pupils attend less effective schools than their white counterparts? There has not, as yet, been a sufficiently large national empirical study of schools sensitive to the wide range of relevant variables. Drew and Gray concluded that:

> Neither of these studies relating to schools effectiveness provides convincing evidence about the school's contribution to the existence of the black–white gap in achievement ... Schools certainly differ to some considerable extent in their effectiveness, but whether they are *the* major contributing factor remains unclear. To date we lack a study with a sufficient number of pupils and schools, covering a sufficient range of variables, with a nationally representative sample, combining both qualitative and quantitative forms of data gathering to answer the questions Swann posed
>
> (Drew and Gray, 1991, p. 171)

9.4 Special schools, disruptive units, suspensions and expulsions

Estimates in the early 1980s indicated Afro-Caribbeans to be five times more likely than 'non-immigrant' groups to be placed in ESN establishments (Tomlinson, 1981) and more likely than white pupils to be located in disruptive units, withdrawal classes and guidance units (Tattum, 1982, ch. 2). A CRE inquiry into school suspensions in Birmingham found that Afro-Caribbean pupils were four times more likely to suspended from schools for a given level of disruptive behaviour (CRE, 1984d). ILEA figures for 1986 to 1987 reveal that pupils from Afro-Caribbean backgrounds were heavily over-represented among those suspended from schools: 33 per cent of pupils suspended were of Afro-Caribbean origin, yet Afro-Caribbeans were only 14 per cent of the ILEA school population. The research showed that Afro-Caribbean pupils were more likely than other pupils to be suspended for a single severe offence.[9] Evidence also suggests some minority ethnic groups may be more prone to expulsion from schools than whites. Between 1986 and 1987, of 27 pupils expelled in Brent, 18 were black, 8 were listed as having 'unknown' ethnic identities, and only one was white.[10]

In July 1991 Nottingham County Council's Advisory and Inspection Service found that nearly one in four of the 449 pupils given formal warnings, suspensions or expulsions in the city's secondary schools was black. Fewer than 1,000 of Nottingham's 14,000 secondary school children are black. Their service's survey concluded that Afro-Caribbean children's body language leads teachers to think they are 'looking for trouble'. The survey also pointed to the important role played by teachers' cultural misunderstanding and ignorance in the exclusion and disciplining of Afro-Caribbean pupils.[11]

9.5 Teacher recruitment and career progression

The following are the comments of practising teachers:

> I have noticed very few people from ethnic minorities who are in positions of responsibility. Amongst students there is a lot of evidence of racial discrimination – for example, verbal abuse, graffiti. It is difficult to pin down and to deal with.

> I knew a coloured teacher on a temporary one year contract. She was told at her interview (initially) that senior staff were not sure that the school was ready for a black teacher – mainly because there were very few ethnic minority children in the school.

> The very first day I came to the school a teacher remarked that coloured people should be lined up and shot. After that I have kept with staff who I know are not racially biased.

> Ethnic minority teachers are only given jobs when they find no better teachers – all promotions go to others while we do all the donkey work and are nowhere today.

> I think there is much more awareness of the needs and cultures of ethnic minorities than before. Teaching staff are aware of ethnic minorities' cultures and needs, and it is becoming a multi-cultural society.

> (CRE, 1988d, pp. 54–60)[12]

In the mid-1970s the Caribbean Teachers Association estimated that only 0.15 per cent of teachers were of Caribbean origin (Select Committee on Race Relations and Immigration, 1977b). By the beginning of the 1980s, the estimated number of black teachers (of Caribbean, African and Asian origin) was less than 1,000 out of 500,000, or around 0.2 per cent. The proportion of pupils of Afro-Caribbean and Asian origin at this time was estimated to be 6 per cent (see Carr-Hill and Chadha-Boreham in Bhat *et al.*, 1988, p. 154).

In 1986 a recruitment drive for 140 primary school teachers in the London Borough of Ealing resulted in only three minority ethnic group teachers being appointed, despite the borough's commitment to an equal opportunities policy. 'Black' teachers (Afro-Caribbean and Asian) were found to be systematically denied jobs, refused promotion and confined to teaching certain subjects. The study revealed no minority ethnic group heads, one deputy head and no senior managers in the borough education department. Out of 2,400 teaching staff, only 200 were classified as 'black' and most of these were in low-scale posts (London Borough of Ealing, 1988). In the mid-1980s, 30 per cent of Ealing's population and over half of the school pupils came from Afro-Caribbean and South Asian backgrounds. One black teacher working in the multi-cultural support service told the Ealing investigating panel:

> I have often been mistaken for the cleaner or the dinner lady; anything but a teacher. You're not allowed in the staff room because they think you are a parent.

> (London Borough of Ealing, 1988)

The CRE, disturbed by the high level of individual complaints from minority ethnic group teachers and general allegations about their recruitment and relative failure to progress, examined minority ethnic group teacher distribution and career development in primary and secondary education (the levels where most minority ethnic group teachers are employed). Eight local education authorities were investigated (excluding ILEA), representing a broad geographical spread, with local minority ethnic group populations ranging from 2.4 per cent in Avon to 33.5 per cent in Brent. The total number of teachers in the 1,189 schools surveyed was 20,246, of whom only 431 were of minority ethnic group origin: teachers of Caribbean, African and Asian origin accounted for barely 2 per cent of the profession (see *Tables 9.1 and 9.2*).

The survey also pointed to barriers to career progression for minority ethnic group teachers and confirmed career difficulties experienced by female teachers. Black teachers generally remained on the lowest rungs of the professional ladder. They were also passed over for promotion. The CRE found that 70 per cent of black male teachers were on scales 1 and 2 compared with 38 per cent of white males, while 84 per cent of black females were on scales 1 and 2 compared with 71 per cent of white females. Over half of the teachers

Table 9.1: ethnic origins of teachers in Great Britain, by sex

	Total No.	Total %	Male No.	Male %	Female No.	Female %
Base: all teachers (20,246)						
Total minority ethnic group	431	*	192	100	239	100
African	58	*	20	10	38	16
Caribbean	87	*	33	17	54	23
Pakistani	29	*	17	9	12	5
Bangladeshi	2	*	–	–	2	1
Indian	212	1	103	54	109	46
Other	43	*	19	10	24	10
Total white	19,285	95	7,657	100	11,371	100
UK origin	18,513	91	7,376	96	10,885	96
European	675	3	249	3	421	4
Other	97	*	32	*	65	1
Not known	530	3	–	–	–	–

* Less than 1%.
(CRE, 1988d, p. 15)

Table 9.2: ethnic origins of teachers in primary and secondary schools in Great Britain

	Primary No.	Primary %	Secondary No.	Secondary %
Base: all teachers in primary and secondary schools	(8,494)	(100)	(11,383)	(100)
Total minority ethnic group	149	2	240	2
African	18	*	34	*
Caribbean	31	*	49	*
Pakistani	8	*	19	*
Bangladeshi	1	*	1	*
Indian	77	1	114	1
Other	14	*	23	*
Total white	8,096	95	10,862	95
UK origin	7,812	92	10,379	91
European	238	3	435	4
Other	46	*	48	*
Ethnic origin not given	249	3	281	3

* Less than 1%.
(CRE, 1988d, p. 15)

reported experiencing racial discrimination. Two out of three white teachers thought there was racial discrimination in teaching compared with four out of five minority ethnic group teachers. Over half of the minority ethnic group teachers reported a personal experience of racial discrimination in teaching: over three-quarters felt racial discrimination had adversely affected their careers.

Minority ethnic group teachers were more likely than white teachers to be located in schools where there were high proportions of minority ethnic group pupils. Only 4 per cent of white teachers taught in schools where there were 76 per cent or more minority ethnic group pupils (see *Table 9.3*). Minority ethnic group teachers were also more likely to be employed in far higher percentages than white teachers in schools where there were pupils of their own ethnic origin.

Table 9.3: proportion of minority ethnic group pupils and teachers in schools in Great Britain

| | Teachers | | | |
| | Minority ethnic group | | White | |
	No.	%	No.	%
Base: all teachers*	(431)		(19,285)	
Minority ethnic group pupils:				
1–25%	136	32	14,369	76
26–50%	60	14	1,676	9
51–75%	85	20	1,069	6
76% or more	106	25	754	4
None	4	1	1,293	7
Not known	40	9	124	1

* Excludes those whose ethnic origins were not given.
(CRE, 1988d, p. 21)

The CRE concluded that:

> The overall picture which emerges ... is that minority ethnic group teachers are few in number, that they are disproportionately on the lowest salary scales, and that they are concentrated in subjects where there is a shortage of teachers or where the special needs of ethnic minority pupils are involved. They do not enjoy the same career progression as white teachers, even when their starting scales and length of service are similar, nor do their headteachers encourage them in the same way as they do white teachers to apply for vacancies within their school. Over half of the minority ethnic group teachers believed they had personally experienced racial discrimination in teaching. There is little likelihood of a significant increase in the number of minority ethnic group teachers. In 1986 only 2.6 per cent of students in final year teacher training were of minority ethnic group origin.
>
> (CRE, 1988d, p. 65)

Minority ethnic group teachers can also face problems in redeployment. According to the Inner London Black Teachers' Group and the Inner London Teachers' Association, Afro-Caribbean and Asian teachers were twice as likely as white teachers to be moved against their wishes.[13]

9.6 Teacher training

Throughout the 1980s a series of studies examined the shortage in minority ethnic group enrolments at teacher training colleges. This is of particular concern because a higher proportion of the minority ethnic group population of Britain is in the age range from which teacher trainees come than is the case for the white majority. In England and Wales the CRE found that students of Afro-Caribbean and Asian origin made up only 1 in 40, or 2.6 per cent, of all students on PGCE, final year BEd and other degree courses leading to qualified teacher status. In the appropriate teacher-trainee recruitment age group, an estimated 5.3 per cent of the population belong to Afro-Caribbean and Asian minority groups, twice the proportion registered for courses. About one-third of the PGCE courses and a little over two-fifths of BEd courses had no minority ethnic group representation at all. Moreover, over half of the teacher-training institutions studied in 1986 had either none or only one black student teacher in preparation and only 5 per cent of such institutions had 10 or more such students (see CRE, 1988d, pp. 63–5; Searle and Stibbs, 1989).

> The absence of such role models for black children is a major contributory factor to black under-achievement. There is also the growing recognition of the value of black teachers in predominantly 'white' schools for altering negative values and attitudes held of black people and for eventually leading to a fairer and juster society ... The profession needs black teachers. The principle of equality in education cannot be achieved without an expansion of their supply.
>
> (Carlton Duncan, 'The barriers must fall', Education Guardian, 30 January 1990)

A 1990 study of 70 UK teacher-training institution showed that the positive perceptions of teaching that minority ethnic group students often bring with them can be systematically undermined by the training they receive. They reported experiencing direct and indirect racism within teacher-training establishments and on teaching practice: 40 per cent of minority ethnic group students reported experiencing 'racism' from initial teacher education (ITE) lecturers, 64 per cent from fellow students and 60 per cent from staff and pupils in teaching-practice schools (Siraj-Blatchford, 1990).

9.7 Higher education

According to Labour Force Survey (LFS) data published in February 1991 the proportion of minority ethnic group young people staying on in full-time education was more than double that of the white population.[14] The differences were most marked among males aged 16–24, where 33 per cent were involved in study compared with 11 per cent of whites. For females the figures were 24 per cent and 12 per cent respectively. The figures showed that all minority ethnic groups had higher proportions of students staying in full-time education than the white majority population. More white young people entered the labour force directly after the minimum school leaving age: 80 per cent of the white 16–24 age group were economically active compared with 58 per cent for minority ethnic groups.

Evidence on the distribution of minority ethnic groups in higher education – as staff or students – is, however, still relatively limited. Such evidence that does exist suggests that minority ethnic group students, along with women and students of working class origin, were significantly under-represented at degree level.

> The belief that there are too few black students in Britain's universities and polytechnics is widespread and shared by the National Union of Students and the Commission for Racial Equality. But with no proof of a shortfall and with discrimination being hard to prove ... under-representation has been a silent problem.
>
> (Vikram Dodd, 'Some are far less equal', *Education Guardian*, 30 January 1990)

A 1987 study of first degree Council for National Academic Awards graduates, excluding education degrees, showed that 6 per cent of graduates came from minority ethnic group backgrounds (CRE, 1987c).[15] In 1989 a study of ethnic differences in further and higher education courses at ILEA colleges found that black students tended to enrol on 'low-status' courses and that Asian women were particularly under-represented in further and higher education, especially on schemes involving block release or part-time day release courses (Sammons and Newbury, 1989). The Association of University Teachers (AUT) and the National Association of Teachers in Further and Higher Education (NATFHE) have argued for increased representation from minority ethnic groups on both student and staff intakes (see AUT, 1985; NATFHE, 1986).

A 1989 CRE report showed how slow higher education had been to formulate equal opportunities policies. Thirty out of 42 universities and 14 out of 26 polytechnics studied could provide no policy statement on equal opportunities. Only 5 universities and 7 polytechnics indicated that they had a policy or were operating some form of equal opportunity policy. Nearly half the universities cited their charter as sufficient evidence of a commitment to equal opportunities (Williams *et al.*, 1989).[16]

In July 1991 Oxford University announced its intention to offer easier entry for black and economically disadvantaged students. Two colleges initially joined the Oxford access scheme which was launched following staff and student concern at the lack of British-born black undergraduates at Oxford colleges.[17]

In April 1990 the Polytechnic Central Admission System published its first breakdown of the ethnic origins of applicants who live permanently in the United Kingdom (see *Table 9.4*).

Table 9.4: ethnic origins of applicants to polytechnics, 1990

Ethnic origin	Number	%
White	131,452	76.7
Black Caribbean	2,441	1.4
Black African	2,072	1.2
Other Black	653	0.4
Indian	7,146	4.2
Pakistani	3,434	2.0
Bangladeshi	501	0.3
Chinese	1,365	0.8
Other Asian	1,512	0.9
Other origin	2,097	1.2
Unknown origin	9,872	5.8

Figures refer to applications for degree courses. Overseas students (8,739, 5.1%) are excluded from the table.
(The Times, *23 April 1990*)

Data emerging from the first ethnic monitoring of polytechnics showed these institutions were admitting fewer white students compared with applicants and greater proportions of almost all minority ethnic groups.

How students are funded could be a crucial factor influencing access. Research in Avon and Lancashire revealed that one in three aspiring black higher education students would not go to college if they had to take out a loan: another third said the introduction of a student loan system could act as a deterrent. Of all the black groups studied, Asians were most favourably disposed towards loan schemes.[18]

But the issue is not simply one of access. Evidence is beginning to emerge that Afro-Caribbean students are more likely to *drop out* of degree courses than white and Asian undergraduates. They may also receive *lower status* degrees. In the spring of 1991 the preliminary findings of a research study into the progress of 1,500 students who entered higher education without traditional qualifications was published. This revealed that more than one-quarter of Afro-Caribbeans failed to take their final examinations. The drop-out figure for Asian students was 15 per cent and for white students 17 per cent. The research, based on data from Leeds and Bradford Universities, Leeds and Manchester Polytechnics, and Bradford and Ilkley Community College, also showed disparities between groups in level of degree awarded. South Asian students were less likely than whites to get first or upper seconds, but twice as successful as Afro-Caribbeans.[19]

The findings of the first ethnic monitoring of university applicants by the University Central Council on Admissions (UCCA) was published in 1991.[20] According to UCCA's figures, black students made up just 1 per cent of the university population. (This compares with 4 per cent for polytechnics – see *Table 9.4*.) Universities admitted lower proportions of all minority ethnic groups compared to proportions of applicants, but slightly higher proportions of white students than applications received. The UCCA data also revealed that universities rejected half of all their black applicants. More black applicants applied to their local university than whites, a trend which effectively reduced their chances of gaining university acceptance. UCCA claimed that any bias caused by 'race' factors disappeared if applicants of similar examination performance were compared.

Great care must be taken with these preliminary results of monitoring. First, certain differences may be obscured. For example, black women may do better than black men; Afro-Caribbean and Asian applicants may fare differently; the locality, recruitment policies and course provision of different institutions can influence the extent of minority ethnic group demand. Polytechnics may be recruiting from catchment areas that have far higher proportions of minority ethnic groups than the 5 per cent national average – 14 per cent of the economically active population of greater London are from minority ethnic groups – while universities recruit more nationally. Polytechnics also provide more vocational courses, and courses that are attractive to minority ethnic groups, such as legal studies, are not available at all institutions. Secondly, the figures quoted often do not take into account the form of some of the findings. The minority ethnic group population in Britain is younger than the white group and comparisons with the total population figure can produce potentially misleading results. Thirdly, the quality of service is not analysed. Such data tell us little of the black experience of higher education.

9.8 'Race' and qualifications

Table 9.5 uses LFS data for 1987, 1988 and 1989 to compare the qualification levels held by people aged 16 to 64 (59 for women) for different minority ethnic groups in Great Britain. Both males and females of Pakistani and Bangladeshi origin were not as well qualified as those from other groups: women from these groups were also more likely to be economically inactive.

Table 9.5: highest qualification levels in Great Britain, by ethnic origin and sex, 1987–9

	White	West Indian/ Guyanese	Indian	Pakistani/ Bangladeshi	Other*	All**
Males						
Higher	14	–	17	7	23	14
Other	56	54	50	36	54	55
None	30	41	32	56	22	30
Females						
Higher	12	16	12	–	20	13
Other	49	49	45	24	50	49
None	38	35	44	72	30	38
All persons						
Higher	13	11	15	6	22	13
Other	53	52	48	30	52	52
None	34	38	38	64	26	34

* Includes African, Arab, Chinese, other stated and mixed origin.
** Includes don't knows and those who did not state their ethnic origin.
(Central Statistical Office, 1991, p. 60)

9.9 Developments since 1992

The Government White Paper on *Education, Choice and Diversity,* published in July 1992, contained no reference to current sex or 'race' legislation (Runnymede Trust, 1993a, p. 10). The White Paper formed the basis of the 1993 Education Act, which was subsequently amended to ensure that funding arrangements would be subject to the Race Relations Act (*Independent*, 22 September 1992).

The CRE and Runnymede Trust made several recommendations to the Government. First, they urged the Government to guarantee that the new

School Curriculum and Assessment Authority would consider the ethnic and cultural diversity of British society and emphasized the importance of the curriculum in promoting equal opportunity for all pupils regardless of ethnic origin and gender. Second, they argued for equitable resourcing to avoid the creation of a two-tier education system in which minority ethnic groups could be disproportionately disadvantaged. Third, they urged the introduction of guidance for schools in order to prevent the use of sanctions, particularly school exclusions, from being unlawfully discriminatory, and to enforce rigorous ethnic monitoring in order to identify and evaluate discrimination (Runnymede Trust, 1993a, p. 10).

In November 1993, the National Commission on Education published a blueprint for change in education which proposed enhancements to nursery and 16–18-year-old education provision. The proposals were welcomed by the Association of Metropolitan Authorities (AMA). One of the conclusions of the report was that education spending had not increased in real terms since 1982–3 (National Commission on Education, 1993). In 1991, it was estimated that £2 billion was needed to refurbish our schools, a figure that in 1995 was thought to be nearer £4 billion. Of 6,500 schools surveyed by the National Union of Teachers (NUT) in 1995, one in four had closed dilapidated buildings (*Independent*, 17 March 1995; BBC Radio 5, interview with Doug McEvoy, NUT, 16 March 1995). *Social Trends 25* showed that total Government education expenditure had increased by just over half in real terms between 1970 and 1993 (CSO, 1995, p. 45, Table 3.27), but these data disguise the neglect of funding in real terms since 1982. For example, Nottinghamshire County Council (NCC) asked the Government for £18.63 million for capital building and repairs in 1995: it received £1.67 million. A disappointed spokesperson for NCC commented: 'We actually needed £80 million to do everything that needs to be done' (*Independent*, 17 March 1995).

The underfunding also affected Higher Education. The 1995 *Review of Higher Education* report revealed that public funding per full-time student in Higher Education had fallen very rapidly in real terms between 1989 and 1994 by 28 per cent, and is projected to fall by a further 9 per cent by 1998 (HEFCE, 1995, para 37).

In 1994, the Government vacillated over its contribution to Section 11 funding, which considerably supports minority ethnic group education. At the beginning of the year cuts were announced in Section 11. The cuts, 18 per cent in 1994–5 and 25 per cent in 1995–6, reduced Section 11 funding by 40 per cent, from £130 million to £98 million. The cuts have adversely affected the job prospects of ethnic minority teachers. It was estimated that the jobs of 4,000 teachers would be lost out of 10,000 employed on Section 11 funding. Growing numbers of Section 11 teachers were reported to have left the profession, causing damage even before the proposed cuts took hold (*Guardian*, 15 March 1994; *Independent*, 2 November 1994). In some areas LEAs acted with alacrity to minimize the effect of Government reductions. Two of the largest urban areas of minority settlement are acutely affected. Bradford, with a minority ethnic group school population of 27 per cent, decided to make up the £1.5 million resource loss. Bradford anticipates that by the year 2000 over half of its school leavers will be from minority ethnic groups. Elsewhere, Tower Hamlets identified 130 Section 11 posts out of 410 for cutting (in 1993 the borough received the largest slice of Section 11 funding).

The announcement of such severe funding reductions led to fierce debate, and pressure from education and 'race' voluntary bodies and the LEAs, for the Government to reconsider these proposals (Runnymede Trust, 1994b; *Guardian*, 15 March 1994). The Government's new Single Regeneration Budget (SRB) was established, and poor LEAs were alarmed to be told that they could only apply to the SRB for funding for teachers, and no longer bid for Section 11 funds. By September 1994, the Home Office reversed the decision to stop applications for Section 11 funding: LEAs could apply for both SRB and Section 11 finance, but were told that the overall budget would still be cut, with £60 million transferred to the SRB, which was specifically established to rekindle life in areas of greatest need (*Guardian*, 24 September 1994). The Government announced further cuts in the SRB – by 8 per cent over 1994–6 and speculation grew that no bidding would be possible in 1996–7.

In November 1994, Michael Howard, responding to public outcry over the cutbacks, announced in Parliament that the Government would be doubling the amount it spends on Section 11 funding to minority ethnic communities to £30 million, the extra money to be allocated over a two-year period, beginning in April 1995 (*Independent*, 23 November 1994). In the spring of 1995, however, the Government once more created further unease by announcing another 33 per cent cut in Section 11. Further Treasury cuts in LEA funding in 1995 have compounded the problems faced by schools, especially in inner cities, as education budgets are squeezed. Seven out of ten schools in England and Wales face debilitating cutbacks to staff and material resources (*Independent*, 3 May 1995). The European Commission is to make funds available to UK schools with large black and Asian populations in the form of EC grants to replace the flow of white pupils from UK schools. The proposed 'Socrates' programme arises from concern to desegregate inner-city areas, and to reduce racial conflict and violence (*Guardian*, 11 April 1994).

The new SRB is 'of great potential benefit to black and ethnic minority communities' (Runnymede Trust, 1994d), although the Trust warned it could turn out to be the 'Savage Reduction' Budget. The SRB is administered through ten regional offices. The staffing of these offices is multi-ethnic: 129 staff out of 2,589 are black or Asian (5 per cent). Of these, 44 will hold senior posts: Asian staff are twice as likely as black to hold senior positions in the SRB (*Hansard*, 1994a).

The CRE, in a 1993 national survey of schools, disclosed that children with English language difficulties, especially those of black and Asian backgrounds, were treated as though they had learning difficulties; that Afro-Caribbeans in Birmingham schools were four times more likely to be suspended; that black and Asian pupils were often expected to fail by their teachers; that black pupils were encouraged to go for the 'soft' subjects such as sport; and that of 20,000 teachers in 8 cities, only 400 were from minority ethnic groups, with 80 per cent of these staff at the bottom of the wage scale. The survey also found that to the question 'do schools treat ethnic minorities worse?' 13 per cent of white respondents said 'yes', compared with 15 per cent of Asians, and 38 per cent of black respondents (CRE, 1993c; Donnellan, 1993, pp. 26–7).

A CRE investigation into Hertfordshire County Council in 1992, following complaints from Asian parents that they could not gain access to the secondary school of their choice in Watford, recommended that every school should establish effective ethnic monitoring procedures for admissions, eliminate any unlawful discrimination, and, in the case of Watford, report the results of its analysis to the CRE until 1998 (CRE, 1992).

The 1993 Education Act instructs local education authorities to ensure that all children receive education even if they have been excluded from school. DES figures on school exclusions revealed that minority ethnic group pupils were disproportionately represented. As long ago as 1985 the CRE found that black pupils were four times more likely than white pupils to be suspended for similar offences. In 1991, for instance, it was reported that, in Brent, black children comprised 17 per cent of the school population but formed 85 per cent of exclusions (*Observer*, 18 October 1991). In 1993, the National Exclusions Reporting System revealed that Afro-Caribbeans accounted for 8.1 per cent of exclusions despite making up only 2 per cent of pupils (exclusions for other minorities were in line with pupil numbers) (Runnymede Trust, 1993a). Research into 336 Birmingham primary schools found that while black pupils of Caribbean origin formed only 7.5 per cent of the school-age population, they formed 30–40 per cent of all expulsions. Research by the Office for Standards in Education (OFSTED) found that one in four excluded pupils were of Caribbean origin, though they made up only one in fourteen of the school population (*The Times Educational Supplement*, 9 April 1993). The OFSTED report claimed that an increasing number of schools in Britain – even those with satisfactory discipline records – were turning to temporary and permanent exclusions. Between 1990 and 1992, the number of children permanently excluded from school rose from 2,910 to 3,833. OFSTED noted that unequal treatment was being applied both within and between schools, especially in relation to black pupils. This was most noticeable in the disproportionate numbers of Afro-Caribbean boys excluded for incidents where boys had retaliated against racial harassment (OFSTED, 1993; *Guardian*, 14 December 1993). Reactions to the OFSTED report were mixed. The NUT welcomed the report, the National Association of Schoolmasters Union of Women Teachers dismissed it as a 'waste of space' and called it 'a counsel of perfection in a very imperfect world' (*Guardian*, 14 December 1993).

Since OFSTED, several other research studies have highlighted the extent to which black pupils are disproportionately excluded. Stirling pointed to the ways in which schools have been given greater powers through the 1988 and 1993 Education Acts to shape their own populations, 'weeding out' unwelcome pupils in attempts to improve league table status. Stirling also found evidence to suggest that black children react to the white, male-dominated European curriculum presented at school, against which a pupil's own culture is seen as inferior and subordinate. Mayet examined the post-Education Act 1993 situation which distinguished between two types of exclusion: fixed term (technically a suspension), and permanent, subject to governor monitoring. Mayet found that since 1987–8, permanent exclusions (expulsions) had risen by 20 per cent a year. Mayet examined ethnicity and found that the exclusion rate for white pupils matches its distribution in the school population (approximately 56 per cent). The African-Caribbean position is a 32 per cent exclusion rate from a school population of 9 per cent. The Asian exclusion figure is a 21 per cent exclusion rate from a school population of 30 per cent (Stirling, 1993; Mayet, 1993).

An Institute of Race Relations report estimated that 66,000 children are excluded or suspended from school each year and Afro-Caribbean boys are four times more likely than white pupils to be excluded (Bourne *et al.*, 1994). School Inspectors were reported to be extremely worried by the escalation in official expulsions, despite Government directives that expulsion should be a last resort – it was estimated that expulsions rose from 3,000 in 1990/91 to over 8,000 in 1994/95, while suspensions could be running as high as 90,000 pupils a year (*Independent*, 14 November 1994; Family Policy Studies Centre, 1994). In February 1995, the Government ordered further research into why more pupils are being excluded, and why increasing proportions of them come from Afro-Caribbean backgrounds (*Independent*, 11 February 1995).

Black children with special educational needs have also been wrongly assessed by local authorities through the failure to use translators and interpreters (*The Times Educational Supplement*, 23 April 1993). Strathclyde local authority faces CRE investigation following disclosures of 'excessive' numbers of black children being allocated to special schools (*Weekly Journal*, 8 April 1993). Lindsey's research in an Ealing primary school suggested that the education system could be failing young black boys by stereotyping them as troublesome and stupid (*Independent*, 30 December 1993).

In 1990, ILEA reported further on their longitudinal analysis of children's performance in the old O-level and CSE examinations, confirming the promising performances of pupils of Indian origin. English, Scottish, Welsh and Caribbean pupils fared less well, while pupils of Bangladeshi and Turkish origin fared worst of all (Nuttall and Varlaam, 1990). Since 1991, there has been a series of important research projects which have focused on minority ethnic group educational outcomes. An NFER survey of 300 primary schools in 1992 found that 74 per cent of 7-year-olds from Afro-Caribbean families achieved science targets for their ages, compared with 69 per cent of white and 67 per cent of Asian pupils. Afro-Caribbean children also scored highly in the oral English tests with 75 per cent reaching their target compared with 66 per cent of white and 61 per cent of Asian pupils (*Evening Standard*, 23 December 1992). Chinese pupils at nine London secondary schools performed more than twice as well as pupils of English, Scottish and Welsh backgrounds in the 1992 GCSE examinations, according to Islington Council's Education Department. Pupils with Indian and Pakistani backgrounds performed almost as well as Chinese (*Evening Standard*, 4 March 1993). Further research by the London University Institute of Education into GCSE results in 12 metropolitan areas revealed that Chinese, Indian, Bangladeshi and Pakistani are far more successful than white pupils, with black-Caribbean pupils faring worst of all. The research called for the Government to launch a detailed research programme into the reasons for these disparities in educational achievement, especially since the findings for Bangladeshis seem inconsistent with previous work (*The Times*, 27 June 1994).

The new list of authors to be used on the national English curriculum from the autumn of 1995 will have dropped authors from the United States, India and the Caribbean. The new list of twelve twentieth-century authors are all British and all male, except one. Based on recommendations by Sir Ron Dearing, the chair of the School Curriculum and Assessment Authority, the list is exemplary rather than compulsory. V.S. Naipaul, Derek Walcott and Grace Nichols have been dropped (*Independent*, 8 October 1994). In June 1995, the Major Government's chief adviser on the school curriculum, Dr Nick Tate, called for the development of a British cultural identity regardless of ethnic background to be taught in schools. He emphasized a curriculum characterized by Christianity and the classical world, the English language, and English history and literary heritage. Tate denied he intended to denigrate multi-cultural educational perspectives, but his comments stimulated concern among minority ethnic groups, Muslims and headteachers in schools serving areas of high minority ethnic group populations (*Guardian*, 19 July 1995).

The NUT has emphasized every child's right to the national curriculum in their anti-racist guidelines (NUT, 1992). The National Union of Headteachers (NUHT) has also produced a code of practice to ensure that overt and covert forms of racial discrimination are discouraged (NUHT, 1992).

Racism in the playground

From Miss Sneh Shah

Sir: On a recent visit to Preston Park, my friend Deepa and I rode up to the play area on our bikes. Since there were a lot of children between the ages of seven and 15 in the park's play area, we decided to return when it was less crowded. Instead, we rode around the park on our bikes.

As Deepa passed the play area, one of the children called her a Paki. She rode quickly towards me and warned me. She looked worried, so I said: 'Don't worry, they are probably mucking around.'

The second time she passed by, another one of the children shouted to her: 'Too scared to come in here!'

At this point, I got angry and rode towards them. Deepa caught up with me and told me not to do anything stupid. Although I calmed down, I was still asking myself questions: why do people make such stupid remarks?

I, and many other people, would like this changed. We can see from the past that racism has caused unhappiness, permanent injuries and even death. At school, I think it should be law to study racism, discuss the reasons behind it, and so help understand people's ignorance.

Yours faithfully,

SNEH SHAH
(12 years old)

Wembley, Middlesex

(Independent, *10 April 1995*)

Table 9.6 confirms earlier findings that white men and Indian men are better qualified than their women counterparts (the gender difference is reversed for people of Caribbean and Guyanese origin). Caribbean men and Pakistani and Bangladeshi women are more disadvantaged than other groups. Indians are slightly better qualified than whites. Other analysis of this data has shown that Asian groups with high levels of educational attainment are predominantly middle class (Abercrombie *et al.*, 1994, p. 360).

Table 9.6: highest qualification level of the population of Great Britain[1], by ethnic origin and sex, 1988–90[2], in percentages

Highest qualification held[5]	White	West Indian/ Guyanese	Indian	Pakistani/ Bangla- deshi	Other[3]	All[4]
Males						
Higher	15	–	19	8	22	15
Other	57	58	51	40	56	57
None	29	36	30	52	21	29
Females						
Higher	13	16	13	–	20	13
Other	51	52	46	20	52	51
None	36	32	41	68	28	36
All persons						
Higher	14	11	16	6	21	14
Other	54	55	49	34	54	54
None	32	34	36	60	25	32

[1] Aged 16 to retirement age (64 for males and 59 for females).
[2] Combined data from 1988, 1989 and 1990.
[3] Includes African, Arab, Chinese, other stated and Mixed origin.
[4] Includes those who did not know or did not state their ethnic origin.
[5] Excludes those who did not know or did not state their qualifications.
(CSO, 1992, p. 65)

Department of Education research into minority ethnic group teacher employment found that only 3.3 per cent of full-time teachers in England and Wales came from minority ethnic groups. Relatively few were found in senior positions (*The Times Educational Supplement*, 12 March 1993). The situation is particularly poor in areas with high minority ethnic group populations. For example, in Bradford, about one third of pupils, but only 1 per cent of teachers, are from minority ethnic groups. The NUT debated the issue at their National Conference in 1994, following research findings that only 1 per cent of new teachers recruited in 1993 were from minority ethnic groups. Competition with other professions (law and accountancy) and discrimination within the profession were cited as the main reasons for the fall in minority group recruitment (*BBC Radio 5 Magazine*, 22 June 1994). In higher and further education overall figures are difficult to obtain. National Association of Teachers in Further and Higher Education (NATFHE) 1994 data showed that of their union membership in higher education, 2.3 per cent were of Afro-Caribbean origin (NATFHE, 1994).

An Economic and Social Research Council (ESRC) study reported that black school governors experienced racism from many headteachers and other school governors, and were often excluded from the 'inner-circle' of governors that form the power base in schools (*The Times Educational Supplement*, 23 April 1993).

Department of Employment research has revealed a high proportion of young black people remaining in full-time post-16 education compared with whites – while 37 per cent of whites stayed on in full-time education, 51 per cent of Afro-Caribbeans and 67 per cent of Asians did so. Further differences emerged between the type of courses pursued with white and Asian students tending to take A-level type courses, while Afro-Caribbeans took vocational courses (Drew *et al.*, 1992). Drew concluded that many black and Asian students stayed on because of the extent of racial discrimination in the labour market or because minority group parents valued higher education more than whites, a conclusion supported by research by the Policy Studies Institute (PSI) in 1994 (*Independent*, 12 September 1994).

Figures released in 1991 by UCCA revealed that less than half of all minority ethnic candidates, 44.7 per cent, gained admission to universities, compared with 53 per cent of white applicants. Only one in three Afro-Caribbeans were accepted (*Guardian*, 13 July 1991).[21]

One-seventh of applicants to polytechnics and colleges in 1990 were of minority ethnic group origin. Data for home applicants to polytechnics and colleges (updating *Table 9.4*) show that of applicants with known ethnic origin, 1.7 per cent were black Caribbeans, 1.6 per cent black Africans, 0.5 per cent other black applicants, 4.7 per cent Indians, 2.3 per cent Pakistanis, 0.3 per cent Bangladeshis, 0.9 per cent Chinese, 1.1 per cent other Asian origin, and 1.4 per cent other group status (10 per cent of applicants did not reveal their ethnic group origin; and 11,626 overseas applicants have been excluded from the analysis) (Polytechnics Central Admissions System, 1991). Gender analysis shows that Caribbean women are twice as likely as Caribbean men to apply (gender differences are not as acute for other minority ethnic groups).

Modood's research looked at the experience of minority ethnic groups in higher education more broadly. While his research confirms differences between groups, institutions and subjects, the claim of minority ethnic under-representation was not proved for 1990 and 1991. On the contrary, Modood found, after controlling for overseas students, that in the PCAS system Africans had a representation of more than 300 per cent, closely followed by Indians, East African Asians and Chinese; even black Caribbeans and Pakistanis were over-represented; only the Bangladeshis and the 'other blacks' had an under-representation greater than that for whites. In the UCCA sector, acceptance rates showed a hierarchy with whites at the top, closely followed by the Chinese, with the Indians and Bangladeshis 5–10 per cent below, Pakistanis about 15 per cent, Africans around 20 per cent below and Caribbeans 25 per cent below. Only half as many Caribbean applicants as whites were likely to succeed. Modood also found that minority ethnic groups tended to apply to a limited range of courses and institutions compared with whites. His most interesting conclusion was that despite minority ethnic groups having worse class profiles than whites, they generated larger proportions of applications and admissions in the national higher education system (Modood, 1993).[22]

A report commissioned by the Department of Employment found that one in three people from Britain's minority ethnic groups participates in adult learning, though rates varied widely between groups. More women were studying than men. The rate of participation in education and training for the population as a whole was 29 per cent, for people of African origin it was 60 per cent. Over 50 per cent of the minority ethnic group sample were unemployed (National Institute of Adult Continuing Education, 1993; *The Times Higher Education Supplement*, 16 August 1993).

The AUT and the Committee of Vice Chancellors and Principals (CVCP) issued guidance to university admissions departments to ensure that minority ethnic candidates were not disproportionately penalized (*AUT Bulletin*, March 1992). In July 1993, Leeds Metropolitan University was found guilty of race and sex discrimination at an Industrial Tribunal, by failing to appoint a black Asian lecturer (The 1990 Trust, 1994). At the time of writing, the CRE is investigating Leeds Metropolitan University after a second racial discrimination case – in which an Afro-Caribbean woman was passed over for two administrative posts which were awarded to less-qualified white candidates – was won at an industrial tribunal (*Guardian*, 3 August 1995).

A PSI report registered further concern over black students' access to universities. The study, based on 1992 data, and after taking into account academic performance, revealed that Pakistanis and black Caribbeans appeared to be disadvantaged, and concluded that there was 'a strong possibility of direct or indirect discrimination' in admissions systems and procedures. The PSI report identified the 'old' universities as showing the widest disparities on black and Asian entry, and was based on analysis of 500,000 entrants to both 'old' universities and polytechnics (before the sector was restructured) (Shiner and Modood, 1994; *Independent*, 6 July 1994).

In 1993, the Commission on University Career Opportunity (CUCO), the higher education equal opportunities body, was launched. The first Commission survey into equal opportunities practices in Higher Education revealed that almost all 109 institutions had some form of equal opportunities policy, but that for most the resources were often inadequate to support action. Only 42 per cent of the university sector provided equal opportunity training, while only a fifth made this compulsory (*AUT Bulletin*, November 1994). In 1995, the Higher Education Statistics Agency will carry out the first comprehensive survey of academic staff. We will not know the minority ethnic group profile until 1996 (*The Times Higher Education Supplement*, 7 April 1995).

The Open University began ethnic monitoring in 1989 and introduced an equal opportunities policy in 1991. The Executive Report from the University Equal Opportunities Unit in late 1994 examined student and staff data from 1992 to 1993, and revealed that the percentage of black and Asian students entering the University undergraduate and associate programmes was firmly established at 8 per cent and 5 per cent (Open University, 1994a). The Unit reported an increase in the percentage of black and Asian students registered on the MA in Education programmes, from 4 per cent to 6 per cent, and on the MBA from 6 per cent to 9 per cent. The Unit also registered its concern that black students might be dropping out of University courses in greater proportions than other groups. Analysis of Open University full-time staff revealed that out of over 3,000 employees, only 59 were of black or Asian origin (ethnic monitoring of part-time staff and staff at University residential schools has only just been introduced). The staff report (Open University, 1994b) revealed that there were no black regional academics, and only small percentages of black and Asian employees among central academics and non-academic Universities Authorities Panel staff (the total amount of unknown data concerning staff ethnic origin was 16 per cent in 1994).

In 1994, Trinity College Cambridge appointed its first black President in 450 years, and Doreen Cameron was installed as the first black President of the NATFHE. Ms Cameron is the first black leader of a major teaching union (*Independent*, 16 February 1994; 31 May 1994). In June 1995, the AUT launched its Charter for action on race equality to develop policy designed to eradicate racial disadvantage.

Longsight Youth Club, Manchester, 1987. Photograph by Clement Cooper.

Notes

1   Our focus here is on patterns of racial inequality, but you should bear in mind that social class, gender, locality, policy formulation and implementation, levels of funding and provision, the curriculum and the management of education all have significant impacts on the educational life chances of minority ethnic groups. Only some of these can be illustrated.

2   In examining this data you should remember that the terms 'achievement' or 'performance' have been used in a restricted sense. The scores or points referred to are for tests designed for and within a white British curriculum in a structure still dominated by white personnel.

3   'The Bradford story', *The Times,* 6 October 1988.

4   F. Abrams, 'GCSE fails to eliminate inequality', *The Times Educational Supplement,* 15 February 1991.

5   D. Nuttall and H. Goldstein, 'A parents' guide of real value', *The Times Educational Supplement*, 15 February 1991.

6   *Independent*, 29 October 1991.

7   We are very grateful to Drew and Gray's review of a decade of research on 'race' and achievement in the 1980s (see 1991, pp. 159–72). For a fuller account of multi-level modelling see Goldstein (1987).

8   Nuttall and Goldstein, 'A parents' guide of real value', *The Times Educational Supplement*, 15 February 1991.

9   See *Independent*, 10 September 1988.

10 See *Voice*, 3 October 1989.

11 *Independent*, 11 July 1991.

12 Teachers in evidence to a CRE survey into eight LEAs. The overall picture varies between the eight LEAs and the information presented here is very much the general impression from all. The CRE report found evidence for good as well as bad practice.

13 Information gathered by ILEA in 1989. See *Independent*, 6 September 1989.

14 See *Independent*, 7 February 1991.

15 For an analysis of graduate access to the labour market see Brennan and McGeever (1990).

16 In January 1991 a content analysis of university prospectuses concluded that their visual multi-ethnic presence appeared to reflect a wish to attract a lucrative overseas market rather than a conscious effort to implement equal opportunity strategies by reflecting a multi-cultural Britain. See Jewson *et al.* (1991) pp. 183–99.

17 *Mail on Sunday,* 21 July 1991.

18 See *Independent*, 9 August 1990.

19 Ramindar Singh, reported in the *Guardian*, 14 January 1991.

20 *The Times Higher Educational Supplement*, 21 June 1991, reported the main findings ahead of publication of the UCCA report.

21 'Synthesis trends', *The Times Higher Education Supplement*, 16 July 1993, provides the first detailed breakdown of minority group access into university education.

22 See also 'Synthesis trends', ibid., p. iv.

10 'RACE' AND THE LABOUR MARKET

▼ ▬▬▬▬▬▬▬▬▬▬▬▬▬▬▬▬▬▬▬▬▬▬▬▬▬▬▬▬ ▼

Racism and racial discrimination accounts for most of the discrepancies in the employment statistics for black people. Generally, the over-representation of blacks on the unemployed register and in low-paid jobs still prevails, and now there is consistent research data to verify this in the private as well as public sectors ... there will no doubt be a steady growth in black businesses, but this is not going to resolve the economic crisis faced by the black community.

(Bhat *et al.*, 1988, pp. 95–7)[1]

▲ ▬▬▬▬▬▬▬▬▬▬▬▬▬▬▬▬▬▬▬▬▬▬▬▬▬▬▬▬ ▲

10.1 *'Race' and the professions*

In the mid-1980s investigations showed that while most large British employers professed to be attempting to operate equal opportunities policies, positive effects were only visible among younger and more junior recruits. For example, in an investigation into the progression of black people into middle management in 1986 the *Observer* reported that British Airways, ICI, the Bank of England, British Rail, British Gas, British Telecom and Abbey Life Assurance did not keep records of black recruitment or career advancement. Of the companies surveyed, only the Littlewoods Group at that time monitored all stages, from job application, appointment to promotion, and they reported that black people were 'barely visible in senior management ranks'.

> Many employers still discriminate racially at interviews and blacks are often dissuaded from applying for jobs with organisations which have an overwhelmingly white image ... When it comes to recruiting for middle management jobs, word-of-mouth announcements or internal advertising can also exclude blacks.
>
> (Sue Ollerenshaw of the Commission for Racial Equality's employment promotion department)[2]

In 1988 Elizabeth Burney argued that black workers were no better off than they were before the second Race Relations Act became law in 1968. Colin

Brown drew similar conclusions in his two influential studies in the early 1980s (Brown, 1984; 1985); the first examined racial discrimination in labour recruitment, the other explored inequalities in the labour market in the context of broader life chances and opportunities. The Burney Report concluded that without positive action members of minority ethnic groups would forever fail to join mainstream economic life and that equal opportunity practices were of 'little use if there are still too few members of minority groups able to take advantage of the opportunities, because they are held down by their position in society' (Burney, 1988, p. 1).[3]

Advances have been made during the 1980s, especially in public-sector employment where councils, despite severe financial constraint, developed positive action programmes, established race relations units, improved training schemes and introduced monitoring of recruitment and employment practices. At the beginning of the 1990s a more mixed picture can be seen in the private sector, with many employers proclaiming themselves committed to equal opportunities but substantial numbers still not keeping records to monitor the progress of their efforts. In a 1990 report on minority ethnic group graduates in the job market, the Commission for Racial Equality (CRE) concluded that serious lack of opportunities in the private sector for black and Asian groups forces many Asians into self-employment and Afro-Caribbeans into the public sector (CRE, 1990g).

The civil service and the armed forces are both popular career aspirations for young people. A study of these institutions highlights the problem of career advancement and illustrates the potential impact that perceived levels of racism within an institution may have on minority ethnic group recruitment and retention

10.1.1 The civil service

In May 1990, following a national minority ethnic group monitoring survey, the civil service announced an official racial equality programme to ensure fair treatment for minority ethnic groups in recruitment and promotion. Although there were some regional disparities, the survey revealed that minority ethnic group employment patterns in the civil service broadly matched the distribution of these groups in the general working populations, although there were significant differences in terms of gender equality. However, striking discrepancies were found in the distribution of staff above low grade categories. Variations in age and length of service could not explain why only 2.3 per cent of minority ethnic group staff were found in executive officer posts and only 1.5 per cent at principal grade and above.[4] In August 1989 a separate survey by Greville Janner, Labour MP for Leicester West, showed that black people occupied just 207 of the 18,644 posts in the top seven civil service grades.[5]

10.1.2 The armed forces

In the 1990s the number of 15–24 year olds is projected to fall by 20 per cent. However, the proportion of blacks and Asians in this age cohort is growing. They will thus form an increasingly significant part of the armed forces' recruitment pool. Recruitment data, however, show considerable under-representation for such groups. In 1988 it was revealed that only 1.6 per cent of all applicants to the armed forces came from minority ethnic groups, although at that time they accounted for 5.7 per cent of the population in the 15–24 age range (Runnymede Trust, 1989, p. 8). Within the armed forces, only 1.2 per cent were then from minority ethnic groups and these recruits faced barriers to career advancement.[6] When they rose through the ranks to become officers, they ended up with second-rate postings compared to their white contemporaries. One senior Guard non-commissioned officer told a special inquiry into racial prejudice in the army, 'There are no blacks in the Guards. There have never been and never will be. People do not want to see a black face under a bearskin. Blacks are generally persuaded to go elsewhere' (P. Lashmar and A. Harris, 'The thin white line', *Observer*, 8 June 1986).

In October 1987 the Ministry of Defence had no black Youth Training Scheme (YTS) trainees out of 918 YTS trainees on its books. Two years later this figure had risen to 1 per cent (Runnymede Trust, 1988–9, p. 9). In 1988 a Defence Committee report urged that if an individual wished to join a particular regiment, his or her 'race' must be irrelevant. The report recommended the introduction of ethnic monitoring of forces recruitment, but did not recommend the monitoring of career advancement, despite finding little evidence for the beginnings of any Asian representation at officer cadet academies.[7]

The Ministry of Defence has denied accusations of widespread racial discrimination in the services. In 1990 Lord Arran, Under Secretary of State for the Armed Forces, was reported as saying, 'I firmly do believe there is not an enormous amount of discrimination in the services. I believe there is scarcely any at all' (S. Barwick, 'Blacks shun forces because of race bias', *Independent*, 24 January 1990).

A report in January 1990 by Peat Marwick McLintock revealed that racially offensive views and language existed in all ranks of the services and that many members of minority ethnic groups, especially Asians, dropped out. The report – involving a study of 500 Asians, 500 Afro-Caribbeans and 500 young whites – also found that minority ethnic groups were less likely than whites to consider a career in the armed forces because they feared the forces would be racist (S. Barwick, ibid.). In a Commons written reply in response to the Peat Marwick McLintock investigation, Archie Hamilton, then the armed forces minister, commented:

The services are equal opportunity employers under the Race Relations Act, and we will continue to make clear that no form of racial discrimination will be tolerated and that all complaints will be properly investigated.

(S. Tirbutt, 'Services to take positive anti-racist line', *Guardian*, 24 January 1990)

In another comment on the report, Colonel Donald Campbell, commanding officer of the Parachute Regiment's training depot at Aldershot, observed, 'If you call someone Blackie it is not meant to be a derogatory term. It is just an expression' (A. Culf, 'Paras jump to dismiss overstated problem of prejudice', *Guardian*, 24 January 1990).

10.1.3 The Church of England

No institution is immune from racism and its effects. In October 1991 the first reported study of minority ethnic group outcomes in a religious institution revealed that racial prejudice was 'rife' in the Church of England (Sentamu, 1991). A three-year study of all England's 43 dioceses found black clergy to be under-represented at all levels of the Church of England structure. The level of racism was partly responsible, the report claimed, for the increase in all-black churches in Britain.

10.2 Evidence from the workplace

10.2.1 The use of psychological tests in recruitment and promotion

At the beginning of the 1990s concern was particularly focused on the use of standardized aptitude and psychological tests in recruitment and promotion processes. For example, in 1991 London Underground Ltd (LUL) were found to have discriminated against applicants for middle management vacancies (CRE, 1991c). Nearly one-third of LUL's 20,000 workforce were of minority ethnic group origin at the time of the CRE investigation, compared with only 3 per cent of LUL management grade staff. After the King's Cross disaster in 1988, LUL created 250 new management posts. The selection process included psychometric tests and structured interviews. Of 963 applicants, 29 per cent came from minority ethnic groups, but only 11 per cent of the minority ethnic group applicants were appointed. The CRE found that the psychometric tests particularly disadvantaged Afro-Caribbean candidates.

In the same year, British Rail (BR) changed their testing procedures for promotion following a case brought under the Race Relations Act by eight Asian guards who failed BR's aptitude tests for promotion. The tests were found to discriminate against people for whom English was a second or other language. The case attracted considerable interest from other companies, as many of the principles behind BR's aptitude tests were common across industrial recruitment and promotion procedures.[8]

10.2.2 The Ten Company Group of the West Midlands

In the mid-1980s the Rover Group decided to increase the number of trainees from minority ethnic groups after monitoring had revealed that their annual trainee intake was only 9 per cent at a time when 20 per cent of school leavers in the West Midlands were from minority ethnic groups. By 1989 Rover's intake had risen to 22 per cent. The rise was in part due to Rover's involvement with a group of ten companies committed to increasing the minority ethnic group content of their workforces. Since the Ten Company Group was formed in 1985 – members include J. Sainsbury and the TSB – the average proportion of minority ethnic group recruits in the ten has risen from 4 per cent to more than 10 per cent. The Ten Company Group advertise widely in ethnic media such as *Voice* and *Caribbean Times*. They have also forged links with schools and adopted far more flexible recruitment criteria, dropping an insistence that applicants meet specified academic standards.[9]

10.2.3 Government training schemes

A series of government training schemes were created during the 1980s to broaden access and increase skills and employment opportunities. Evidence from these schemes suggests that they failed to respond to minority ethnic group needs. In 1979 the education and labour market status of all 16–17 year olds revealed that 34 per cent were in full-time education, 7 per cent were unemployed, 55 per cent were in work and 4 per cent were on Youth Opportunity Programmes (YOP). In 1988, 39 per cent were in full-time education, 9 per cent were unemployed (a fall from a peak of 15 per cent in 1985), 30 per cent were in employment and 24 per cent were on Youth Training Scheme (YTS) (Department of Employment, 1987, p. 460; see also Ball, 1989, p. 15). At its inception, one of the major hopes for YTS was that it would help to redress inequalities in the labour market, especially in relation to minority ethnic groups, and open up new areas of work for young black people. Early evidence, however, revealed significant levels of under-representation. In October 1987 the first published data on the ethnic origin of YTS trainees showed that fifty companies had no black trainees and twelve supermarket chains accounted for only 21 young black people out of

2,685 YTS trainees – less than 0.8 per cent – when in March of that year black trainees represented 3.8 per cent of all registered YTS trainees (see Gore, 1987; Runnymede Trust, 1988–9, p. 9).

In the late 1980s evidence emerged of considerable differences between the experiences on YTS for black and minority ethnic group trainees and white trainees. A YTS-leaver study in Sheffield by the Manpower Services Commission (MSC) disclosed that 29.6 per cent of black YTS trainees obtained work compared with 45.2 per cent of white trainees, and that one in three black trainees became unemployed compared with one in four white trainees (Manpower Services Commission, 1987).

In September 1989 approximately one in five trainees on YTS schemes in Greater London was black. Yet three months after leaving YTS black trainees were three to four times more likely to be in full-time education than their white peers and twice as likely to be unemployed. The average unemployment rate for YTS leavers in London was 16.3 per cent. For white young people it was 13.5 per cent: for black young people the rate ranged from 20.4 per cent for Asians to 28.6 per cent for Afro-Caribbeans (Mizen, 1990, p. 2). Young black people were also marginally more likely than young white people to leave training before completion (see *Table 10.1*).

Table 10.1: number and percentage of YTS leavers in each ethnic group who left YTS before the end of their training entitlement

	White	Afro-Caribbean	Asian	Other
Greater London	16,912	4,314	1,685	729
	67%	78%	76%	74%
Manchester	27,018	637	547	181
	73%	81%	80%	77%
Birmingham and Solihull	11,165	1,266	1,527	240
	74%	79%	82%	82%
Coventry and Warwickshire	7,327	141	413	40
	67%	71%	69%	67%

(Hansard, 1990)

A study of YTS in London during the period July 1987 to June 1989 found that while 20 per cent of all YTS trainees in London were black, many major employers running YTS had no black trainees at all. While some employers were active equal opportunity employers, many others had less than 10 per cent of black YTS staff (Mizen, 1990, pp. 1–7).

In 1989 the Youth Employment and Training Unit (YETRU) alleged that racial discrimination was widespread on YTS. This was particularly the case among the type of prestigious employers – the high street stores, financial institutions and manufacturers – most likely to offer full-time jobs and high-quality training. These employers generally have outlets in the big cities where black communities tend to live (YETRU, 1989; de Sousa, 1989).

YTS's own figures showed that of those training on 31 December 1988, very few were from minority ethnic groups. Stores such as Safeway, Waitrose and Woolworths had no black trainees at all; the Co-op had 1 out of 158 trainees, Asda 6 out of 303, Gateway 2 out of 519, Sainsbury's 2 out of 232 (despite membership of the Ten Company Group), Lunn Poly 1 out of 564, Mothercare 1 out of 183 and Boots 4 out of 452.[10] In May 1989 a survey of the careers service in London by the Greater London Action for Racial Equality (GLARE) found that almost 60 per cent of respondents said that some employers and YTS managing agents did not take black youngsters.[11]

The situation gradually improved, largely through the efforts of a few pioneering firms (for example, the Ten Company Group – see section 10.2.2) who were among the first to take equal opportunities more seriously. Some transformed recruitment practices, advertised widely in minority ethnic group media, and increased liaison with schools and career services. Other companies began to improve their black trainee intakes. By 1989 black trainees at Dixons had increased from only 1 young person in 1987 to 5.88 per cent of their intake, Abbey National had increased from 1.6 per cent to 5.8 per cent and Marks and Spencer from 1.4 per cent to 5.4 per cent. By autumn 1989 many firms had begun to increase the number of black people on their YTS schemes. Nationally, 4 per cent of all YTS trainees were black, but still the scheme's Large Company Unit (LCU) reported that many firms recruited no young black people at all (Unemployment Unit and Youth Aid, 1990). Wide variations within sectors persisted (see *Table 10.2*).

By 29 May 1990, when YTS ended and was replaced by Youth Training (YT), black young people were still far less likely than white young people to be trained in employer-led schemes – the ones that led to jobs. In terms of gender, young women were consistently trained in lower-paid occupations compared to young men (Unemployment Unit, 1990, pp. 1–4). In 1989–90 public spending on YTS was £50 a week per trainee. Under the revised YT scheme it was scheduled to fall to £33 a week per trainee based on government spending plans released in January 1990 (HM Treasury, 1990, ch. 6, table 6.5).

Employment Training (ET) was similarly affected by cuts in funding and the recession. ET was designed for people between 18 and 59, but targeted particularly at those aged 18–24 who had been unemployed for more than six months but less than twelve months. A survey of all ET leavers between August 1989 and July 1990 showed that 40 per cent of the people who had completed their training were in work three months later. However, 55 per cent were unemployed. ET participants from minority ethnic groups were marginally less likely to obtain jobs than whites. While 38 per cent of white ET leavers had obtained work, only 30 per cent of Afro-Caribbean and 33 per cent of Asian participants had (Unemployment Unit and Youth Aid, 1991).

	31 December 1988		31 October 1989			31 December 1988		31 October 1989	
	Black	All	Black	All		Black	All	Black	All
ancial sector					Marks & Spencer	21 (6%)	371	2 (1%)	207
tionwide Anglia	3 (4%)	77	0 (0%)	152	Safeway	2 (1%)	227	1 (1%)	218
lifax	3 (1%)	190	4 (2%)	178	Tesco	6 (4%)	148	4 (1%)	465
B	8 (3%)	272	22 (3%)	677	Rumbelows	5 (1%)	370	8 (2%)	392
yds Bank	14 (5%)	316	9 (4%)	256	B&Q	11 (2%)	503	7 (2%)	474
BA	16 (8%)	197	6 (4%)	143	Littlewoods	2 (1%)	147	3 (3%)	115
bey National	13 (6%)	225	11 (5%)	228	ASDA	6 (2%)	303	6 (3%)	230
t West Bank	14 (7%)	193	10 (6%)	170	Texas	2 (3%)	64	7 (3%)	265
rclays	31 (9%)	367	19 (7%)	285	Granada TV	2 (1%)	294	9 (3%)	357
dland Bank	21 (1%)	224	22 (9%)	239	Debenhams	23 (3%)	736	14 (3%)	434
ort and leisure					Sainsburys	3 (1%)	232	12 (3%)	453
nn Poly	3 (1%)	564	6 (1%)	790	Comet	3 (2%)	144	8 (4%)	205
vere Group	0 (0%)	85	1 (2%)	67	BHS	2 (2%)	87	3 (5%)	59
TA	61 (3%)	2,491	43 (2%)	2,002	Burton	27 (3%)	802	35 (6%)	628
usthouse Forte	7 (7%)	92	6 (6%)	110	**Hairdressing**				
anufacturing sector and ITBs					Steiner	2 (1%)	157	2 (1%)	142
H Burgess	0 (0%)	88	0 (0%)	70	Hairdressing TA	17 (1%)	1,468	24 (2%)	1,234
essey	1 (1%)	226	1 (1%)	240	BAPHE	44 (3%)	1,486	39 (3%)	1,290
mpey Group	1 (4%)	161	2 (3%)	80	Essanelle	21 (5%)	419	13 (4%)	368
OSSF	7 (12%)	59	3 (3%)	98	**Public sector utilities and services**				
rd	17 (4%)	442	10 (3%)	351	CEGB	2 (1%)	526	0 (0%)	150
itish Cas	32 (3%)	655	36 (3%)	1,272	PSA3	3 (1%)	181	2 (1%)	235
MW	2 (1%)	157	10 (4%)	271	British Nuclear Fuels	5 (1%)	440	3 (1%)	443
hitbread	12 (4%)	343	12 (4%)	280	MOD	12 (1%)	929	8 (1%)	852
ustin Rover	28 (6%)	467	35 (7%)	526	Electricity Council	28 (2%)	1,546	22 (1%)	1,576
lington Motor	4 (5%)	84	7 (7%)	103	MOD BFG	7 (1%)	415	6 (2%)	352
M	25 (11%)	213	22 (12%)	184	BR	50 (3%)	1,730	41 (2%)	1,716
TB	280 (1%)	21,662	n/a	n/a n/a	**Training associations**				
TB	7 (3%)	239	2 (1%)	271	Arrow	0 (0%)	102	0 (0%)	122
APITB	150 (3%)	5,869	137 (3%)	4,455	Timber Trades	0 (0%)	172	1 (1%)	224
etail sector					Class Training	1 (1%)	179	1 (1%)	186
o-op	1 (1%)	157	0 (0%)	100	Remploy	5 (3%)	166	2 (2%)	129
ster Menswear	2 (2%)	103	0 (0%)	115	BPIF	14 (1%)	1,152	24 (2%)	1,252
ER	6 (4%)	137	0 (0%)	136	Motor Agents	85 (2%)	3,974	56 (3%)	2,151
ateway	2 (1%)	519	0 (0%)	440	Nat. Computing	36 (7%)	499	16 (5%)	316
it All	3 (4%)	92	1 (1%)	87	Sight and Sound	361 (11%)	2,772	395 (15%)	2,661
					BET Public	10 (11%)	92	11 (18%)	61

ote: Black trainees as a percentage of all trainees shown in brackets.
nemployment Unit and Youth Aid, 1990, pp. 7–9)

10.2.4 Industrial tribunal claims

In April 1990 the Department of Employment (DoE) revealed that the number of 'race discrimination' industrial claims completed in 1988–9 rose by 18 per cent, from 709 in 1987–8 to 839 in 1988–9. Applicants were successful in 54 cases compared with 61 in 1987–8, a marginal fall from 23 per cent to 22 per cent. The proportion of withdrawn or otherwise disposed of cases, without the need for tribunal decision, remained at around 60 per cent (DoE, 1990c).[12]

A 1991 Policy Studies Institute (PSI) report, sponsored by the Home Office, concluded that the 1976 Race Relations Act had largely failed to achieve its aim of reducing discrimination and promoting equality of opportunity in employment. The report found that in 'race' cases made under the 1976 Act, industrial tribunals significantly failed to provide the benefits that were originally expected. The report concluded that new laws, a radically over-hauled CRE and more public money were needed before discrimination in the workforce could be reduced (McCrudden *et al.*, 1991).

10.3 Trade unions

On 7 June 1991 Bill Morris was elected general secretary of the Transport and General Workers Union (TGWU), Britain's biggest union. He was the first black leader of a trade union in this country. The TGWU had 160,000 black and Asian members in 1991, a greater proportion than any other union.

In 1987 Bill Morris was reported as saying:

> Black people are losing faith and confidence in institutions generally, whether political parties, trade unions, the established church, or government bureaucracy, because they have failed both black people and ethnic minorities over such a long period and with such regularity. People are almost opting out of the system and searching for their own solutions.

('Restoring black faith in Unions', *Guardian*, 17 September 1987)

Nevertheless, government figures show that people from minority ethnic groups are still more likely than white people to belong to trade unions. In 1990 almost half of employees of black and Asian origin belonged to unions, compared with 40 per cent of the white workforce. Only a third of unions, however, had any full-time black officials. Why is this? In 1988 Gloria Mills, a black official of the National Union of Public Employees (NUPE), informed the 1988 Trades Union Congress (TUC) black workers conference:

There are many black workers who would testify their experience about how trade union structures militate against them ... sometimes it may be easier to convince management than your trade union colleagues of the need for change.

(*Independent*, 9 September 1988)

In 1988 only two of the 100 motions at the TUC conference referred to 'race' issues.

10.4 Equal opportunities and the careers service

The largest 'race' equality survey of careers services was conducted in 1988–9 in London. Although 41 per cent of responding careers services claimed to have a statement as well as a programme of action for achieving equality, only one of the responding careers services – that provided by the former ILEA – actually produced a written document that was considered by the researchers from GLARE to be a programme for working towards 'race' equality.

A quarter of services did not communicate their equal opportunities policies to their own employees. Over one-third did not communicate the policies to the employers they referred young people to. Less than half regularly reported 'race' equality matters to their education committee and of these 12.5 per cent did so only on an *ad hoc* basis.

Only a third of the services evaluated the effectiveness of their policies. No careers service had ever made use of Section 38 of the Race Relations Act 1976 to encourage applications from black people for posts in which they are under-represented in the careers service. Only two services had taken up Section 11 of the Local Government Act 1966 to employ specialist staff. Less than half of the services could produce figures on the ethnic make-up of their client groups. Nearly 80 per cent were unable to provide information on the ethnic origins of 1987 school leavers. The survey found only twenty Afro-Caribbean and nine Asian careers service officers in Greater London. Black staff were confined to junior administrative positions. The report concluded that the careers service of Greater London lacked appropriate strategies for dealing with racial discrimination. It made a dozen recommendations, including the adoption of a 'race' equality policy, the creation of a programme of action in collaboration with local black organisations and Community Relations Councils (CRCs), and the establishment of 'race' equality working groups comprising representatives of schools, minority ethnic group organizations, the CRC and local employees (GLARE, 1989). In 1991 a survey of 1,500 young black people by *Voice* highlighted their low opinion of the careers advice they received at school: 75 per cent thought their career guidance had been inadequate.[13]

10.5 Is there a black middle class?

Analysis of the Labour Force Survey (LFS) data for 1987, 1988 and 1989 reveals that 41 per cent of men in employment of Indian origin were found in managerial and professional occupational groupings, compared with 35 per cent for the white population. The relatively high proportion for Indian men in this occupational band is partly explained by the significantly larger proportions of people of Indian origin in self-employment. The LFS figures for this occupational band are reproduced in *Table 10.3*.

Table 10.3: employees in managerial and professional occupational groups, by ethnic origin and sex, 1987–9

	Men	Women
White	35%	27%
All ethnic groups	34%	29%
West Indian/Guyanese	17%	31%
Pakistani/Bangladeshi	27%	23%
Indian	41%	Not available
All other orgins	43%	30%

(Department of Employment, 1991)

The *Voice* survey referred to above also raised questions about upwardly mobile tendencies among young black people. The majority of respondents were single people under 35 in the London area who had been born in the UK of Afro-Caribbean parents. The survey revealed a tendency for young black people to be in white collar jobs; nearly 30 per cent of respondents were qualified to degree level, while a quarter held professional or vocational qualifications. Nearly two-thirds of the men and half the women surveyed said they had suffered discrimination at work and in promotion.[14]

10.6 'Race', unemployment and employment

10.6.1 Unemployment: the national context

January 1991 saw the biggest monthly rise in unemployment since the depth of the recession in May 1981. In February 1991 manufacturing firms employed fewer than 5 million people for the first time since records began. March 1991 saw unemployment in Britain rise by 112,900 to over 2 million, the biggest monthly increase since the DoE unemployment index began in 1971.[15] In April 1991 unemployment rose by a further 84,100 – the highest official April rise since 1945. In May 1991 the DoE unemployment figure stood at 2.2 million.[16] The Unemployment Unit's (UU) index measures 'broader' unemployment levels, based on pre-1982 criteria before the DoE changed their index to a count of unemployment benefit claimants only, and taking into account some of the thirty identified changes to benefit regulations and other adjustments made since. According to the UU the *real* level of unemployment in March 1991 was nearer 3 million. Whereas the DoE data put the proportion of people unemployed in March 1991 at 7.4 per cent, the UU estimate was over 10 per cent (UU, 1991). Using the DoE index, city forecasters estimated that unemployment would rise to an average of 2.4 million during 1992 (UU, 1991, p. 10). In July 1991 the EC revealed that the rise in unemployment among Britain's young people was more than double that of any other EC country – a 37 per cent increase in under-25-year-olds out of work in the year to April 1991.[17]

In October 1991 the UU estimated that the number of school leavers with no job, no training place and no entitlement to benefit had more than doubled in the previous twelve months to a total of 65,000 under-18-year-olds.[18]

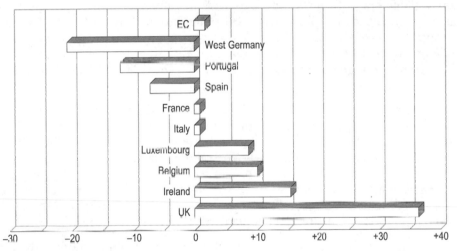

Figure 10.1: unemployment in the EC: percentage change for under-25-year-olds, April 1990 to 1991
(Guardian, 18 July 1991)

Many of the industries worst affected by the recession of the early 1990s are significant employers of minority ethnic groups – motor vehicles, textiles, footwear and clothing, metal goods manufacture, mechanical engineering and electrical and electronic engineering (UU, 1991, p. 10). The proportion of long-term unemployed (claimants out of work for more than a year), which peaked at over 42 per cent in 1987 (DoE figures), was 29 per cent and rising in October 1990. Here, there were strong regional differences, ranging from 18.1 per cent in the non-London south east to 35.5 per cent in Scotland (UU, 1991, p. 9). During the 1980s, youth unemployment rose by one-third.[19]

10.6.2 'Race' and unemployment

The true figure of minority ethnic group unemployment is unknown because the DoE no longer provides a breakdown by ethnic group. Instead, we have to rely on LFS to estimate regional and national trends and patterns. Evidence from the 1970s and 1980s has shown that as unemployment rises, minority ethnic group unemployment rises faster (Ohri and Faruqi, 1988, p. 69). If black people were hit hard by the recession of the early 1980s, young black people were hit harder. Black women were especially vulnerable. The recession of the early 1980s had a dramatic effect on levels of black unemployment. Between 1978 and 1983, for example, the number of black women registered as unemployed rose from 14,900 to 74,000, an increase of 397 per cent, compared with an increase of 137 per cent in the total number of women, both black and white, registered as unemployed during the same period (Ohri and Faruqi, 1988, pp. 68–74).[20]

The latest LFS analysis of unemployment available at the time of the first edition covered averages for the years 1987 to 1989 (see also Section 4).[21] The unemployment rate for young people from minority ethnic groups was nearly twice that for the young white population. Among the 16–24 age group, 21 per cent of the minority ethnic group population were unemployed, compared with 12 per cent of whites. The highest rates were found in the Pakistani or Bangladeshi groups (27 per cent) and the West Indian/Guyanese group (25 per cent).

Unemployment among 16 and 17 year olds rose to 90,500 in 1991, an increase of 57.4 per cent on the previous year, according to the UU. The south east of England saw the largest increase – 151 per cent. Since 1988 government employment figures have excluded those under 18 because the age group 'is "guaranteed" a job on youth training schemes'. But the UU claimed that the recession led to insufficient numbers of training scheme places. It warned of a return to the mass youth unemployment of the mid-1980s. In 1984 some 159,000 people aged 16 and 17 were out of work.[22]

According to LFS data for 1987–9, the overall unemployment rate for minority ethnic groups was 14 per cent compared with 9 per cent for whites. The highest rates were found in the Pakistani or Bangladeshi groups (25 per cent) and the West Indian group (16 per cent). The higher unemployment rates for black people across age and gender cohorts cannot be explained by differences in qualification levels. Unemployment rates were generally higher among minority ethnic groups than among whites with the same level of qualifications (DoE, 1991, Table 9, p. 68). Full details are given in *Tables 10.4* and *10.5* and *Figure 10.2*.

In August 1991 Professor Robert Moore, a sociologist from Liverpool University, was reported as saying that 'racism is wasting some of the most talented people'. Young West Indians with O-levels were three times more likely and Asians with degrees twice more likely than whites to be unemployed.[23]

Table 10.4: unemployment rates in Great Britain, by sex, age and ethnic origin: average, 1987–9

| | All origins* | White | Minority ethnic groups | | | | |
			All	West Indian/ Guyanese	Indian	Pakistani/ Bangladeshi	All other origins
All							
All aged 16–59/64	9	9	14	16	11	25	11
16–24	13	12	21	25	16	27	17
25–44	7	7	13	11	12	30	–
45–59/64	6	6	–	–	–	–	–
Males							
All aged 16–64	9	9	15	18	10	25	11
16–24	14	13	22	27	–	–	–
25–44	8	7	12	–	8	21	–
45–64	8	8	15	–	–	–	–
Females							
All aged 16–59	9	8	13	14	13	–	11
16–24	12	11	10	–	–	–	–
25–44	9	8	12	–	12	–	–
45–59	6	6	–	–	–	–	–

– Less than 10,000 in cell.
* Includes 'not known'.
(Department of Employment, 1991)

Table 10.5: *unemployment rates in Great Britain, by highest qualification level, ethnic origin, age and sex: 1987–9*

Age group and level of highest qualifications held	All			Males			Females		
	All origins*	White	Minority ethnic groups	All origins*	White	Minority ethnic groups	All origins*	White	Minority ethnic groups
16–59/64									
All*	9	9	14	9	9	15	9	8	13
Higher	3	3	6	3	3	–	4	4	–
Other	8	7	14	7	7	13	8	8	15
None	14	13	19	16	15	21	11	11	15
16–24									
All*	13	12	21	14	13	22	12	11	19
Higher	5	5	–	6	6	–	–	–	–
Other	10	10	18	10	10	18	10	9	18
None	25	25	31	26	25	34	24	24	–
25–44									
All*	8	8	12	8	7	12	9	8	12
Higher	3	3	–	2	2	–	4	4	–
Other	7	7	12	6	6	11	9	8	14
None	14	13	16	16	16	17	11	11	–
45–59/64									
All*	7	7	13	8	8	15	6	6	–
Higher	3	3	–	4	3	–	2	–	–
Other	6	6	–	7	7	–	5	5	–
None	9	9	17	12	11	21	7	7	–

Higher = degree/BTEC Higher level; Other = any other qualification
* Includes 'not known'.
– Less than 10,000 in cell.
(Department of Employment, 1991)

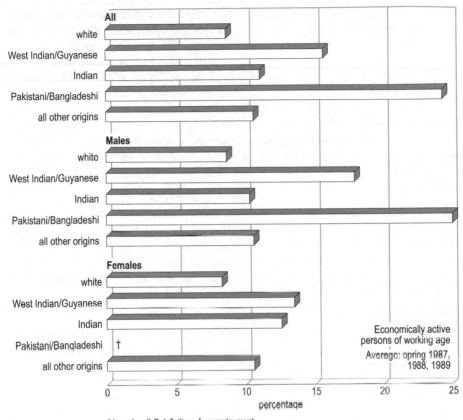

* based on ILO definition of unemployment
† less than 10,000 in cell: estimate not shown

Figure 10.2: unemployment rates* in Great Britain: percentages by ethnic origin and sex (Department of Employment, 1991, p. 67)

10.6.3 'Race' and employment

LFS averages for 1987–9 revealed that minority ethnic groups comprised 4.7 per cent or 1.6 million of the population of working age in Britain (16–64 for men, 16–59 for women). Of these, 32.1 per cent were of Indian origin, 21.4 per cent of West Indian or Guyanese origin, 18.1 per cent of Pakistani or Bangladeshi origin, and 28.3 per cent of mainly Chinese, African, Arab or mixed origin (DoE, 1991, p. 60).

White people, at 80 per cent, were more likely than people from minority ethnic groups, at 68 per cent, to be *economically active* – that is, in or looking for employment. A wide variation was found among minority ethnic groups: 80 per cent of West Indian/Guyanese were economically active compared with 51 per cent of Pakistani/Bangladeshi (DoE, 1991, Table 1, p. 61).

The data showed that for young people aged between 16 and 24 the economic activity rates for whites was 80 per cent compared with 58 per cent for all ethnic groups (the lowest rate was for Pakistani/Bangladeshi at 44 per cent). These differences are partly explained, according to the *Employment Gazette*, by the different proportions of young people aged 16–24 staying on in full-time education (33 per cent for young minority ethnic group men and 24 per cent for women, compared to 12 per cent and 11 per cent respectively for young white men and women), and partly by the different proportions of young women 'whose domestic and family activities meant that they were not available for work' (40 per cent of the Pakistani/Bangladeshi young women in this age band were in this category) (DoE, 1991, Tables 2 and 3, pp. 61–2).

People from minority ethnic groups were more likely than white people to be *self-employed* (16 per cent compared with 12 per cent), the proportion of self-employed people being especially high among men of Indian origin (27 per cent) and of Pakistani/Bangladeshi origin (23 per cent). Working *part-time* was more common among white women: 40 per cent worked part-time compared with 27 per cent of minority ethnic group women (DoE, 1991, Figure 3, p. 63).

Marked variations between minority ethnic groups and whites were found in their *industrial distribution*. For example, 29 per cent of minority ethnic group men in employment were in distribution, hotels, catering and repairs, compared with 16 per cent of white men. Minority ethnic group men were also strongly represented in health services, as were minority ethnic group women. Overall, the sectoral profile of the 375,000 women from the minority ethnic groups in employment was broadly similar to that for the employed in the white female population (DoE, 1991, Table 4, p. 64).

LFS analysis of *occupational distribution* showed little difference as a whole between minority ethnic groups and the white population: 53 per cent of each group of employees were in manual occupations and 47 per cent in non-manual. Significant variations emerged, however, between ethnic groups. Around one-third of West Indian and Pakistani/Bangladeshi men were non-manual workers, compared to over half of those of Indian or other origins. In manual occupations a converse pattern was found, with West Indian men accounting for the highest proportion – 29 per cent – working in craft occupations (DoE, 1991, Figure 4 and Table 5, pp. 64–5).

The LFS data revealed that the regional distribution of economically active members of minority ethnic groups of working age showed marked variations. Fifty-eight per cent of economically active members of the minority ethnic population lived in the south east region, including nearly two-thirds of the West Indians, more than half of the Indians, and nearly two-fifths of the Pakistani/Bangladeshis, and 31 per cent of the white population. Fifteen per cent of the economically active population of working age in Greater London and 10 per cent in the West Midlands were from minority ethnic groups, compared with 1 per cent or less in Scotland, Wales, the North, and those parts of the West Midlands, Yorkshire and Humberside and the north west outside metropolitan county areas. The figure as a whole for Great Britain was 4 per cent (DoE, 1991, Table 11, pp. 68–9).

Mr Bernard, Manchester, 1986. Photograph by Clement Cooper.

10.7 Developments since 1992

10.7.1 Labour market context

Official unemployment trends reveal that between 1991 and 1994 unemployment in Britain rose by 13 per cent. Long-term unemployment rose by 84 per cent. Estimates from the UU showed that the numbers out of work topped 4 million at the beginning of 1993, and put the proportion of those unemployed at one in eight of the workforce (Unemployment Unit, 1993a). In April 1994 the Government, under attack from Labour, accepted the possibility that real unemployment could be as high as five million (*Independent*, 21 April 1994; CSO, 1995; *Independent on Sunday*, 26 March 1995).[24] In July 1995 Government figures showed the first increase in unemployment following two years of gradual decline.

Since 1975 the proportion of the working population in full-time employment has declined by 35 per cent, and 15 per cent of British households now have no member in employment (*Guardian*, 3 April 1995). More people are working part-time. Between 1984 and 1994, nearly a million part-time jobs have been created for women, and the number of male part-time workers has nearly doubled to one million. In the last three months of 1994, 75,000 full-time jobs were lost and 174,000 part-time jobs created. Eight out of nine of jobs created since March 1993 have gone to women, mostly in low-paid part-time retailing and service work. Manufacturing firms continue to announce large job losses and plant closure (a fall from 41 per cent in 1971 to 28 per cent in 1994). Nearly 1.2 million British workers earned less than £2.50 an hour in 1994 (CSO, 1995; *Independent on Sunday*, 26 March 1995).

10.7.2 Minority ethnic group unemployment

Trends in minority ethnic group unemployment continue to reveal disproportionate disadvantages for black and Asian groups. In January 1995, LFS estimates revealed in the Commons showed that 62 per cent of black people between 16 and 24 were unemployed, and that more than a third of black men of all ages in the capital were out of work. *Social Trends 25* confirmed that in spring 1994, fewer than one in ten white people were unemployed, compared with 27 per cent of black people, and 28 per cent of Pakistanis and Bangladeshis (see *Figure 10.3*) (CSO, 1995; Runnymede Trust, 1995c). The trends in black and Asian unemployment are shown in *Figure 10.4* and *Table 10.6*. Particularly affected are Pakistani and Bangladeshi men and women, with more than three times the average unemployment rate. *Table 10.6* provides a detailed gender breakdown by ethnic group.[25]

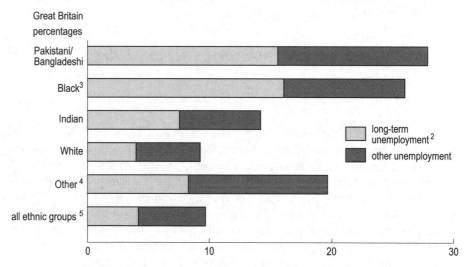

[1] Unemployed based on the ILO definition as a percentage of all economically active.

[2] Unemployed for more than 52 weeks.

[3] Includes Caribbean, African and other black people of non-mixed origin.

[4] Includes Chinese, other ethnic minority groups of non-mixed origin, and people of mixed origin.

[5] Includes ethnic group not stated.

Figure 10.3: unemployment rates[1], by ethnic group, spring 1994
(CSO, 1995, p. 78)

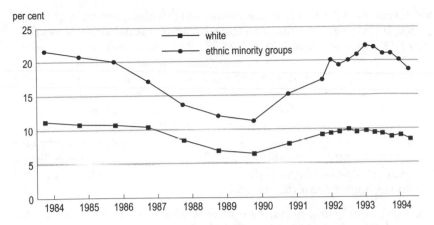

Figure 10.4: trends in ILO unemployment rates, by ethnic origin, spring 1984 to autumn 1994 (not seasonally adjusted)
(Employment Gazette, *June 1995*)

Research by the Equal Opportunities Commission (EOC) shows that skilled minority women are twice as likely as white women to be unemployed. Black Caribbean women are twice as likely to be without a job; Pakistani and Bangladeshi women five times as likely to be unemployed. EOC found that black and Asian women work longer hours than whites for lower pay, often in ancillary jobs in hotel and catering, manufacturing and textiles. Minority women were also more likely to be overqualified for inferior employment, and twice as likely as whites to be on Government training schemes (Owen, 1994). Owen concluded that black and Asian women's unemployment was more likely to be hidden from official statistics because of factors such as home-working, or working in a family business, and their participation in the professions of the contracting welfare state. In 1995 over one fifth (22 per cent) of black and Asian women in London were unemployed (Runnymede Trust, 1995d).

Table 10.6: unemployment[1], by ethnic origin and gender, summer 1994

	White	Black-Caribbean	Black African	Black – Other	Indian	Pakistani	Bangladeshi	Chinese	Other/na	All
en and omen	2,456,300	55,700	40,900	8,900	61,000	42,700	15,300	8,500	47,300	2,736,500
	9.4%	22.5%	37.2%	21.2%	14.4%	27.2%	31.2%	11.8%	21.2%	9.9%
en	1,646,100	35,500	25,700	5,300	37,400	33,600	11,600	4,600	32,700	1,832,500
	11.2%	27.4%	41.0%	21.5%	15.6%	29.1%	33.8%	12.3%	25.1%	11.9%
omen	810,200	20,200	15,200	3,600	23,600	9,000	3,700	4,000	14,600	904,000
	7.0%	17.0%	32.1%	20.8%	12.9%	21.6%	25.2%	11.5%	15.7%	7.5%

Unemployed category is 'standard' LFS unemployed plus those on Government employment and training schemes.
Jnemployment Unit, *1994*)

The 1990s' recession hit young black people hard. Youth unemployment for people aged 16–24 years old, doubled from 497,900 in April 1990, to over one million in 1993 (*Independent*, 5 March 1993). The proportion of unemployed black 16–17-year-olds is around four in ten, compared with the overall percentage of 17.6 per cent, or one in five. In the summer of 1994, Norman Fowler, then the Chairman of the Conservative Party, revealed in the House of Commons that while 88,000 school leavers are unemployed, 76,000 of them received no income at all, and had slipped through the training and benefits net (1 June 1994). Black and Asian long-term unemployment also increased significantly (Unemployment Unit, 1993b; Runnymede Trust, 1993h). *Social Trends 25* revealed that long-term Caribbean unemployment was four times higher than that of whites (CSO, 1995).

The latest data analysing minority ethnic origin, unemployment and age showed that in the autumn of 1994, in the 16–24 age group, 51 per cent of Afro-Caribbean, 33 per cent of Bangladeshi and 30 per cent of Indian men were unemployed compared with 18 per cent of white men aged 16–24. In other age categories, minority ethnic group men were twice as likely as white men to be unemployed (Runnymede Trust, 1995g).

Department of Employment analysis has also demonstrated that minority ethnic group unemployment rates were higher for ethnic groups within the same broad level of qualifications, controlling for age (*Employment Gazette*, May 1994, Table 7). Census analysis has showed that minority ethnic groups have greater chances of being out of work than similarly qualified whites (*Independent*, 16 July 1994). Voluntary groups are expressing growing concern over the Conservative Government's move towards job-seekers' allowances, which they believe will lead to massive loss of benefits for the black and Asian unemployed (*Independent*, 23 March 1995; *Guardian*, 31 March 1995).

10.7.3 Employment

A 1993 PSI national study revealed greater variation between minority ethnic groups in employment: 'Certain groups – the African Asians and Indians in particular – have come to occupy a labour market position hardly inferior to that of whites. Other groups – especially Bangladeshis and to a lesser extent Pakistanis – continue to occupy a much poorer position' (R. Chote, 'Ethnic poor need pay as well as jobs', *Independent on Sunday*, 29 August 1993; J. Jones, 'NHS to check ethnic origins', *Independent*, 12 August 1993). Two reasons are primarily responsible, the growth of the service sector, and the development of self-employment. Important differences exist between minority ethnic groups in relation to work status and the increasing shift from manufacturing to a service sector economy has had implications for job losses and opportunities for minorities. Between 1984 and 1993, the proportion of white people in manufacturing showed a 9 per cent decline, while for ethnic minorities this proportion was 18 per cent. For services, during the same period, the proportion of minority ethnic people's jobs rose by 50 per cent compared with 15 per cent for white people (Runnymede Trust, 1994a, p. 25).

The 1991 census and the 1991 LFS survey demonstrate the variations in class structure of different ethnic communities. *Table 10.7* provides a breakdown of people in employment by ethnic group, gender and socio-economic status.

Pakistani and Bangladeshi workers are disproportionately represented in the skilled manual group. The highest proportion of professional males was among Indians, with 14 per cent compared with the white figure of 8 per cent. Indian and Pakistani people are far more likely to be self-employed than others; there is very little self-employment among Caribbean people. Over a third of Afro-Caribbean men work in the public sector, compared with 18 per cent of white men and 18 per cent of Indian men. The figure for Afro-Caribbean women employed in the public sector is 51 per cent (Runnymede Trust, 1995g).

Table 10.7: people in employment in Great Britain[1], by ethnic group, socio-economic group[2] and gender, spring 1994, in percentages

	Black	Indian	Pakistani or Bangladeshi	Other ethnic minority groups	All ethnic minority groups	White persons	All
Males							
Professional	–	13.7	–	19.5	11.7	8.2	8.4
Intermediate	25.2	30.5	18.3	28.2	20.3	31.1	30.0
Skilled non-manual	13.7	13.5	15.7	16.8	14.7	11.6	11.8
Skilled manual	28.6	22.3	33.5	19.2	25.3	31.6	31.3
Partly skilled	17.2	17.0	22.9	11.1	16.9	13.4	13.5
Unskilled	9.4	–	–	–	5.1	4.1	4.1
All males (thousands) (=100%)[3]	144	190	110	126	571	12,887	13,458
Females							
Professional	–	7.0	–	–	4.8	2.6	2.6
Intermediate	35.1	23.2	28.7	30.9	29.4	30.3	30.3
Skilled non-manual	28.8	34.2	40.7	35.9	33.5	37.0	36.8
Skilled manual	9.6	–	–	–	8.1	8.1	8.1
Partly skilled	14.2	26.7	–	13.0	18.7	15.5	15.7
Unskilled	9.7	–	–	–	5.5	6.6	6.5
All females (thousands) (=100%)[3]	147	152	45	103	443	10,272	10,715

Males aged 16–64, females aged 16–59.
Based on occupation.
Includes members of the armed forces and those who did not give ethnic group or occupation.
(CSO, 1995, p. 20)

Two thirds of minority ethnic group residents of working age were economically active according to the 1991 census, compared with over three-quarters of the total population (Pearce and White, 1994). LFS activity rates in late 1993 were 79 per cent for white and 43 per cent for Bangladeshi/Pakistani people of working age. LFS analysis revealed that rates for minority ethnic groups in the 16–24 age band were lower than for whites (56 per cent compared with 78 per cent). There was little variation in the rates from the prime working-age range of 25–44, while older Pakistani and Bangladeshi men experienced a relatively low activity rate (61 per cent). Activity rates for minority group women were lower than for whites (54 per cent compared with 72 per cent) (*Employment Gazette*, May 1994).

The growth in part-time work among women has impacted on the minority ethnic group communities, but it is white people who are more likely to find work in the sector. The 1989–91 LFS showed that 26 per cent of all minority group women worked part-time compared with 40 per cent of white women (*Hansard*, 1992).

Britain's ethnic minorities produced 25 per cent more entrepreneurs than the UK white population. Minority ethnic groups accounted for over 8 per cent of the six million small business owners and self-employed people in the UK though they comprise only 4 per cent of the workforce (*Mail on Sunday*, 5 July 1992; *Employment Gazette*, May 1994). In spring 1994, LFS analysis showed that 15 per cent of all ethnic groups were self-employed, compared with 12 per cent of the white workforce. The figures for male self-employment were: 17 per cent white; 21 per cent all ethnic groups; 11 per cent black; 26 per cent Indian and 25 per cent Pakistani (*Employment Gazette*, October 1993, May 1994, January 1995).

One in 17 Afro-Caribbeans were running their own companies in 1993. Crucially, Afro-Caribbeans are much more reliant on mainstream banks for start-up capital; the survey revealed that inappropriate measures were used in assessing lack of collateral, surplus cash and business track record, and that these disadvantaged Afro-Caribbeans (MBS Associates, 1993; *Independent on Sunday*, 26 September 1993). Further ESRC research has revealed that banks were failing small businesses, and that genuine gaps in minority ethnic group funding did exist, especially where minorities wanted to finance business which ran against the corner-shop stereotype of food retailing, tobacconists and news agency. ESRC found manufacturing capital especially difficult to locate for black and Asian people (Hughes, 1994; *Guardian*, 26 August 1994).

A study by Jones and McEvoy of self-employment amongst Asians denounces the basic stereotypes of self-employment, first by arguing that self-employment is forced on many Asian households by other factors, not least discrimination in the job market and decline in UK manufacturing and textiles base. Second, by suggesting that the successful 'Open All Hours' corner shop is a myth for the majority of Asian small businesses. A small group of mega-business successes (Joe Bloggs Jeans; Patak's Foods; The Happy Shopper, etc.) have emerged. There are more than 200 Asian millionaires living in Britain. But Jones and McEvoy argue that the vast majority of Asian self-employed are struggling to survive against recession and racism, often in the same marketplace. Jones and McEvoy found that two thirds were concentrated in seven Asian wards, with an annual weekly turnover of about £1,000. One half of those businesses studied ceased trading, many went bankrupt (*Independent on Sunday*, 12 July 1994; *Financial Mail on Sunday*, 8 January 1995; Jones and McEvoy, 1994).

Department of Employment findings on training outcomes for minority ethnic groups show variations between groups. On Youth Training in 1993, the proportion gaining a qualification was 48 per cent for white young people, 42 per cent for Asian, but only 39 per cent for Afro-Caribbeans. Larger differences were found in those getting jobs: whereas half the white group obtained employment, only 31 per cent of Asian young people and 24 per cent of Afro-Caribbean young people did. Training for Work, which targeted long-term adult unemployed, revealed little difference between groups getting a qualification, but wide differences in job success-rates (one in three white adults obtained work compared with one in five Afro-Caribbeans) (TUC, 1994).

The LFS reports that people from minority ethnic groups in employment were as likely to be members of trade unions as were white workers, with densities of 32 per cent and 33 per cent respectively. Union density was highest, however, among people of Afro-Caribbean and Guyanese background with 46 per cent membership, compared with 33 per cent for Indian, and 25 per cent for Bangladeshis (*Employment Gazette*, January 1993, p. 685; minority group descriptions are those of the LFS). Forty-three per cent of black women were union members compared with less than 1 per cent of those of Bangladeshi and Pakistani origin (CSO, 1994, p. 147). TUC membership fell by 30 per cent from its peak in 1979 of 13.3 million (*Employment Gazette*, June 1994). In 1994, the TUC elected three black members to sit on its ruling general council (Runnymede Trust, 1994g).

Enquiries answered by the EOC and CRE covering a range of issues, including 'race' related concerns, rose from 3,132 in 1981 to 39,557 in 1993 (EOC), and from 864 in 1981 to 1,630 in 1993 (CRE) (CSO, 1995, Table 9.34). In each of the years 1991–1994, two thirds of the racial discrimination cases brought to industrial tribunals were either withdrawn, disposed of, or conciliated without the need to proceed. Soaring costs and cuts in legal aid deterred complaints. Complaints of racial discrimination taken to industrial tribunals rose by 24 per cent in 1991, and increased a further 19 per cent during 1992 (*Guardian*, 21 April 1993; Runnymede Trust, 1994a).

A 1993 Department of Employment survey showed that Asian and Afro-Caribbean applicants comprised only 4 per cent of complainants at industrial tribunals. The survey also revealed discrepancies in tribunal outcomes regarding ethnicity (*Employment Gazette*, June 1994). The Government responded by approving a fast-tracking strategy to speed racial discrimination complaints through industrial tribunals. However, CRE recommendations to extend the Race Relations Act 1976 to introduce compulsory ethnic monitoring of workforces, recognize discrimination on religious grounds and set up tribunals specifically to deal with 'race' cases, were rejected by the Government (*Guardian*, 5 July 1994).

There have been several 'landmark' industrial tribunal cases since 1992. Twenty black crew managers won a total of £60,000 as compensation from London Underground (LU). The finding, in the biggest 'race' case brought before an industrial tribunal, involved claims that black staff received smaller bonuses than their white colleagues (Runnymede Trust, 1993e; *Independent*, 6 April 1993). Bradford Metropolitan Council received five judgements against it involving racial discrimination between 1988 and 1993, and paid out £100,000 in compensation (*Equal Opportunities Review*, May/June 1993). In 1993, a black trade union official accepted £10,500 in settlement of a claim of racial discrimination against the shop workers' union USDAW (Runnymede Trust, 1993i).

In June 1993, a British Rail inquiry found that only 2 per cent of its drivers came from ethnic minorities (341 drivers out of 15,000). Guards and station staff, however, made up 10 per cent of those employed in these categories. The results followed complaints of discriminatory recruitment and promotion practices in BR (*Independent on Sunday*, 27 June 1993). In Ashford, Kent, a college lecturer successfully won a tribunal, the first against an educational establishment for racial abuse. In London, Harrods faced a series of tribunals brought by staff claiming unfair dismissal and racial discrimination (*Guardian*, 24 September 1994). In Leeds, a group of Muslim workers were awarded £1,000 compensation each for racial discrimination against a company who would not let them take leave to celebrate a religious festival (*Independent*, 18 February 1994). There have also been several successful tribunals against police forces on the grounds of racial discrimination, including the first successful case against the Hendon Police Training College, in 1994, and a record award of £32,000 to PC Sarah Locker on grounds of both racial and sexual discrimination, thirty times more than the police's initial offer (*Daily Mail*, 13 January 1994; *Guardian*, 6 December 1993; *Independent*, 23 March 1994; 7 May 1994).

A survey of Britain's biggest private companies revealed that most still refused to co-operate with ethnic monitoring strategies (including ICI, British Airways and the Prudential). Only four companies could provide a detailed breakdown of the ethnic origin of their workforce (NatWest bank, the Royal Bank of Scotland, Marks and Spencer and United Biscuits) (ECCR, 1992). In April 1993, a survey of 166 companies revealed that only 3 had adopted Department of Employment recruitment targets for ethnic minorities. This reluctance was due to fears that targets might be regarded as discriminatory quotas. Just over half the companies, however, had set up equal opportunity policies and action plans which emphasized new training and recruitment policies, but most had no overall strategy on equal opportunities for ethnic minorities (*Personnel Management Plus*, April 1993; *Equal Opportunities Review*, 1993).

In 1995, the CRE reported that of 300 leading companies, only one half were beginning to put racial equality policies into practice, and called it a 'disappointing failure'. Nine of ten of the top 300 firms had, however, established racial equality policies, but very few had moved from commitment to action (*The Times*, 19 January 1995; *Searchlight*, March 1995). A survey of 41 councils found that over 66 per cent employed a smaller proportion of people from minority ethnic groups than the proportion of minority ethnic population that lived within travelling distance: one in four councils could provide no ethnic breakdown of their workforce (*Searchlight*, March 1995).

The CRE is planning the first full-scale inquiry into racial discrimination in the armed services, following a series of successful claims against racial discrimination. Recruitment among ethnic minorities fell dramatically between 1989 and 1992: black recruits from 146 to 53, and Asian recruits from 56 to 14. Between 1990 and 1992, no ethnic minority officer entered the Army. The Royal Air Force accepted one ethnic minority officer, the Navy and Marines six. Of the 12,044 people accepted into the armed forces in 1991–2, only 112 were of minority ethnic group origin (*Daily Telegraph*, 7 July 1993). Ethnic monitoring is still not fully practised in the armed forces: the Ministry of Defence is still involved in a seven-year period of protracted negotiation (*Guardian*, 2 December 1993). In August 1995 the first Afro-Caribbean soldier to join the Household Cavalry Sovereign's Escort rode alongside the Queen at the VJ Day ceremony (*Independent*, 12 August 1995).

The civil service revealed that 5.6 per cent of white civil servants, 0.9 per cent of black and 2.3 per cent of Asians had now reached senior grades. However, 50 per cent of white civil servants, 80 per cent of black and 71 per cent of Asian were still located in non-managerial clerical grades. An analysis of the civil service grade structure showed gradual improvements for minorities between 1989 and 1993 (Runnymede Trust, 1994a, pp. 20–1). In February 1993, the Cabinet Office disclosed that private companies bidding to maintain Government services run by the civil service will not be required to operate equal opportunities policies (*Independent*, 28 February 1993). The Advisory Panel on Equal Opportunities is due to report in the summer of 1995 on black and ethnic minority recruitment into the civil service (*Employment Gazette*, November 1994).

In March 1995, several years after fieldwork had been conducted, the findings of a study of black and Asian access to media employment were published. The study, undertaken at the end of the 1980s by Beulah Ainley, showed that print journalism was behind broadcasting in the employment of black and Asian staff. Only 5 per cent of those black and Asian journalists who had received training found work in the mainstream media. The majority were turned down by white media employers. Of 4,000 national newspaper journalists only 20 were black or Asian. Of 8,000 provincial journalists only 15 per cent were black or Asian. Of 3,700 editorial staff in broadcasting, an estimated 100 were black or Asian. Ainley argues that black and Asian journalists are severely under-represented in white mainstream media jobs. During the 1990s, the launch of the *Weekly Journal*, the increasing use of mainstream television and radio for 'exploring race' issues – through documentary, drama, soap opera and comedy – and the expansion in black radio have improved on the 1980s situation. Racism reached the Ambridge of *The Archers* in 1995. However, the role of the media in affirming racial attitudes still persists, especially in the tabloid press and through the presentation of fashion, where, for example, black models still mirror white model stereotypes (Runnymede Trust, 1995d).

Studies in Sheffield and London have shown significant discrepancies in white and black employment in service industries, particularly computing and banking (Benson, 1989; Amin and Oppenheim, 1992). The Fire Service has also come under attack from the Home Office, following accusations of racial discrimination in recruitment policies, and for racial abuse in the workplace (*Independent*, 10 April 1994).

The National Association of Citizens Advice Bureaux (NACAB) reported that discrimination is rooted in the policies, practices and attitudes of companies, and that there had been an increase in complaints of racial discrimination in companies. Poor legislation, loss of employment rights and reduced job security provided employers with 'increasing freedom to act on prejudice'. Enquiries to Citizens Advice Bureaux in England and Wales rose by 31 per cent to 882,257 a year between 1990 and 1994 (NACAB, 1994).

In 1995 a 'Race for Opportunity' initiative was launched, to raise further the profile of 'race' amongst employers, under the 'Business in the Community' scheme. The CRE also announced a Standard for Racial Equality with the support of the TUC and CBI. It is designed to help employees meet their needs and to promote good business practice. Though the Standard is voluntary and carries no legal status, it is designed to improve 'race' relations in workforces. Employers are encouraged to develop a public plan of action, collecting and evaluating ethnic monitoring data, enhancing training, improving outreach work with communities, and improving black and Asian representation in the boardroom (CRE, 1995b).

Notes

1 Students of Open University course ED356 *'Race', Education and Society* should note that this section has strong links to Reader 3 (Braham *et al.*, 1992).

2 Quoted in G. Neale and C. Fitzsimmons, 'Wealth of talent along the slow road to equality', *Observer*, 2 November 1986.

3 See Section 5 where evidence for the relationship between 'race', poverty, and employment/unemployment is explored.

4 *Independent*, 23 May 1990 and 29 January 1989. While women occupy nearly 50 per cent of civil service posts, they occupy only 7 per cent of principal grade officer posts or above.

5 Reported in the *Independent*, 26 September 1989.

6   *Independent*, 2 September 1989.

7   See Defence Committee (1988). A form of ethnic monitoring did operate in the armed forces between 1959 and 1968 by which a quota system limited the number of people 'not of European descent' or barred them from some regiments. The 1968 Race Relations Act led to the abolition of this practice. See Runnymede Trust (1988) p. 7.

8   *Independent*, 23 March 1991.

9   *Financial Times*, 8 November 1989.

10 K. Hyder, 'Large stores reject blacks for YTS', *Observer*, 21 May 1989.

11 *Observer*, 21 May 1989.

12 See also *Equal Opportunities Review*, May/June 1990, p. 31.

13 *Education*, 7 June 1991, p. 459.

14 *Education*, 7 June 1991, p. 459.

15 Department of Employment figures are quoted here. See *Employment Gazettes*, February to April 1991.

16 *Independent*, 17 May 1991.

17 *Guardian*, 18 July 1991.

18 *Independent*, 28 October 1991.

19 *Breadline Britain in the 1990s*, London Weekend Television, 13 May 1991.

20 Ohri and Faruqi provide an excellent survey of 'race' and unemployment in the early 1980s. See also Clough *et al.* (1988), for an interesting case study of young black unemployment, and Brown (1985).

21 See 'Ethnic origins and the labour market', *Employment Gazette*, February 1991. See also *Equal Opportunities Review*, 36, March/April 1991, pp. 4–5. The *Employment Gazette* now publishes an annual analysis on this subject each spring (February or March issue).

22 Alex Renton, *Independent*, 13 September 1991.

23 *Independent*, 30 August 1991.

24 The Conservative Government continues to change official statistics. Of more than 36 changes made to the official statistics since 1979, only one failed to lower the total. A comparison of census returns and official unemployment figures disclosed that nearly 400,000 more people were out of work in April 1991 than the Department of Employment official returns calculated (*Independent*, 22 April 1993). The introduction to *Social Trends 25* was removed partly because of the author's stance on official data. Research and voluntary groups have maintained pressure on the Government for new standards of measurement to be introduced, to reduce public lack of confidence in official data, and to establish a central statistical office independent of Government control (*Independent*, 16 October 1994).

25 The 'standard' LFS (ILO) definition of unemployment includes persons who have looked for work within the previous four weeks. It differs both from the broader LFS count which excludes the looking for work criteria, and from the crude claimant count introduced in 1995. The LFS does control for class factors in producing its findings.

11 RACIAL ATTITUDES
IN BRITAIN

▼ ▼

The pervasiveness and deep rootedness of racism requires us to be continually vigilant and to understand that, simply because it no longer finds the same expression, it has not been erased.

(CRE, 1991a, p. 7)

▲ ▲

In 1984 the first British social attitudes survey described a British society that was seen by more than 90 per cent of the adult population to be racially prejudiced against its black and Asian members (Jowell *et al.*, 1984). More than one-third classified themselves as racially prejudiced: 42 per cent thought racial prejudice would be worse in five years' time. Two years later, the 1986 British social attitudes report offered an equally pessimistic picture of the perceived extent of racial prejudice for the 1990s (Jowell *et al.*, 1986, pp. 149–50). In July 1991 the Runnymede Trust and National Opinion Poll (NOP) produced the findings of the largest national study of attitudes to racism conducted in Britain since the British social attitudes studies of the mid-1980s and the Policy Studies Institute's third national survey.[1]

Two out of every three white people thought Britain was a very or fairly racist society compared with four out of five Afro-Caribbeans and 56 per cent of Asians. Almost half the white respondents agreed with the proposition that 'non-white' people were treated worse than white people by the police, a similar response to the Asian sample. This compared with three-quarters of the Afro-Caribbean respondents. Two-thirds of Afro-Caribbeans believed employers discriminated in favour of white workers, compared with four out of ten from white and Asian samples. All these figures were significantly higher than those reported by the PSI in their third national survey (see Brown, 1984, chs 7 and 10). The 1991 survey disclosed that over 60 per cent of Afro-Caribbeans thought that British laws against racial discrimination were not tough enough, compared with 45 per cent of Asians and 31 per cent of whites. It concluded that confidence in black and Asian people getting fair treatment from the police and the courts had 'plummeted in the past decade' (see *Figure 11.1*).

Most whites surveyed thought that social security offices, council housing departments and schools treated non-whites the same as or better than white people. However, while only 13 per cent and 18 per cent of whites and

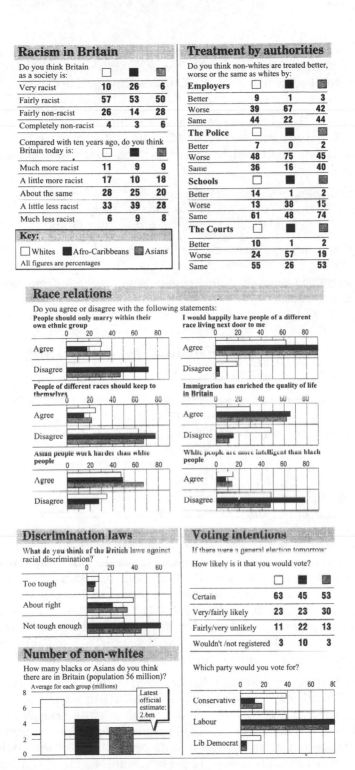

Racism in Britain

Do you think Britain as a society is:

	Whites	Afro-Caribbeans	Asians
Very racist	10	26	6
Fairly racist	57	53	50
Fairly non-racist	26	14	28
Completely non-racist	4	3	6

Compared with ten years ago, do you think Britain today is:

	Whites	Afro-Caribbeans	Asians
Much more racist	11	9	9
A little more racist	17	10	18
About the same	28	25	20
A little less racist	33	39	28
Much less racist	6	9	8

Key:
☐ Whites ■ Afro-Caribbeans ▦ Asians
All figures are percentages

Treatment by authorities

Do you think non-whites are treated better, worse or the same as whites by:

	Whites	Afro-Caribbeans	Asians
Employers			
Better	9	1	3
Worse	39	67	42
Same	44	22	44
The Police			
Better	7	0	2
Worse	48	75	45
Same	36	16	40
Schools			
Better	14	1	2
Worse	13	38	15
Same	61	48	74
The Courts			
Better	10	1	2
Worse	24	57	19
Same	55	26	53

Race relations

Do you agree or disagree with the following statements:

People should only marry within their own ethnic group

Agree / Disagree

I would happily have people of a different race living next door to me

Agree / Disagree

People of different races should keep to themselves

Agree / Disagree

Immigration has enriched the quality of life in Britain

Agree / Disagree

Asian people work harder than white people

Agree / Disagree

White people are more intelligent than black people

Agree / Disagree

Discrimination laws

What do you think of the British laws against racial discrimination?

Too tough / About right / Not tough enough

Voting intentions

If there were a general election tomorrow:

How likely is it that you would vote?

	Whites	Afro-Caribbeans	Asians
Certain	63	45	53
Very/fairly likely	23	23	30
Fairly/very unlikely	11	22	13
Wouldn't /not registered	3	10	3

Which party would you vote for?

Conservative / Labour / Lib Democrat

Number of non-whites

How many blacks or Asians do you think there are in Britain (population 56 million)?

Average for each group (millions)

Latest official estimate: 2.6m

Figure 11.1: attitudes concerning racism in Britain
(Independent on Sunday, 7 July 1991)

Asians thought that non-whites received worse treatment in schools, the figure for Afro-Caribbeans, at 38 per cent, was much higher. One in four white people believed that social security offices gave preferential treatment to non-white people: one in five did not want a neighbour of a different 'race'.

All groups over-estimated the numbers of black or Asian people living in Britain. The true figure was around 2.6 million (see Section 1). Over half the white sample thought the true figure was 5 million: a quarter thought it was 10 million.

The survey also revealed that over one-fifth of Afro-Caribbeans said they would be fairly or very unlikely to vote 'if there were a general election tomorrow', twice as many as those from the other groups.

Finally, the survey found that racial prejudice amongst white people correlated highly with social class and age. There were also indicators that racial prejudice against Asian people was stronger than against Afro-Caribbean groups.

11.1 Developments since 1992

A range of surveys has assessed the general attitudes of the British people towards 'race' and racism since 1991, with conflicting and often contradictory findings. The ninth British Social Attitudes survey (BSA) revealed that racism was still perceived to be widespread, but that it was beginning to decline (Young, 1993). Over 50 per cent of those surveyed believed there was a lot of prejudice against Afro-Caribbeans and slightly more against Asians. The study reported a small decrease in reported prejudice. It did, however, reveal that over one third of the sample were either 'very prejudiced' or 'a little prejudiced' against minority ethnic groups. The 1992 BSA, for the first time, revealed that more people were optimistic about the future of 'race' relations in Britain than were pessimistic. Moreover, people who believed themselves to be free from the effects of racial prejudice has also increased. The BSA confirmed, however, that the public still perceived Britain as a racially prejudiced society (Jowell et al., 1992; Guardian, 7 November 1992). This finding might be related to increasing media coverage of the extent of 'racial violence' and harassment in British society. The BSA reported that three-quarters of the sample supported anti-discrimination legislation.

In 1993, further analysis into British racism, by Gallup for the American Jewish Committee, focused more upon the attitudes of specific minority ethnic groups, and also examined the range of attitudes between minority ethnic groups. This survey revealed a more disturbing report about the levels of racism. Gallup showed that 25 per cent of Britons would object to living next to non-white people, 10 per cent wanted anti-discrimination laws to be abolished and 45 per cent thought that anti-Semitism was not a problem. The survey, based on a sample of 959 people, found that 20 per cent would not want Chinese neighbours, 25 per cent would not want African, 27 per cent would not want West Indian, and 30 per cent would not want Pakistani (the terms used are Gallup's). The 'most racist respondents' tended to be from working class, elderly and least educated backgrounds. Over three-quarters of respondents felt that race relations in Britain were 'only fair' or 'poor'. Over 40 per cent thought that anti-racist laws should be strengthened (American Jewish Committee, 1993; *Independent*, 26 October 1993).

The BSA surveys of 1993 and 1994 tended to support the BSA 1992 survey trends of a society taking a slightly more liberal turn in attitudes during the 1990s, despite the reported increase in racial violence and harassment. They perhaps underestimate the political shifts to far right agendas (see Section 12). The surveys also confirmed an increasing awareness and acceptance of the extent to which Britain was a racist society (Jowell *et al.*, 1993, 1994). In 1992 Yasmin Alibhai-Brown observed that 'racism has got worse and society cares less' (*Guardian*, 29 January 1992). She returned to her theme in 1993:

> It must be because it is fashionable to attribute a problem to individual failure rather than social and political forces ... [that there] is a backlash against any attempt to tackle inequality. The attacks follow a pattern: derision on the one hand and cataclysmic warnings on the other ... Anyone who pushes for equality, or criticises the male Anglo-Saxon world is ... discredited and silenced.
>
> (*Guardian*, 11 August 1993)

An ICM representative multi-ethnic survey in July 1995, in which 1,042 adults aged 18 and over were interviewed in 52 randomly selected constituencies, revealed that two-thirds of the population admitted to being racist, and only one in ten said that people they knew were not racist. The majority of the sample – weighted to the profile of adults aged 18 and over – reported supporting a variety of repatriation strategies for non-whites. Over half the sample believed there was racial discrimination in the labour market. Just under half of the black and Asian respondents reported that 'coloured people felt British'. On the more positive side, the younger respondents were reported to be more open-minded about racial differences (*Daily Express*, 8 August 1995).

Note

1   *Independent on Sunday,* 7 August 1991. NOP used a representative quota
    sample and conducted face-to-face interviews between 22 and 25 June 1991
    across Britain. 766 'white' people aged 18 and over were interviewed at 48
    sampling points. 472 Asian people and 572 Afro-Caribbean people were
    interviewed, each at 44 sampling points. The minority ethnic group
    samples were selected from the 100 constituencies with the highest
    concentration of people from the New Commonwealth and Pakistan. The
    terms 'white' and 'non-white' here are NOP's. The samples were almost
    evenly balanced between males and females. 38 per cent of the sample
    belonged to social classes ABC1 (white collar) and 62 per cent to social
    classes C2DE (blue collar). One-third of all the males and half of all the
    females were not working full-time.

The survey is reviewed in the Runnymede Trust Bulletin (1991b). A report,
'Race issues opinion survey', is available on request from the Runnymede
Trust (see 'List of useful addresses').

12 THE BRITISH POLITICAL SCENE: DEVELOPMENTS SINCE 1992

Findings from the 1992 General Election emphasized how important the 'race' card may have been, especially in relation to immigration. The *Daily Star*'s editorial the day before the election spoke about 'the threat of unbridled immigration', while the *Daily Mail* featured a story linking immigrants with rising crime. Two days before voting, the *Daily Express* carried the headline, 'Baker's Migrant Flood Warning', while the *Sun*'s editorial spoke of a 'threat of massive immigration under a Labour government'. The *Sun* (readership 10 million) later claimed responsibility for the Conservative victory (Billig and Golding, 1992).

The parties of the far right fared less well in 1992 than they did in 1979 and 1983 (they did not fight the 1987 election). Even in the two Tower Hamlets constituencies, the British National Party (BNP) leaders who stood, Tyndall and Edmonds, did not together attract as many votes as the 1,480 gained by another BNP member in a council ward by-election (Le Lohe, 1994).

In 1979, the National Front (NF) fielded 303 candidates and secured 1.4 per cent of the vote. In 1992 the NF and the BNP fielded 27 candidates and their vote share fell to 0.9 per cent (Le Lohe, 1992). There was, however, a by-electoral warning of things to come at local level in the performance of the BNP candidate for Millwall, who came third in the October by-election with 20 per cent of the votes (in a low turn-out of 30 per cent).

Twenty-four black and Asian candidates stood in the 1992 General Election – five fewer than in 1987. To be representative of minority ethnic distribution in the general population, 00 black and Asian candidates would have to have stood.

Opinion polls for the 1992 General Election showed that most minority ethnic groups would be likely to vote for the Labour Party (*Independent on Sunday*, 2 August 1992). In June 1992, research by Back and Solomos claimed that Asian Labour Party members either acted as vote brokers for powerful whites or suffered politically if they challenged the system. These factors impinged upon Asian opportunities to become candidates themselves. A year later, Labour groups in constituencies with more than a 15 per cent black and Asian vote were asked to support all-black and Asian shortlists to aim for at least 36 black and Asian MPs to fight the next election (*The Times*, 14 May 1993).

All four of the black and Asian MPs elected in 1987 were re-elected in 1992 with increased shares of the vote, but black Conservative candidates did slightly worse than average (Geddes, 1993). The Labour Party sought new initiatives to improve black and Asian representation. In 1983, it was estimated that 81 per cent of Asians voted Labour, in 1987, 64 per cent, and in 1992, this proportion had fallen to 41 per cent (*Independent*, 10 March 1992; 16 March 1992; *Independent on Sunday*, 2 August 1992). In 1994, Diane Abbott became the first black or Asian woman to be elected by Labour's grassroot membership on to the Party Executive. In 1995 (following the death of Lord Pitt) there were six black and Asian MPs, and three black and Asian peers in the House of Lords.

In autumn 1994, the Labour Party introduced new rules to prevent minority ethnic groups from seizing control of some of Labour's safest inner-city seats (Runnymede Trust, 1994h; *Independent*, 25 September 1994). The move followed the application of 625 Asians in the Manchester Gorton constituency (the total membership was 900). The rules gave the Party greater powers to rescind membership in certain cases, such as where applicants were not on the electoral register. In Gorton, 492 of the Asian applicants were accepted. Labour were reported to have rejected one in four Asians for party membership (*Independent*, 30 August 1994; *Independent on Sunday*, 25 September 1994). Similar surges in Asian recruitment to the Labour Party were reported in Nottingham East, Bradford West, Rotherham, Birmingham and in inner London. Roy Hattersley, the retiring MP for Sparkbrook, spoke of his concern that his successor should be from one of the minority ethnic communities in the ward. Sparkbrook, in 1995, was represented by eight Labour councillors, of these four were Muslim and one a Sikh. Hattersley remained committed to introducing a policy of affirmative action for minority ethnic candidature:

> Muslims, despite their increasingly important role in British life do not have a representative in Parliament. They want to remedy that omission ... Becoming a Labour candidate is a complicated business. And, for the initiated, it is easy to manipulate (as distinct from break) the rules in a way that provides an unreasonable advantage. That must not be allowed to happen when my successor is chosen.

> (*Independent*, 2 March 1995)

Despite Birmingham's 200,000 minority ethnic group population, no black or Asian candidate has ever represented a Birmingham constituency in a Westminster election. The Conservative Party's One Nation Forum was also designed to capture the black and Asian vote. However, BBC2's *Open Space* reported that the Conservatives were encountering prejudice in constituency organisations and from their selection procedures (BBC2, 'New Blues', 1993). Black barrister John Taylor, who lost the Cheltenham seat for the Tories in 1992, commented:

> Conservative central office has to realise that three or four receptions a year for Asian millionaires is not a race relations policy.

> (*Independent*, 13 December 1993)

In the autumn of 1994, a leading Asian Conservative One Nation Forum member resigned on the eve of the Party's National Conference claiming that she had been placed in double jeopardy because of her Asian origin and gender (Runnymede Trust, 1994h). Other One Nation Forum minority group members remained in the Party, however, although acknowledging that most black and Asian Tories still played a peripheral role (*Voice*, 18 October 1994).

Geddes looked at the national picture of local election black and Asian representation in the early 1990s at district, borough and county levels. He found that in 1992, 107 out of 124 black and Asian councillors in London boroughs represented the Labour Party (54 were of Afro-Caribbean origin, and 70 of Asian). Two out of three of the Afro-Caribbean councillors were women compared with one in six Asian councillors. There were only six black and Asian Conservative councillors in the capital. Geddes' survey (see *Table 12.1*) found that of 18,778 local councillors nationally, only 287 (1.5 per cent) were from minority ethnic group backgrounds. Of these 287, 248 (or 86 per cent) represented the Labour Party.

Table 12.1: members of local councils in England, by party and ethnicity, 1992

Type of authority	Total councillors	Total b and em*	Affiliations of b and em councillors			
			Labour	Cons	LD	Ind
District	12,368	104	88	8	5	3
County	2,849	26	21	1	0	4
Metropolitan	2,079	33	32	1	0	0
London	1,482	124	107	6	7	4
Totals	18,778	287	248	16	12	11

* Black and Asian ethnic minority.
(*Runnymede Trust, 1994a, p. 19; from Geddes, 1993*)

Geddes also examined gender differences in black political representation. Afro-Caribbean women were much more likely to be councillors than South Asian women. Geddes revealed that there were eleven times as many Asian male councillors as Asian female (185 compared with 17), but that three in eight of Afro-Caribbean councillors were women (32 out of 85). Overall Geddes found that 64 per cent of all minority ethnic group councillors (185 out of 287) were South Asian men (Geddes, 1993).

After the May 1994 elections, further analysis by the Runnymede Trust revealed that in London 10.5 per cent (202) of its 1,917 councillors were of South Asian, Afro-Caribbean or African origin. This was a significant improvement on the 1986 figure of 134, but remained unrepresentative in relation to their population distribution. Approximately a quarter of all councillors in Tower Hamlets (28 per cent), Newham (28 per cent), Hounslow (27 per cent), Brent (25 per cent), Haringey (24 per cent), Lewisham (23 per cent) and Ealing (21 per cent) were of black or South Asian origin. The boroughs of Bexley, Bromley, Enfield, Havering and Richmond had no minority ethnic representation (Runnymede Trust, 1994d). Despite the fact that Afro-Caribbeans form the largest minority in London boroughs, and there are slightly more black people in London than South Asian (535,000 compared with 520,000), 70 per cent of all minority ethnic group councillors in London are of South Asian background (Runnymede Trust, 1994a, p. 19).

Outside London, at the 'shire' level, black and Asian political representation has increased since the 1980s, especially in shires with a relatively high ethnic minority population – for example in Derby, Luton, Slough, Nottingham and Leicester. In Leicester the county council representation in 1993 was 6 out of 28 (21.4 per cent) (Le Lohe, 1993). Geddes' study found that of 21,065 councillors in England and Wales, 342 (1.6 per cent) were of Asian and Afro-Caribbean origin; of these 342 councillors, only 6 per cent were women, while 85 per cent represented the Labour Party (Geddes, 1993).

Research by the Runnymede Trust for the seminal 1994 conference on multi-ethnic Britain contained a detailed analysis of minority ethnic group appointments to public bodies, based on Cabinet Office data. The analysis, in 1993, showed that 1,300 'non-department public bodies' (NDPBs), spending between them £12 billion of public money, had 42,000 members. Of these, 98 per cent were white. Exactly 1,000 members (2.3 per cent) were from black and minority ethnic communities.

Le Lohe's analyses of political issues and 'racist parties' show how they are susceptible to periods of 'surge and decline' (Le Lohe, 1994), with the surges being associated with an increased focus on housing concerns (one BNP slogan for the 1993 local election in Millwall was 'Rights for Whites'), or immigration issues, which attract considerable tabloid publicity, and/or racist sentiment. Le Lohe's thesis is that surges in far right support electorally follow the reporting of issues with 'racist' emphases. A few days before the BNP success in autumn 1993, Conservative MPs John Carlisle and Winston Churchill had made speeches about immigration and preferential housing treatment for persons of ethnic origin, while the tabloid press coverage of protests about the 'racist' attack on Quaddas Ali included such headlines as 'Riot flares as race protesters go on rampage', 'Cops hurt in race mob battles', 'Race riot injures 25 PCs', five days before election day (*Daily Express*, *Daily Star*, *Sun*, all 11 September 1993).

Le Lohe concludes that the possibility of an increase in racist attitudes, particularly in relation to immigration, has to be faced. The evidence from opinion polls appears to support his argument. An ICM poll indicated that 81 per cent of people believed they were right to be concerned about the scale of immigration to the UK, while over a third supported the idea of sending immigrants home; 50 per cent of those over 65 in the survey favoured forcible repatriation (*Sunday Express*, 26 September 1993). A survey for Channel 4 in 1994 found that 51 per cent believed racial tension in Britain was increasing. A further Gallup survey revealed that the elderly and the working class were more racist than the young and the middle class but that a distinction had to be drawn between Jews, Chinese, Pakistanis, black people and gypsies (65 per cent of respondents said they preferred not to have gypsies in their neighbourhood, 30 per cent would not have Pakistanis, 27 per cent West Indians, 19 per cent Chinese, and 12 per cent would not have Jews (Le Lohe, 1994).

Since the 1992 General Election there has been a gradual shift to the far right, especially in some inner London boroughs. The NF, the BNP, the Blood and Honour Party, and the Third Way Party each reported rising membership (*Guardian*, 13 October 1992). In the winter of 1992, the BNP pushed the Tories into fourth place in the Millwall ward of the Isle of Dogs. The BNP candidate finished third with 20 per cent of the vote – the turn-out was only 13 per cent (BBC2, *First Sight*, 14 January 1993). It was in Millwall, in 1901, that the British Brothers League was first established to oppose Jewish immigration.

In autumn 1993, the BNP achieved 34 per cent of the vote when they won the Isle of Dogs seat on Tower Hamlets council by seven votes from the Labour candidate (Runnymede Trust, 1993h; *Economist*, 18 September 1993). The BNP victory generated considerable speculation, not least about the election campaigns run by the political parties. Subsequently the Liberal Democrats dismissed three members of the local party for 'pandering to racism' in the campaign literature – although they were later reinstated (*Independent*, 18 December 1993).

In local elections in May 1994, the BNP councillor lost his Tower Hamlets seat, despite receiving an increased 28 per cent of the vote. BNP support was highest in the Beckton ward (32 per cent). In the Midlands the BNP increased its vote in pockets such as the Lye and Wollescote ward of Dudley and Sandwell, where their proportion of the vote reached double figures. BNP activists claimed that rises in support – despite the failure to secure electoral victory – were consolidating the BNP base in the East End as a whole. In the Dagenham by-election in July 1994, won by Labour, BNP leader John Tyndall won almost as many votes as the Liberal Democratic candidate and gained 7 per cent of the poll. It was the first time the BNP – formed in 1982 – had saved its deposit in a by-election (*Independent*, 14 June 1994).

The local elections of May 1994 did witness a growth in support for the BNP. Its policy of contesting only 30 out of 5,000 council seats appeared to meet with qualified success (by specifically targeting racially sensitive areas of the East End, the East Midlands, West Yorkshire and the West Midlands). The main policies of the BNP were published in the *British Nationalist* (April 1994). The BNP aimed to abolish all race relations laws and make all golliwogs legal again. Liberty, the civil rights group, found this increase in BNP support 'very worrying'. The Newham Monitoring Project commented that for the foreseeable future racially charged elections in the East End of London would continue to be the norm. However, Ivor Crewe, Professor of Government at Essex University, dismissed claims that the far right were making significant progress into mainstream British politics: 'The far right is not making serious inroads in Britain despite the economic situation', he observed (*Independent*, 7 May 1994).

One progressive outcome in the 1994 local election campaign was the agreement of all the main political parties (including the Green Party, Plaid Cymru and the Scottish National Party) to support a CRE initiative to take action against any candidates publishing racist material during campaigning. The parties were encouraged not to endorse any materials which 'cause or invite hostility or division between people of different racial or national groups' (Runnymede Trust, 1994c).

The fear after 1994 BNP local election defeats was that there would be an increase in racial violence and harassment (*Guardian*, 7 May 1994). In October 1994, it was reported that the BNP had increased its involvement with Combat 18, a neo-Nazi group formed in 1991 that carries out violent attacks on minorities, after splits between the BNP and Combat 18 had been healed. The number 18 stands for the first and eighth letters of the alphabet, Adolf Hitler's initials. Its publication, *Combat 18*, argues that all non-whites should be 'shipped back to Africa, Asia, Arabia, alive or in body bags'. Members are urged to 'execute' homosexuals and 'white-race mixers' and 'weed out Jews in Government, the media, arts, and professions' (*Observer*, 6 March 1994; *Guardian*, 5 May 1994; 26 October 1994; Channel 4, *Dispatches*, 26 October 1994). It was also reported that the Klu Klux Klan had formed what was believed to be their first three groups in Britain. (*Guardian*, 12 February 1994). Research in the 12 months since the BNP victory in the Millwall by-election of 1993, has shown that racist attacks increased in the East End by one-third (*Guardian*, 11 April 1994).

In July 1995, the BNP were ordered by John Gummer, then the Environment Secretary, to close down their 'Nazi Bunker' Welling headquarters following a planning inspector's report that the building's use was unacceptable. Gummer instructed the BNP to remove the shuttered fortification and return the building to its lawful use as a shop with a home above (*Guardian*, 20 July 1995). Also in July, the National Front announced it had changed its name to the National Democrats (*Independent*, 17 July 1995).

Cabinet Office policy was not to reveal the differing involvements of Afro-Caribbean and South Asian people in public bodies, and Government departments. Inquiries by Keith Vaz MP have established that over two-thirds of minority ethnic appointments to NHS bodies were Asian (98 out of 143); that the Home Office made 79 Asian appointments and 68 black; and that nearly all appointments (92 out of 96) made by the Department of Environment were of black people. The Cabinet Office did reveal that the male–female ratio for minority ethnic group appointments was 72:28 compared with an overall ratio of 83:17 (Runnymede Trust, 1994a, p. 22). *Table 12.2* shows the black and minority ethnic appointments to public bodies in 1993.

Table 12.2: black and ethnic minority appointments to public bodies, 1993

Department	White	B and em*	Total
Cabinet Office	68	1	69
Education	166	6	172
Employment	3,336	98	3,434
Environment	3,206	96	3,302
Foreign and Commonwealth	138	5	143
Health	4,658	143	4,801
Home	4,148	160	4,308
Lord Chancellor	2,230	63	2,293
National Heritage	642	9	651
Social Security	8,116	379	8,495
Trade and Industry	879	8	887
Other	14,019	32	14,051
Totals	41,606	1,000	42,606

* Black and ethnic minority.
(Runnymede Trust, 1994a, p. 22; from Cabinet Office, 1993)

13 'RACE' AND SPORT: FOOTBALL – A CASE STUDY

Sport reflects the nation. Studies, especially in the 1990s, have focused upon the historical and contemporary extent of racism in athletics, cricket, rugby league and union, football, hockey, tennis, horse racing, show jumping, boxing, and a range of other sports. A picture emerges of increased black and Asian involvement and participation especially at grassroot levels. However, Asian minority participation in cricket, football and rugby appears to be very low, despite significant breakthroughs at the amateur level and at the grassroots. The Asian community in Britain has yet to provide a leading footballer or rugby union player and contributed just 2 out of 392 competitors representing Britain at the last Olympics (*Independent*, 10 February 1995). Black and Asian involvement in sport management and administration, or in the politics of sport, remains negligible. Its publishing outlets remain predominantly establishment-based, especially in cricket, which launched a CRE-sponsored 'Hit Racism for Six!' campaign in 1995. Two England test cricketers, Devon Malcolm and Philip De Freitas, were sueing *Wisden Cricket Monthly* at the time of writing for doubting the ability of black cricketers to play their best at test cricket for England (*Wisden Cricket Monthly*, July 1995; *Independent*, 4 July 1995). This section confines itself to football, the national game.

Black and Asian players have a long history in football. The first black and Asian professional footballers were Darlington's Arthur Warton in 1889, Abdul Salim, who played for Celtic Reserves in the 1930s, and Jamaican-born Giles Heron, who scored twice on his Celtic debut in 1951. The first black manager was Tony Collins, who led Rochdale to victory in the first League Cup Final in 1962.

The 1990s saw the emergence of Afro-Caribbean people into football management (although at the beginning of 1994/95 season the figure of two black and Asian managers out of 92 clubs had fallen back to zero). The 1990s have also seen the first Afro-Caribbean coach, and first Asian player (for Lincoln City in 1995), but there remains little sign of any black and Asian penetration into the higher echelons of football politics (except for Garth Crooks' brief tenure as the first black chair of the Professional Footballers' Association) or club management.

Racial abuse and violence remain a cancer in the game and are important reasons why so few black and Asian spectators watch British football at top level. The failure of people of Asian origin to become more involved in professional football is a paradox which is the subject of much contemporary research and debate. The education system is deemed partly responsible, by sustaining the stereotypes of black athleticism and Asian studiousness. Other factors include the fear of racial discrimination in society, cultural pressures within the home and institutional racism (CRE, 1994b).

The CRE, the PFA and the Football Trust (FT) launched the 'Let's Kick Racism Out of Football Campaign' in August 1993 in England and Wales (1994 in Scotland). At the launch Herman Ouseley, chair of the CRE, spoke of people being 'free of racist abuse', while Richard Faulkner of the FT urged the ending of racist chanting and the cessation of the distribution of racist literature at grounds. 'Football can play, and is playing, a major part in breaking down racial divisions in our society', he said (CRE, 1994b).

Racist chanting was made illegal by the Football (Offences) Act of 1991. In 1991, six people were prosecuted under the Act. In 1992 there were 31 prosecutions and 21 convictions. The Act, however, does have a loophole. It is still legal for one person to hurl racist abuse from the terraces. The Act referred only to acting 'in concert with one or more others'. In summer 1995, the Football Association, following disturbances involving far right groups in an Eire v England international friendly, announced a new drive against racism, with a stricter directive to clubs to ensure that racist chants and behaviour are removed from football matches (*Independent*, 18 March 1995).

In 1995 there is one Asian club chairman, and very few people of black and Asian origin on football club boards of directors. At the player level, 20 per cent of footballers in the 92 clubs are black. Afro-Caribbean players have also succeeded in following Viv Anderson into the full England team. All the seven goals against San Marino in England's failed campaign to qualify for 1994 World Cup were scored by Afro-Caribbean players. The BNP does not recognize black players as representing England, so presumably they believe the result was a 1–0 victory for San Marino.

Black and Asian spectators are under-represented, especially in inner-city clubs where they form substantial proportions of the community around the ground (Millwall, Crystal Palace, Manchester City, Everton and Liverpool). Everton, near Toxteth, and Manchester City, in the heart of multi-ethnic Moss Side, have made only limited progress in attracting a representative crowd from their catchment area. A Liverpool University survey of all black and Asian players in the Premier League in 1994, listed six clubs where black players felt exposed to racism – Everton, Leeds, Newcastle, West Ham, Millwall and Crystal Palace (*BBC Radio 5 Magazine*, 18 June 1995). Black and Asian groups are also under-represented among referees and linesmen, and in the media, where all the main television channels and BBC radio predominantly employ white men as their main commentators and studio experts (though the position is more encouraging at local media level).

One of the more famous commentators, ITV's Alan Parry, himself a director of one of the 92 top-flight football clubs, commentating on the World Cup game between South Korea and Spain in USA 1994, said:

> They are so small. They all looked the same. They were really only very good at martial arts. Their names were a hoot. One of them was even called 'Ha' – Ha? Oh, ha, ha, ha. When Spain scored twice it was really proof that the good old Europeans, nice and tall with not so funny names, are really a class apart.
>
> (Runnymede Trust, 1994d, p. 7)

The Koreans drew 2–2.

It is to be hoped that as black and Asian footballers move into retirement many will stay in the game at a variety of levels. The CRE believes that by the millennium, black and Asian penetration of football at all levels will be more representative. In 1994, Subbuteo, the famous table football game, began manufacturing black and Asian players for the first time.

The 'Kick It' campaign endorsed a nine-point action plan for clubs, encouraging them to: issue a statement saying that they will not tolerate racism and to display it in their club programmes and on posters throughout the ground; make public announcements condemning racist chanting and abuse; take action against the sale of racist literature; take disciplinary action against employees or spectators who commit acts of racist abuse; remove racist graffiti; and adopt an equal opportunities policy in the areas of employment and service provision. By 1995, this action plan had been adopted by 91 of the 92 Premiership and Football League Clubs. Only York City had not joined the campaign. In 1994, several clubs, including Newcastle and Blackburn, banned supporters for racially abusing players.

Millwall, however, have met with less success, despite substantially improved efforts to erase racism from the New Den. The club has been surrounded by controversy for many years (seventeen crowd hooligan incidents in their recent history), with increasing involvement of BNP and Combat 18 activists, and other neo-fascist groups. With several black people in their playing and coaching staff, the club has been trying to build relations with the community, especially at youth level. Several players from opposing teams, however, have complained of racial abuse on the pitch and from the stands (Runnymede Trust, 1994d). The BBC television programme *All Black* posed the question, if one in four footballers is black or Asian, why is only one in 100 spectators from a black or Asian group? *All Black* focused on Millwall, Manchester City and Leyton Orient and found that fear of racism was one of the major reasons why black and Asian supporters (including women and children) did not go to football matches (BBC2, 'Racism in football', *All Black*, 28 September 1994). In 1994, the CRE reminded Everton, a club with no tradition of encouraging black and Asian players, to take greater action to recruit young black and Asian players, especially from the neighbouring Toxteth area of Liverpool. The City of Liverpool has a poor record for developing the football talents of its multi-ethnic communities, despite having the oldest black community in Britain. Elsewhere, Leeds United had a long tradition of racial intolerance on and off the pitch. The London fanzine *When Saturday Comes*, visiting Elland Road in 1993, observed an improvement:

> Looking at Elland Road today, it's hard to remember what the atmosphere was like in 1987. The National Front sellers have disappeared driven away by hostility and lack of sales. Racist abuse has almost disappeared as has violence. The club and police deserve credit for responding to public pressure.
>
> (*When Saturday Comes*, February 1993)

Chelsea, too, responding to speculation that the far right Combat 18 groups had targeted Stamford Bridge, inserted the following message in their programme: 'Just a note for any sympathizers with Hitler and his beliefs … Hitler lost. He died. He blew it. There's no room for losers at this club anymore' (*Searchlight*, March 1995, p. 8).

Things may have improved inside many grounds. Reviewing the 1990s, Hill concluded.

> For every black hero on the pitch and every hardy black or Asian supporter who passes through a turnstile at Everton or West Ham, there are scores who stay away, just as there are dozens of Asian football teams whose talents and enthusiasm are largely neglected by the mainstream.
>
> (D. Hill, 'For those watching in black and white', *Guardian*, 11 May 1994)

One problem which does remain is that while black and Asian players themselves may be receiving less racial abuse, their families and children face abuse when they come to watch their sons play. Two weeks before Andy Cole was transferred to Manchester United, the Newcastle *Sunday Sun* commented:

> We can't tolerate a situation where Andy Cole and Ruel Fox are feted as heroes and their unrecognised parents, brothers and sisters are treated like dirt.
>
> (Quoted in *Searchlight*, February 1995)

14 CONCLUSION: THE NEED FOR RADICAL REFORM

The Home Affairs Committee concluded its third report on racial attacks and harassment with the following statement:

> Racism, in whatever form, is an evil and destructive force in our undeniably multi-racial society. We are in no doubt that racial attacks and racial harassment, and the spread of literature which preaches racial hatred, are increasing and must be stopped. More can be done ... we re-emphasise the importance of all agencies and organisations working together ... As racism is spreading so rapidly, time is short.

(Home Affairs Committee, 1994, p. xxxvii)

What is the nature of British society that has generated the litany of empirical evidence presented in this book? To what extent does it present too negative a picture of black and Asian inequality? How complex and inextricably interwoven are the dimensions of 'race', ethnicity, class and gender? To what degree are these patterns and trends the result of changes and developments in 'capitalist' society? How do these relate to our colonial history, and to contemporary cultural factors in multi-ethnic Britain? How will the diverse minority ethnic groups respond? Will the racialized inequalities and disadvantages be ameliorated in the next millennium? Is racism, as Gilroy has argued, 'a volatile presence at the very centre of British politics, actively shaping and determining the history not simply of blacks but this country as a whole' (Gilroy, 1990). Will European developments push Britain towards introducing more specific legislation directed at racism? To what extent will the political gains of far right parties in France, Belgium, Germany, Austria and Italy reinforce racism in Britain? What impact might a change in Government in Britain have on these issues?

These questions can only be posed here. Some answers to them are provided in the three readers (Braham *et al.*, 1992; Gill *et al.*, 1992; Donald and Rattansi, 1992), the study guides, the broadcasts, the introduction and the conclusion to ED356 *'Race', Education and Society*, the OU course for which this book is a resource reference. Just because the sections in this book have been prefixed with the word 'race' does not mean that the evidence here is either conclusive or explained. Neither is education itself a panacea: it cannot compensate for society.

We are living in a complex and rapidly changing multi-ethnic Britain, where there are no simple answers, but where old divisions seem resistant to change. We live in a society whose Governments, especially Conservative

Governments since 1979, have lacked the political will to tackle inequalities, to transform rhetoric into action, and to confront British racism. There are real dangers of complacency as resources continue to contract: slippage in resolve and commitment may occur. We need to be increasingly vigilant and pro-active as a society, as communities and as individuals, to ensure that the positive changes that have occurred since 1992 are sustained and built upon, especially through legislation. The slowness of our progress, the persistence, and in some areas the increase, of social and economic disadvantage and racialized inequalities is testimony to past neglect, and the historical rootedness of British racist values. We need a Bill of Rights, but we need more than this to combat state, institutional and individual racism.

The VE Day celebrations in May 1995 provided an illuminating symbolic representation of just how blind Britain is to its multi-ethnic heritage. Of how, in Gilroy's terms, 'there ain't no black in the Union Jack'. Lost in the celebrations was any real acknowledgement or understanding of the contributions of black British and ex-colonial people to victory in 1945. Apart from one BBC East feature on the contribution of British muslims, we were left with *The Dam Busters* and Guy Gibson's dog 'Nigger' to bear the burden of representation. Paul Gilroy has argued that we increasingly face more sophisticated forms of racism which, chameleon-like, avoid being recognised as such because they are able to hide behind a 'respectable' image of national culture. Is this racism becoming more established during the 1990s? Have we, as Gilroy suggests, produced a metaphysics of Britishness which has acquired racial referents (Gilroy, 1990)?

Racial attacks do not occur in a vacuum. They occur in a political system in which people from different cultures are said to constitute 'a problem'. What is needed is the political courage to emphasize the positive contributions that minority ethnic groups have made to the wellbeing of British society (CRE, 1995). The new millennium is surely a time to embrace this diversity, to recognize difference and to respond to change through understanding.

The 1990s have witnessed a gradual shift from rhetoric to action. There have been practical attempts throughout the past 30 years to tackle social inequalities, but they have been patchy and uncoordinated. Therefore there needs to be a radical programme of reform to tackle racism and the intrinsic divisions in British society, between rich and poor, to empower all the British people, irrespective of 'race', ethnicity, gender or class. The needs of multi-ethnic Britain may best be served by substantial reforms delivering social justice and increased life chances for all, but we must not fail to meet the challenge of the 'racism' within.[1]

Note

1   For an excellent guide to action for the future see Runnymede Trust (1995a), especially pp. 42–5.

REFERENCES

Abercrombie, N., with Soothill, K, Urry, J. and Walby, S. (1994) *Contemporary British Society*, Cambridge, Polity Press.

Action Group on Immigration and Nationality and Immigration Laws (AGIN) (n.d.) *Background Briefing on Reform of Nationality and Immigration Laws*, London, AGIN.

Adams, N. (1981) *Black Children in Care*, SS208/80–8, London Borough of Lambeth Social Services Committee.

Ahmed, W. and Sheldon, T. (1991) '"Race" and statistics', *Radical Statistics Newsletter*, June, pp. 27–33.

Alibhai, Y. (1988) 'Broken and by-passed: mental health and ethnic minorities', *New Society*, 6 May.

American Jewish Committee (1993) *British Survey, October, 1993*, American Jewish Committee, London.

Amin, K. and Oppenheim, C. (1992) *Poverty in Black and White: deprivation and ethnic minorities*, London, Child Poverty Action Group with the Runnymede Trust.

Amnesty International (1994) *Prisoners without a Voice*, London, Amnesty International.

Anionwu, E., Walford, D., Brozovic, N. and Kirkwood, B. (1981) 'Sickle cell disease in a British urban community', *British Medical Journal*, **282**, pp. 283–6.

Arnold, E. (1982) 'Finding black families for black children in Britain' in Cheetham, J. (ed.) *Social Work and Ethnicity*, London, Allen and Unwin.

Ashford, M. (1993) *Detention Without Trial*, London, Joint Council for the Welfare of Immigrants (JCWI).

Association of University Teachers (AUT) (1985) *Ensuring Equal Opportunities for University Staff and Students from Ethnic Minorities*, London, AUT.

Atkinson, A. (1990) *DSS Report on Households Below Average Income, 1981–87*, paper for Social Services Select Committee, London, DSS.

Back, L. and Solomos, J. (1992) *Who Represents Us? Racialised Politics and Candidate Selection*, London, Birkbeck College.

Bailey, J. (1993) '1991 Census results for local authority districts in Great Britain', *Population Trends 72*, OPCS, London, HMSO.

Baldwin, J. and McConville, M. (1979) *Jury Trials*, Oxford, Oxford University Press.

Ball, L. (1989) 'What future for YTS?', *Unemployment Bulletin*, **30**, pp. 14–16.

Barn, R. (1990) 'Black children in local authority care: admission patterns', *New Community*, **16**(2), pp. 229–47.

Barn, R. (1993) *Black Children in the Public Care System*, London, Bamford.

Barnardos (1994) *Unfair Shares*, Ilford, Barnardos.

Benson, C. (1989) *An Investigation of the Access the Black Community Has to Employment and Training in Information Technology*, London Voluntary Service Council.

Bentley, S. (1982) 'A bureaucratic identity: a note on the "racialization" of data', *New Community*, **10**(2), pp. 259–68.

Bethnal Green and Stepney Trades Council (1978) *Blood on the Streets*, London, Bethnal Green and Stepney Trades Council.

Bhat, A., Carr-Hill, R. and Ohri, S. (eds) (1988) *Britain's Black Population: a new perspective*, 2nd edition, Aldershot, Gower.

Billig, M. and Golding, P. (1992) 'Did the race card tip the balance?', *New Community*, **19**(1), pp. 161–3.

Bolton, P. (1984) 'Management of compulsorily admitted patients', *International Social Psychiatry*, **30** (1/2), pp. 77–84.

Booth, H. (1988) 'Identifying ethnic origin' in Bhat *et al.* (eds) *Britain's Black Population: a new perspective*, 2nd edition, Aldershot, Gower.

Bourne, J., Bridges, L. and Searle, C. (1994) *Outcast England: how schools exclude black children*, London, Institute of Race Relations.

Bowling, B., Graham, J. and Ross, A. (1994) 'Self-reported offending among young people in England and Wales', London, Home Office unpublished report.

Bradshaw, J. (1990) *Child Poverty and Deprivation in the UK*, London, National Children's Bureau/UNICEF.

Braham, P., Rattansi, A. and Skellington, R. (eds) (1992) *Racism and Antiracism: inequality, opportunities and policies*, London, Sage/Open University.

Brent Social Services (1985) *A policy regarding transracial adoptions and foster care placements*, Document no. 24685, London, Brent Borough Council.

Brimacombe, M. (1991) 'Room to grow', *Roof*, March/April, pp. 30–2.

British Council of Churches (1990) *Return to Justice*, London, Community and Race Relations Unit, British Council of Churches.

Britton, M. (1989) 'Mortality and geography', *Population Trends 56*, OPCS, London, HMSO.

Brown, C. (1984) *Black and White Britain: the third PSI Survey*, Aldershot, Gower.

Brown, C. (1985) *Racial Discrimination: 17 years after the Act*, London, Policy Studies Institute.

Bryan, B., Dadzie, S. and Scafe, S. (1985) *The Heart of the Race: black women's lives in Britain*, London, Virago.

Burney, E. (1988) *Steps to Racial Equality: positive action in a negative climate*, London, Runnymede Trust.

Burns, G. (1990) 'Education, training and black offenders', *Voices*, 3, London, Forum for the Advancement of Training and Education for the Black Unemployed (FATEBU).

Byron, M. (1995) 'Return migration to the Caribbean', paper presented at the National Conference of the Institute of British Geographers.

Cabinet Office (1993) *Public Bodies 1993*, London, HMSO.

Campaign Against Racism and Fascism (CARF) (1992) 'Racism in special hospitals', *CARF Newsletter*, Nov/Dec.

Carpenter, L. and Brockington, I. (1980) 'A study of mental illness in Asians, West Indians and Africans living in Manchester', *British Journal of Psychiatry*, **137**, pp. 201–5.

Carter, B., Harris, C. and Joshi, S. (1987) 'The 1951–55 Conservative government and the racialisation of black immigration', *Policy Papers in Ethnic Relations*, No. 11, Centre for Research in Ethnic Relations, University of Warwick.

Carter, E. P. *et al.* (1990) 'Material deprivation and its association with childhood hospital admission in the East End of London', *Community Medicine*, 15 (6).

Central Council for Education and Training in Social Work (CCETSW) (1983) *Teaching Social Work for a Multi-Racial Society*, London, CCETSW.

CCETSW (1991a) *One Small Step Towards Racial Justice: the teaching of anti-racism in social work programmes*, Improving Social Work Education and Training Series, London, CCETSW.

CCETSW (1991b) *Paper 30: Rules and Requirements for the Diploma in Social Work*, 2nd edition, London, CCETSW.

CCETSW (1991c) Press Release 11/91: 'Precise and comprehensive definitions of social work competences now available', 3 October, London, CCETSW.

Central Statistical Office (CSO) (1990a) *Social Trends 20*, London, HMSO.

CSO (1990b) *Annual Abstract of Statistics, 1990*, London, HMSO.

CSO (1991) *Social Trends 21*, London, HMSO.

CSO (1992) *Social Trends 22*, London, HMSO.

CSO (1993) *Social Trends 23*, London, HMSO.

CSO (1994) *Social Trends 24*, London, HMSO.

CSO (1995) *Social Trends 25*, London, HMSO.

Chambers Community Consultants (1989) *Fear and Crime in the Inner City*, Leicester, Chambers Community Consultants.

CHAR (1992) *Plans Not Action – the Children Act and homeless young people*, London, CHAR.

Child Poverty Action Group (CPAG) (1987) *The Growing Divide*, London, CPAG.

CPAG (1991) *Windows of Opportunity*, London, CPAG.

Churches Commission for Racial Justice (1994) *Breaking Up the Family*, London, Churches Commission for Racial Justice.

Citizens Advice Bureaux (1994) *In Work and Out of Pocket*, London, CAB.

Clough, E., Drew, D. and Jones, B. (1988) 'Ethnic differences in the youth labour market in Sheffield and Bradford', *New Community*, 14 (3), pp. 412–25.

Cochrane, R. (1977) 'Mental illness in immigrants to England and Wales: an analysis of mental hospital admissions, 1971', *Social Psychiatry*, 12, pp. 2–35.

Cohen, R., Coxhall, J. Craig, G. and Sadiq-Sangster, A. (1992) *Hardship Britain: being poor in the 1990s*, London, CPAG and Family Service Units.

Coleman, D. A. (1987) 'UK statistics on immigration: development and limitations', *International Migration Review*, 21, winter, pp. 1137–52.

Coleman, J. (1994) 'Black children in care: a crisis of identity', *Runnymede Bulletin*, October, pp 4–5.

Commission for Racial Equality (CRE) (1981) *Racial Harassment on Local Authority Estates*, London, CRE.

CRE (1983a) *CRE's Submission to the House of Commons Social Services Select Committee Inquiry into Children in Care*, London, CRE.

CRE (1983b) *Ethnic Minority Hospital Staff*, London, CRE.

CRE (1984a) *Race and Council Housing in Hackney: report of a formal investigation*, London, CRE.

CRE (1984b) *Race and Housing in Liverpool*, London, CRE.

CRE (1984c) *Racial Discrimination in a London Estate Agency*, London, CRE.

CRE (1984d) *Birmingham Local Authority and Schools – Referral and Suspension of Pupils: report of a formal investigation*, London, CRE.

CRE (1985a) *Immigration Control Procedures: report of a formal investigation*, London, CRE.

CRE (1985b) *Race and Mortgage Lending*, London, CRE.

CRE (1987a) *Living in Terror: a report on racial violence and harassment in housing*, London, CRE.

CRE (1987b) *Overseas Doctors: experiences and expectations*, London, CRE.

CRE (1987c) *Employment of Graduates from Ethnic Minorities: a research report*, London, CRE.

CRE (1988a) *Learning in Terror: a survey of racial harassment in schools and colleges*, London, CRE.

CRE (1988b) *Homelessness and Discrimination: report of a formal investigation into the London Borough of Tower Hamlets*, London, CRE.

CRE (1988c) *Investigation into St George's Hospital Medical School*, London, CRE.

CRE (1988d) *Ethnic Minority School Teachers*, London, CRE.

CRE (1989a) *Racial Equality in Social Services Departments: a survey of equal opportunity policies*, London, CRE.

CRE (1989b) *Racial Discrimination in Liverpool City Council: report of a formal investigation into the housing department*, London, CRE.

CRE (1989c) *Positive Action and Racial Equality in Housing*, London, CRE.

CRE (1990a) *Director's Annual Report: January–December 1989*, London, CRE.

CRE (1990b) *Racial Discrimination in Property Development: report of a formal investigation into the London Borough of Southwark*, London, CRE.

CRE (1990c), *Putting Your House in Order: estate agents and equal opportunity policies*, London, CRE.

CRE (1990d) *Out of Order: report of a formal investigation into the London Borough of Southwark*, London, CRE.

CRE (1990e) *Racial Discrimination in an Oldham Estate Agency*, London, CRE.

CRE (1990f) *Sorry, It's Gone: testing for racial discrimination in the private rented housing sector*, London, CRE.

CRE (1990g) *Ethnic Minorities and the Graduate Labour Market*, London, CRE.

CRE (1991a) *Annual Report 1990*, June, London, CRE.

CRE (1991b) *Equality in Housing: code of practice for the elimination of racial discrimination and the promotion of equal opportunities*, London, CRE.

CRE (1991c) *Lines of Progress: an inquiry into selection tests and equal opportunities in London Underground*, London, CRE.

CRE (1992) *Secondary School Admissions*, London, CRE.

CRE (1993a) *Housing Associations and Racial Equality*, London, CRE.

CRE (1993b) *Housing Allocations in Oldham*, London, CRE.

CRE (1993c) *Racism through the Nineties*, London, CRE.

CRE (1994a) *Annual Report 1993*, London, CRE.

CRE (1994b) *Kick It*, London, CRE.

CRE (1995a) *Annual Report, 1994*, London, CRE.

CRE (1995b) *Racial Equality Means Business*, London, CRE.

CRE and Association of Chief Police Officers (1993) *Racism Policing and Racial Equality*, Oxford, Oxford University Press.

Community Relations Commission (CRC) (1977) *Evidence to the Royal Commission on the National Health Service*, London, CRC.

Cope, R. (1989) 'Compulsory detention of Afro-Caribbeans under the Mental Health Act', *New Community*, **15**(3), pp. 343–56.

Craig, G. (1989) *Your Flexible Friend? Voluntary organisations, claimants and the Social Fund*, London, Social Security Consortium.

Crawley, J. (ed.) (1994) *Dictionary of Film Quotations*, Ware, Wordsworth.

Dalton, M. and Daghlian, S. (1989) *Race and Housing in Glasgow: the role of housing associations*, London, CRE.

Dame Colet House/Limehouse Fields Tenants' Association' and Tower Hamlets Tenants' Federation (1986) *Tenants Tackle Racism*, London, Limehouse Fields Tenants' Association and Tower Hamlets Tenants' Federation.

Darbyshire, J. (1983) 'We don't have tuberculosis in this country anymore … do we?', *Maternal and Child Health*, **8** (5), p. 181.

Davy Smith, G., Bartly, M. and Blane, D. (1990) 'The Black Report on socio-economic inequalities in health: 10 years on', *British Medical Journal*, **301**, pp. 373–7.

de Bono, D., Shaukat, N. and Cruikshank, J. K. (1993) 'Clinical features, risk factors and referral delay in British patients of Indian and European origin', *British Medical Journal*, **307**, pp. 717–19.

de Sousa, E. (1989) 'YTS: the racism riddle', *Unemployment Bulletin*, **29**, pp. 23–4.

Dean, G., Walsh, D., Downing, H. and Shelley, P. (1981) 'First admissions of native born and immigrants to psychiatric hospitals in south east England, 1976', *British Journal of Psychiatry*, **139**, pp. 506–12.

Defence Committee (1988) *Ethnic Monitoring and the Armed Forces*, HC 391, London, HMSO.

Demuth, C. (1978) *'Sus': a report on the Vagrancy Act 1824*, London, Runnymede Trust.

Department of Economics, Swansea University (1994) *Winners and Losers*, Swansea University.

Department of Education and Science (DES) (1965) *The Education of Immigrants* (Circular 7/65), London, DES.

DES (1973) *Education 1967–1972*, London, HMSO.

DES (1985) *Education for All: the report of the committee of inquiry into the education of children from ethnic minority groups*, Cmnd 9453, London, HMSO (The Swann Report).

DES (1989) *Ethnically-Based Statistics on School Pupils* (Circular 16/89), London, HMSO.

Department of Employment (DoE) (1987) *Employment Gazette*, September, London, HMSO.

DoE (1989) *New Earnings Survey, 1988*, London, HMSO.

DoE (1990a) *New Earnings Survey, 1989*, London, HMSO.

DoE (1990b) 'Ethnic origins and the labour market', *Employment Gazette*, March, pp. 125–37, London, HMSO.

DoE (1990c) *Employment Gazette*, April, London, HMSO.

DoE (1991) 'Ethnic origins and the labour market', *Employment Gazette*, February, pp. 59–72, London, HMSO.

Department of the Environment (1994a) *Index of Local Conditions: an analysis based on 1991 census data*, London, HMSO.

Department of the Environment (1994b) *Homeless Statistics*, London, HMSO.

Department of Health and Social Security (DHSS) (1986) *Health and Personal Social Services Statistics for England*, London, HMSO.

Department of Social Security (DSS) (1988) *Low Income Families: statistics 1985*, London, DSS.

DSS (1990) *Households Below Average Income 1981–87*, London, DSS.

DSS (1993a) *Households Below Average Income*, London, HMSO.

DSS (1993b) *Income Support Statistics, Annual Enquiry, May 1993*, Analytical Services Division, London, DSS.

DSS (1994) *Households Below Average Income*, London, HMSO.

DSS (1995) *Households Below Average Income*, London, HMSO.

Devis, T. (1985) 'International migration: return migrants and re-migration flows', *Population Trends 41*, OPCS, London, HMSO.

Diversity Directory (1995) *Race and Criminal Justice*, Edition 7, Bedford, Diversity UK.

Docklands Forum (1993) *Homelessness in Tower Hamlets*, London, London Docklands Development Corporation.

Donald, J. and Rattansi, A. (eds) (1992) *'Race', Culture and Difference*, London, Sage/Open University.

Donnellan, C. (1993) *How Racist Are We?* Cambridge, Independence Press.

Dorling, D. (1994) 'Visualising the geography of the population with the 1991 census', *Population Trends 76*, OPCS, London, HMSO.

Dorn, A. and Hibbert, P. (1987) 'A comedy of errors: Section 11 funding and education' in Troyna, B. (ed.) *Racial Inequality in Education*, London, Tavistock.

Doyal, L. (1979) 'A matter of life and death: medicine, health and statistics' in Miles, J. and Evans, J. (eds) *Demystifying Social Statistics*, London, Pluto.

Doyal, L., Gee, F. and Hunt, G. (1980) *Migrant workers in the National Health Service*, Report for the Social Science Research Council by the Department of Sociology, Polytechnic of North London.

Drew, D. and Gray, J. (1991) 'The black–white gap in examination results: a statistical critique of a decade's research', *New Community*, 17 (2), pp. 159–72.

Drew, D., Gray, J. and Sime, N. (1992) *Against the Odds: the education and the labour market experiences of black young people*, Sheffield, Employment Department, Research Management Branch.

Duncan, D. (1986) 'Eliminate the negative', *Community Care*, 5 June.

ECCR (1992) *Buried Talents*, Fareham, Hampshire, ECCR.

Edwards, R. (1993) 'Legislation against families', *Runnymede Bulletin* 263, March.

Equal Opportunities Review (1993) 'Action for race equality: an EO survey of employer initiatives', *Equal Opportunities Review*, no. 48, March/April.

Esmail, A., Nelson, P., Primarolo, D. and Toma, T. (1995) 'Acceptance into medical school and racial discrimination', *British Medical Journal*, **310**, pp. 501–2.

European Parliament (1990) *Report drawn up on behalf of the Committee of Inquiry in Racism and Xenophobia*, European Parliament Session Document A3-195/90, 23 July 1990, Brussels, EC.

Family Policy Studies Centre (1986) *Fact Sheet 3*, December, London, Family Policy Studies Centre.

Family Policy Studies Centre (1994) *Excluding Primary School Children*, London, Family Policy Studies Centre.

Federation of Black Housing Organisations (FBHO) (1986) *Furnace in the Pool*, newsletter, autumn, London, FBHO.

Federation of Black Housing Associations (FBHA) (1993) *Housing Black and Minority Ethnic Elders*, London, FBHA.

Fenton, S. (1989) 'Racism is harmful to your health', in Cox, J. and Bostock, S. (eds) *Racial Discrimination in the Health Service*, Penrhos Publications.

Fletcher, H. (1988) 'Black people and the probation service', *NAPO News*, August, London, National Association of Probation Officers (NAPO).

Forrest, R. and Murie, A. (1987) 'The pauperisation of council housing', *Roof*, **12** (1), p. 20.

Forrest, R., Murie, A. and Williams, P. (1990) *Home Ownership: differentiation and fragmentation*, London, Unwin Hyman.

Fothergill, S. and Vincent, J. (1985) in Kidron, M. *The State of the Nation*, London, Pluto Press.

Frances, E., David, J., Johnson, N. and Sashidharan, S. (1989) 'Black people and psychiatry in the UK', *Psychiatry Bulletin*, 13, pp. 482–5.

Frayman, H. (1991a) *Breadline Britain 1990s: the findings of the television series*, London, Domino Films/London Weekend Television.

Frayman, H. (1991b) *Breadline Britain in the 1990s*, London, HarperCollins.

Gaskell, G. and Smith, P. (1985) 'How young blacks see the police', *New Society*, 23 August 1985, pp. 261–3.

Geddes, A. (1993) 'Asian and Afro-Caribbean representation in elected local government in England and Wales', *New Community*, **20** (1), pp. 43–57.

Genders, E. and Player, E. (1990) *Race Relations in Prisons*, Oxford, Clarendon Press.

Gill, D., Mayor, B. and Blair, M. (eds) (1992) *Racism and Education: structures and strategies*, London, Sage/Open University.

Gilroy, P. (1990) 'The end of antiracism', in Ball, W. and Solomos, J. (eds) *Race and Local Politics*, Macmillan, London.

Ginsburg, N. (1992) 'Racism and housing: concepts and reality', in Braham, P., Rattansi, A. and Skellington, R. (eds) *Racism and Antiracism: inequalities, opportunities and policies*, London, Sage/Open University.

Goel, K. *et al.* (1976) 'Florid and sub clinical rickets among immigrant children in Glasgow', *Lancet*, **1**, pp. 1141–5.

Goldstein, H. (1987) *Multi-level Models in Social and Educational Research*, London, Griffin Press.

Goodman, A. and Webb, S. (1994) *For Richer, for Poorer*, London, Institute for Fiscal Studies.

Gordon, D. and Forrest, R. (1995) *People and Places 2: social and economic distinctions in England*, Bristol, School for Advanced Urban Studies.

Gordon, P. (1989a) *Citizenship for Some? Race and government policy 1979–1989*, Runnymede Commentary No. 2, April, London, Runnymede Trust.

Gordon, P. (1989b) 'Hidden injuries of racism', *New Statesman and Society*, 12 May 1989, pp. 24–6.

Gordon, P. (1990) *Racial Violence and Harassment*, London, Runnymede Trust.

Gore, H. (1987) 'Two year YTS: another whitewash', *Unemployment Bulletin* 23, spring, pp. 12–13.

Grandison, K. (1992) 'Health warning: being black', *Social Work Today*, 22 October.

Grant, C. (1989) 'Behind the facade', *Roof*, **14** (2), pp. 10–11.

Greater London Action for Racial Equality (GLARE) (1989) *Life Chance: What Chance?*, London, GLARE.

Greater London Council (GLC) (1984) *A Report of the Panel of Inquiry into Racial Harassment in London*, London, GLC.

Greve, J. and Currie, D. (1990) *Homelessness in Britain*, London, Joseph Rowntree.

Hansard (1963) 27 November, vol. 1685, pp. 439–40.

Hansard (1965) 23 March, vol. 709, pp. 380–1, 437.

Hansard (1987) 16 November, 'Parliamentary debate on the 1987 Immigration Bill', vol. 1428, p. 785.

Hansard (1992) 21 May, cols 249–252.

Hansard (1993) 26 April, vol. 1619, pp. 266–7.

Hansard (1994a) 21 February, cols 9–10.

Hansard (1994b) 11 March, cols 582–585.

Hansard (1994c) 14 March, cols 485–486.

Hansard (1994d) 12 April, cols 47–48.

Harris, C. (1994) 'Les formes d'intervention de l'Etat face à l'immigration dans la Grande-Bretagne d'après-guerre,' conference on Nations, cultures et relations interethniques, organised by Association Française de Science Politique, Centre de Recherches politiques de la Sorbonne, Universite de Paris, 22–24 September.

Haskey, J. (1989) 'Families and households of the ethnic minority and white populations of Great Britain', *Population Trends 57*, OPCS, London, HMSO.

Haskey, J. (1991a) 'The ethnic minority populations resident in private households: estimates by county and metropolitan district of England and Wales', *Population Trends 63*, OPCS, London, HMSO.

Haskey, J. (1991b) 'Estimated numbers and demographic characteristics of one-parent families in Great Britain', *Population Trends 65*, OPCS, London, HMSO.

Health Education Authority (HEA) (1995) *Black and Minority Ethnic Groups in England*, London, HEA.

Heath, S. and Dale, A. (1994) 'Household and family formation in Great Britain: the ethnic dimension', *Population Trends 77*, OPCS, London, HMSO.

Hemans, E. R. (1993) 'Local authorities and racial harassment', unpublished paper, University of Keele.

Henderson, J. and Karn, V. (1984) *Race, Class and State Housing: inequality and the allocation of public housing in Britain*, Aldershot, Gower.

Hesse, B., Rai, D.K., Bennet, C. and McGilhrist, P. (1992) *Beneath the Surface: racial harassment*, Avebury, Aldershot.

Hibberd, M. and Shapland, J. (1993) *Violent Crime in Small Shops*, London, Police Foundation.

Hicks, C. (1982) 'Racism in nursing', *Nursing Times*, 4–12 May.

Higher Education Funding Council for England (HEFCE) (1995) *Review of Higher Education: Submission by the Higher Education Funding Council for England*, London, HEFCE.

Hitch, P. (1981) 'Immigration and mental health: local research and social explanations', *New Community*, **9** (2), pp. 256–62.

Hitch, P. and Clegg, P. (1980) 'Modes of referral of overseas immigrant and native-born first admissions to psychiatric hospital', *Social Scientific Medicine*, **14A**, pp. 369–74.

HMSO (1992a) *On the State of Public Health for the Year 1991*, London, HMSO.

HMSO (1992b) *Aspects of Britain, November 1992*, Par 502, London, HMSO.

HMSO (1993) *Regional Trends 28*, London, HMSO.

HMSO (1994a) *Annual Report of the Police Complaints Authority, 1993*, London, HMSO.

HMSO (1994b) *Her Majesty's Chief Inspector of Constabulary Annual Report 1993*, London, HMSO.

HM Treasury (1990) *Government Expenditure Plans 1990–91 to 1992–93*, London, HMSO.

Home Affairs Committee (1981) *Racial Disadvantage: report and minutes of evidence* (HC 424), London, HMSO.

Home Affairs Committee (1983) *Ethnic and Racial Questions in the Census: report and minutes of evidence*, 2 (HC 33), London, HMSO.

Home Affairs Committee (1985) *Immigration from the Indian Sub-continent*, London, HMSO.

Home Affairs Committee (1986) *Racial Attacks and Harassment*, London, HMSO.

Home Affairs Committee (1994) *Racial Attacks and Harassment*, London, HMSO.

Home Affairs Select Committee (1989) *Racial Attacks and Harassment*, London, HMSO.

Home Office (1981) *Racial Attacks*, London, HMSO.

Home Office (1985) *Control of Immigration: statistics United Kingdom*, Cmnd 9863, London, HMSO.

Home Office (1991) *Control of Immigration: statistics United Kingdom*, Cmnd 1571, London, HMSO.

Home Office (1992) *British Crime Survey*, London, HMSO.

Home Office (1993) *Evidence to the Select Committee of the House of Commons on Racial Attacks and Harassment*, London, HMSO.

Home Office (1994a) *British Crime Survey: Research and Planning Unit Paper 82*, February, London, HMSO.

Home Office (1994b) *Race and the Criminal Justice System*, London, HMSO.

Hood, R. (1992) *Race and Sentencing*, Oxford, Clarendon Press.

Hughes, A. (1994) *Small Business Access to Finance*, London, Economic and Social Research Council.

Ineichen, B. (1980) 'Mental illness among New Commonwealth migrants to Britain' in Boyce, A. (ed.) *Mobility and Migration*, London, Taylor and Francis.

Ineichen, B. (1986) 'Compulsory admission to psychiatric hospital under the 1959 Mental Health Act: the experience of ethnic minorities', *New Community*, **13** (1), pp. 86–93.

Ineichen, B., Harrison, G. and Morgan, H. (1984) 'Psychiatric hospital admissions in Bristol', *British Journal of Psychiatry*, **145**, pp. 206–11.

Inner London Education Authority (ILEA) (1987) *Ethnic Background and Examination Results, 1985 and 1986: Research and Statistics Report*, London, ILEA.

Institute of Race Relations (IRR) (1991) *Deadly Silence: black deaths in custody*, London, IRR.

Jervis, M. (1986) 'Attack on structural racism', *Social Work Today*, 2 June.

Jewson, N., Mason, D., Bowen, R., Mulvaney, K. and Parmar, S. (1991) 'Universities and ethnic minorities: the public face', *New Community*, **17**(2), pp. 183–200.

Johnson, M. (1987) 'Towards racial equality in health and welfare: what progress?' *New Community*, **14**(1/2), pp. 128–35

Johnson, M.D. (1994) 'Health and social services', *New Community*, **20** (4), pp. 678–86.

Jones, T. (1993) *Britain's Ethnic Minorities*, London, Policy Studies Institute.

Jones, T. and McEvoy, D. (1994) *Asian Business*, Liverpool, John Moore's University.

Joseph Rowntree Foundation (1995) *Income and Wealth*, Poole, Joseph Rowntree Foundation.

Jowell, R., Witherspoon, S. and Brook, L. (1984) *British Social Attitudest*, Aldershot, Gower/Social and Community Planning Research.

Jowell, R., Witherspoon, S. and Brook, L. (1986) *British Social Attitudes*, Aldershot, Gower/Social and Community Planning Research.

Jowell, R., Witherspoon, S. and Brook, L. (1992) *British Social Attitudes*, Dartmouth, Dartmouth Publishing.

Jowell, R., Witherspoon, S. and Brook, L. (1993) *British Social Attitudes*, Dartmouth, Dartmouth Publishing.

Jowell, R., Witherspoon, S. and Brook, L. (1994) *British Social Attitudes*, Dartmouth, Dartmouth Publishing.

Karmi, G. and McKeigue, P. (1993) *The Ethnic Health Bibliography*, London, North East and North West Thames Regional Health Authority.

King, M. and Israel, G. (1989) 'The pursuit of excellence, or how solicitors maintain racial inequality', *New Community*, **16**(1), pp. 107–20.

King, M., Israel, G. and Goulbourne, A. (1990) *Ethnic Minorities and Recruitment to the Solicitors' Profession*, London, Law Society and CRE.

Kinsley Lord (1994) *Metropolitan Police*, London, Kinsley Lord.

Kubie, L. (1971) 'Multiple fallacies in the concept of schizophrenia', *Journal of Nervous and Mental Diseases*, **153**(5), pp. 331–42.

Landau, S. (1981) 'Juveniles and the police', *British Journal of Criminology*, **21** (1), pp. 27–46.

Landau, S., Simha, F. and Nathan, G. (1983) 'Selecting delinquents for cautioning in the London Metropolitan area', *British Journal of Criminology*, **23** (2), pp. 128–49.

Lear, J.T., Lawrence, J.E.F., Pohl, A.C. and Burden, F. (1994) 'Myocardial infarction and thrombolysis: a comparison of the Indian and European populations on a coronary care unit', *Journal of the Royal College of Physicians of London*, **28**, pp. 143–7.

Le Lohe, M. (1992) 'Political issues', *New Community*, **18** (3), pp. 469–74.

Le Lohe, M. (1993) 'Political issues', *New Community* **20** (1), pp. 167–72.

Le Lohe, M. (1994) 'Political issues', *New Community* **20** (3), pp. 514–19.

Leech, K. (1989) *A Question in Dispute: the debate about an 'ethnic' question in the Census*, London, Runnymede Trust.

Liberty (1995) *The Last Resort: violations of the human rights of migrants, refugees and asylum seekers*, London, Liberty.

Littlewood, R. and Cross, S. (1980) 'Ethnic minorities and psychiatric services', *Sociology of Health and Illness*, **2** (2), pp. 194–201.

Littlewood, R. and Lipsedge, M. (1982) *Aliens and Alienists: ethnic minorities and psychiatry*, Harmondsworth, Penguin.

Littlewood, R. and Lipsedge, M. (1988) 'Psychiatric illness among British Afro-Caribbeans', *British Medical Journal*, **297**, p. 135.

London Borough of Ealing (1988) *Ealing's Dilemma: implementing race equality in education*, London Borough of Ealing.

London Borough of Newham (1987) *Report of a Survey of Crime and Racial Harassment in Newham*, London Borough of Newham.

London Research Centre (1992) *Social Renters: council and housing association tenants in London*, London, LRC.

London Research Centre (1993) *First Findings, London Housing Survey 1992*, London, LRC.

London Research Centre (1994) *Housing Needs in London*, London, LRC.

Low Pay Network (1994) *Low Pay*, London, Low Pay Network.

Low Pay Unit (1992) *Poor Britain: Poverty, inequality and low pay in the nineties*, London, Low Pay Unit.

McCrudden, C., Smith, D. and Brown, C. (1991) *Racial Justice at Work: enforcement of the Race Relations Act 1976 in employment*, London, Policy Studies Institute.

McDermott, K. (1990) 'We have no problem: the experience of racism in prison', *New Community*, **16** (2), pp. 213–28.

MacDonald, I. (1983) *Immigration Law and Practice in the United Kingdom*, London, Butterworth.

MacEwan, M. and Verity, M. (1989) *Ethnic Minority Experiences of Council Housing in Edinburgh*, Edinburgh, Scottish Ethnic Minorities Research Unit and the CRE.

MacManus, I.C., Richards, P. and Winder, B. (1995) 'Medical school applicants from ethnic minorities', *British Medical Journal*, **310**, pp. 496–500.

Manchester University (1994) *Ethnic Dimensions of the 1991 Census*, Manchester University.

Manpower Services Commission (MSC) (1987), *Two Year YTS: 100 per cent leaver survey, April 1986–May 1987*, Sheffield, MSC.

Mayet, G. (1993) 'Exclusions and schools', *Multicultural Education Review*, **15**, pp. 7–9.

Mayhew, P., Elliot, D. T. and Dowds, L. (1989) *The 1988 British Crime Survey*, Home Office Research Study III, London, HMSO.

MBS Associates (1993) *Understanding Black Enterprises*, MBS Associates, Bristol.

Medical Foundation for Care of Victims of Torture (MFCVT) (1994) *A Betrayal of Trust*, MFCVT , London.

Metropolitan Police (1990) *Report of the Commissioner of Police of the Metropolis 1989: we care for London*, London, Metropolitan Police.

MIND (1993) *MIND's Policy on Black Minority Ethnic People and Mental Health*, London, MIND.

Mizen, P. (1990) 'Race equality in London's Youth Training Schemes', *Unemployment Bulletin* 32, spring, pp. 1–6.

Modood, T. (1993) 'The number of ethnic minority students in British higher education: some grounds for optimism', *Oxford Review of Education*, **19** (2), pp. 167–82.

Modood, T. (1994) *Racial Equality, Colour, Culture and Justice*, London, Institute for Public Policy Research.

Mohammed, S. (1991) 'Improving health services for black populations', *Share*, 1, November, London, King's Fund Centre.

Moore, R. (1995) *Ethnic Statistics and the 1991 Census*, London, Runnymede Trust.

Nanda, P. (1988) 'White attitudes: the rhetoric and the reality', in Bhat *et al.* (eds) *Britain's Black Population*, 2nd edition, Aldershot, Gower.

National Association for the Care and Resettlement of Offenders (NACRO) (1988) *Some Facts and Findings about Black People in the Criminal Justice System*, London, NACRO.

NACRO (1991) *Race and Criminal Justice*, London, NACRO.

NACRO (1992) *Annual Report*, London, NACRO.

NACRO (1995) *Race Policies into Action*, Newsletter of the NACRO Race Unit, May.

National Association of Citizens Advice Bureaux (NACAB) (1988) *Homelessness: a national survey of CAB clients*, London, NACAB.

NACAB (1991) *Barriers to Benefits: black claimants and social security*, London, NACAB.

NACAB (1994) *Unequal Opportunities*, London, NACAB.

National Association of Teachers in Further and Higher Education (NATFHE) (1986) *NATFHE against Racism*, London, NATFHE.

NATFHE (1994) *Annual Report*, London, NATFHE.

National Audit Office (NAO) (1991) *1991 Report*, London, NAO.

National Commission on Education (1993) *Learning to Succeed: a radical look at education today and a strategy for the future*, London, NCE.

National Federation of Housing Associations (NFHA) (1993a) *Using Race Equality Targets*, London, NFHA.

NFHA (1993b) *Accommodating Diversity*, London, NFHA.

National Housing Forum (1994) *Papering Over the Cracks*, London, National Housing Forum.

National Institute of Adult Continuing Education (1993) *Learning for a Purpose*, London, Department of Employment.

National Union of Headteachers (1992) *Managing Equality*, London, NUHT.

National Union of Teachers (1992) *Anti-Racist Guidelines*, London, NUT.

Norwich and Norfolk Race Equality Council (1994) *Not in Norfolk: tackling the invisibility of racism*, Norwich, Norwich and Norfolk Race Equality Council.

Novak, T. (1994) 'Book reviews of CCETSW, *One Small Step Towards Racial Justice* and *Setting the Context for Change*', *Journal of Social Policy*, **23**, pp. 285–7.

Nuttall, D., Goldstein, H., Prosser, R. and Rasbash, J. (1989) 'Differential school effectiveness', *International Journal of Educational Research*, **13**, pp. 769–76.

Nuttall, D. and Varlaam, A. (1990) *Differences in Examination Performance, RS 1277/90*, London, ILEA Research and Statistics Branch.

Oakley, R. (1989) *Employment in Police Forces: a survey of equal opportunities*, London, CRE.

Office for Standards in Education (OFSTED) (1993) *Achieving Good Behaviour in Schools*, London, OFSTED.

Office of Population Censuses and Surveys (OPCS) (1978) *International Migration 1975*, Series MN, 2, London, HMSO.

OPCS (1979) 'Population of New Commonwealth and Pakistani ethnic origin: new projections', *Population Trends*, summer, Immigrant Statistics Unit, London, HMSO.

OPCS (1986) 'Estimating the size of the ethnic minority populations in the 1980s', *Population Trends 44*, London, HMSO.

OPCS (1991a) *Population Trends 63*, London, HMSO.

OPCS (1991b) *Census County Monitor 1991: Great Britain*, London, OPCS.

OPCS (1992) *Census Newsletter*, No. 20, London, OPCS.

OPCS (1994a) *1992 International Migration*, London, OPCS.

OPCS (1994b) 'Long term illness: results from the 1991 census', *Population Trends 75*, OPCS, London, HMSO.

Ohri, S. and Faruqi, S. (1988) 'Racism, employment and unemployment' in Bhat *et al.* (eds) *Britain's Black Population*, 2nd edition, Aldershot, Gower.

Open University (1994a) *Statistical Digest Executive Summary*, Milton Keynes, Open University Equal Opportunities Unit, pp. 3 and 5.

Open University (1994b) *EO Staff Statistics*, Milton Keynes, Open University Equal Opportunities Unit, p. 7.

Oppenheim, C. (1990) *Poverty: the facts*, London, Child Poverty Action Group.

Oppenheim, C. (1993) *Poverty: the facts*, 2nd edition, London, Child Poverty Action Group.

Owen, C. (1993) 'Using the LFS to estimate Britain's ethnic minority population', *Population Trends 72*, OPCS, London, HMSO.

Owen, D. (1993) *Ethnic Minorities in Great Britain: age and gender structure*, CRER, Coventry, University of Warwick.

Owen, D. (1994) *Ethnic Minority Women and the Labour Market*, London, Equal Opportunities Commission.

Parker, J. and Dugmore, K. (1976) *Colour and the Allocation of GLC Housing*, London, Greater London Council.

Patel, N. (1994) 'Developing antiracist education and practice in professional training: an example of a statutory body in social work CCETSW', paper presented to the conference Multi-Ethnic Britain: The Facts, Runnymede Trust, Reading University September 1994.

Pearce, D. and White, I. (1994) '1991 Census of Great Britain', *Population Trends 78*, OPCS, London, HMSO.

Penal Affairs Commission (PAC) (1993) *The Asylum Bill and Detention*, London, PAC.

Phillips, D. (1986) *What Price Equality? A report on the allocation of GLC housing in Tower Hamlets*, GLC Housing Research and Policy Report 9, London, GLC.

Phillips, D. (1987) 'Searching for a decent home: ethnic minority progress in the post war housing market', *New Community*, **14** (1/2), pp. 105–47

Phillips, D. (1989), 'Eliminating discrimination', *Housing Review*, **38** (5), p. 141.

Phillips, R. (1986) 'No coloureds', *Roof*, November/December, pp. 13–15.

Pinto, R. (1970) 'A study of Asians in the Camberwell area', M. Phil. dissertation, unpublished, University of London.

Police Federation (1993) *Evidence to the Select Committee of the House of Commons on Racial Attacks and Harassment*, London, HMSO.

Policy Studies Institute (PSI) (1994a) *Law Student Disadvantage*, London, PSI.

PSI (1994b) *Changing Lives 2*, London, PSI.

PSI (1995) *Nursing in a Multi-Ethnic NHS*, London, PSI.

Polytechnics Central Admissions System (1991) *Statistical Supplement 1989–90*, Cheltenham, PCAS.

Racial Harassment Project (1989) *Because their Skin is Black*, Sheffield City Council.

Rack, P. (1982) *Race, Culture and Mental Disorder*, London, Tavistock.

Rampton, Anthony (Chair) (1981) *West Indian Children in Our Schools: interim report of the Committee of Inquiry into the Education of Children from Ethnic Minority Groups*, Cmnd 8273, London, HMSO.

Rogers, A. and Faulkner, A. (1987) *A Place of Safety*, London, MIND.

Roys, P. (1988) 'Social services' in Bhat *et al.* (eds) *Britain's Black Population: a new perspective*, 2nd edition, Aldershot, Gower.

Ruddock, J. (1994) *Racial Attacks: the rising tide*, London, The Labour Party

Runnymede Trust (1975) *Race and Council Housing in London*, London, Runnymede Trust.

Runnymede Trust (1986) *Racial Violence and Harassment*, London, Runnymede Trust.

Runnymede Trust (1988) Bulletin 216, London, Runnymede Trust.

Runnymede Trust (1988–9) Bulletin 221, London, Runnymede Trust.

Runnymede Trust (1989) Bulletin 224, London, Runnymede Trust.

Runnymede Trust (1991a) Bulletin 248, London, Runnymede Trust

Runnymede Trust (1991b) Bulletin 247, London, Runnymede Trust.

Runnymede Trust (1992a) Bulletin 254, London, Runnymede Trust.

Runnymede Trust (1992b) Bulletin 258, London, Runnymede Trust.

Runnymede Trust (1992c) Bulletin 259, London, Runnymede Trust.

Runnymede Trust (1993a) Bulletin 262, London, Runnymede Trust.

Runnymede Trust (1993b) Bulletin 263, London, Runnymede Trust.

Runnymede Trust (1993c) Bulletin 264, London, Runnymede Trust.

Runnymede Trust (1993d) Bulletin 265, London, Runnymede Trust.

Runnymede Trust (1993e) Bulletin 266, London, Runnymede Trust.

Runnymede Trust (1993f) Bulletin 267, London, Runnymede Trust.

Runnymede Trust (1993g) Bulletin 268, London, Runnymede Trust.

Runnymede Trust (1993h) Bulletin 269, London, Runnymede Trust.

Runnymede Trust (1993i) Bulletin 270, London, Runnymede Trust.

Runnymede Trust (1994a) *Multi-Ethnic Britain: facts and trends*, London, Runnymede Trust.

Runnymede Trust (1994b) Bulletin 271, London, Runnymede Trust.

Runnymede Trust (1994c) Bulletin 274, London, Runnymede Trust.

Runnymede Trust (1994d) Bulletin 276, London, Runnymede Trust.

Runnymede Trust (1994e) Bulletin 277, London, Runnymede Trust.

Runnymede Trust (1994f) Bulletin 278, London, Runnymede Trust.

Runnymede Trust (1994g) Bulletin 279, London, Runnymede Trust.

Runnymede Trust (1994h) Bulletin 280, London, Runnymede Trust.

Runnymede Trust (1995a) *Challenge, Change and Opportunity*, London, Runnymede Trust.

Runnymede Trust (1995b) Bulletin 281, London, Runnymede Trust.

Runnymede Trust (1995c) Bulletin 282, London, Runnymede Trust.

Runnymede Trust (1995d) Bulletin 283, London, Runnymede Trust.

Runnymede Trust (1995e) Bulletin 284, London, Runnymede Trust.

Runnymede Trust (1995f) Bulletin 285, London, Runnymede Trust.

Runnymede Trust (1995g) Bulletin 286, London, Runnymede Trust.

Runnymede Trust (1995h) Bulletin 287, London, Runnymede Trust.

Runnymede Trust and the Radical Statistics Race Group (RSRG) (1980) *Britain's Black Population*, London, Heinemann Educational Books.

Rwgellera, G. (1977) 'Psychiatric morbidity among West Africans and West Indians living in London', *Psychological Medicine*, **7**, pp. 428–32.

Rwgellera, G. (1980) 'Differential use of psychiatric services by West Indians, West Africans and English in London', *British Journal of Psychiatry*, **137**, pp. 428–32.

Sammons, P. and Newbury, K. (1989) *Ethnic Monitoring in Further and Higher Education*, London, ILEA Further Education Unit.

Sarre, P., Phillips, D. and Skellington, R. (1989) *Ethnic Minority Housing: explanations and policies*, Aldershot, Avebury.

Scarman, Lord (1981) *The Brixton Disorders, 10–12 April 1981: report of an inquiry*, Cmnd 8427, London, HMSO.

Scottish Education Department (1989) *Ethnically-Based Statistics on School Pupils* (Circular 8), Edinburgh, Scottish Office.

Searle P. and Stibbs, A. (1989) 'The under-representation of ethnic minority students in post-graduate teacher training', *New Community*, **15** (2), pp. 253–260.

Select Committee on Race Relations and Immigration (1969) *The Problems of Coloured School Leavers*, HC 413, London, HMSO.

Select Committee on Race Relations and Immigration (1973) *Education: report and minutes of evidence*, HC 405, London, HMSO.

Select Committee on Race Relations and Immigration (1977a) *The West Indian Community*, HC 180, London, HMSO.

Select Committee on Race Relations and Immigration (1977b) *Report on Education*, 1, para 69, London, HMSO.

Sentamu, J. (1991) *Seeds of Hope*, London, Church of England.

Sexty, D. (1990) *Women Losing Out*, London, Shelter.

Shaw, C. (1988) 'Components of growth in the ethnic minority population', *Population Trends 52*, OPCS, London, HMSO.

Shelter (1994) *Homelessness, Shelter and the Churches*, London, National Housing Coalition.

Shiner, M. and Modood, T. (1994) *Ethnic Minorities and Higher Education: why are there differential rates of entry?* Poole, PSI.

Sim, J. (1982) 'Scarman: the police counter-attack' in *The Socialist Register 1982*, London, Merlin Press.

Simon, J. (1993) 'The economic effects of immigration', *European Review*, 1(1), pp. 109–16.

Single Homeless in London (SHIL) (1995) *Time to Move On*, London, SHIL.

SHIL and London Housing Unit (LHU) (1989) 'Local authority policy and practice on single homelessness among black and other ethnic minority people', London, SHIL/LHU.

Siraj-Blatchford, I. (1990) 'The experience of black students in initial teacher education', Department of Education, Warwick University.

Sivanandan, A. (1994) 'Race against time' in Spencer, S. (ed.) *Strangers and Citizens*, London, Oram Press.

Skellington, R. (1993) 'Homelessness' in Dallos, R. and McLaughlin, E. (eds) *Social Problems and the Family*, London, Sage.

Smith, D. (1980) *Overseas Doctors in the NHS*, London, Heinemann/PSI.

Smith, D. and Tomlinson, S. (1989) *The School Effect: a study of multi-racial comprehensives*, London, Policy Studies Group.

Smith, S. (1989) *The Politics of 'Race' and Residence*, Oxford, Polity Press.

Smith, S. and Hill, S. (1991) 'Unwelcome home', *Roof*, 16(2), pp. 38–41.

Social Security Committee (1991) *Low Income Statistics: households below average income, 1988, first report*, London, HMSO.

Spencer, S. (ed.) (1994) *Strangers and Citizens*, London, Institute for Public Policy Research.

Statham, J., Donald, M. and Cathcart, H. (1989) *The Education Factfile*, Sevenoaks, Hodder and Stoughton (new edn 1994)

Statistical Monitoring Unit (1991) *Meaningful Statistics on Poverty*, Statistical Monitoring Unit, University of Bristol.

Stirling, M. (1993) 'A black mark against him?' *Multicultural Education Review*, 15, pp. 3–7.

Tattum, D. P. (1982) *Disruptive Pupils in Schools and Units*, Chichester, John Wiley.

Teague, A. (1993) 'Ethnic group: first results from the 1991 census', *Population Trends 72*, OPCS, London, HMSO.

The 1990 Trust (1994) *Black to Black*, December, London, The 1990 Trust.

Tomlinson, S. (1981) *Educational Subnormality: a study in decision making*, London, Routledge and Kegan Paul.

Torkington, N. (1983) *The Racial Politics of Health: a Liverpool profile*, Merseyside Area Profile Group, University of Liverpool.

Torkington, P. (1991) *Black Health: a political issue*, Catholic Association for Racial Justice and Liverpool Institute of Higher Education.

Tower Hamlets Homeless Families Campaign (1993) *Race for Power*, London, THHFC.

Townsend, P. (1991) *The Poor are Poorer*, Statistical Monitoring Unit, University of Bristol.

Townsend, P. and Davidson, N. (eds) (1982) *Inequalities in Health* (The Black Report), Harmondsworth, Penguin.

Townsend, P. and Davidson, N. (1992) *Inequalities in Health*, Harmondsworth, Penguin.

Trades Union Congress (TUC) (1994) *Black Workers in the Labour Market*, London, TUC.

Troyna, B. (1984) 'Fact or artefact? The "educational under achievement" of black pupils', *British Journal of Sociology of Education*, **5** (2), pp. 153–60.

Troyna, B. and Hatcher, R. (1992) 'Racial incidents in schools: a framework for analysis and intervention' in Gill, D., Mayor, B. and Blair, M. (eds) *Racism and Education: structures and strategies*, London, Sage/Open University.

Tuck, S. (1982) 'Sickle cell disease and pregnancy', *British Journal of Hospital Medicine*, August, pp. 123–7.

Unemployment Unit (1990) 'YT: graduating from YTS', *Unemployment Bulletin*, August.

Unemployment Unit (1991) *Unemployment Bulletin*.

Unemployment Unit (1993a) *Unemployment Bulletin*, January.

Unemployment Unit (1993b) Unemployment Unit Working Brief, August.

Unemployment Unit (1994) Unemployment Unit Working Brief, August/September.

Unemployment Unit and Youth Aid (1990) *Unemployment Bulletin*, 32, spring.

Unemployment Unit and Youth Aid (1991) *ET Leavers Survey*.

Utting, D. (1995) *Family and Parenthood*, York, Joseph Rowntree Foundation.

Victim Support (1991) *Racial Attacks in Camden, Southwark and Newham*, London, Victim Support.

Virdee, S. (1995) *Racial Violence and Harassment*, PSE, London.

West Midlands County Council (1986) *A Different Reality: report of the Review Panel into the Handsworth Rebellions of 1985*, West Midlands County Council.

West Midlands Low Pay Unit (1988) *Last Among Equals*, Birmingham, West Midlands Low Pay Unit.

Westwood, S. *et al.* (1989) *Sadness in My Heart: racism and mental health – a research report*, Leicester, Leicester Black Mental Health Group.

White, R. M. (1979) 'What's in a name? Problems in official and legal usages of race', *New Community*, **7** (3), pp. 333–47.

Whitehead, M. (1987) *The Health Divide*, London, Health Education Council.

Wilkinson, A. (1982) *Children who come into care in Tower Hamlets*, Directorate of Social Services, London Borough of Tower Hamlets.

Williams, J., Cocking, J. and Davies, L. (1989) *Words or Deeds*, London, CRE.

Young, K. (1993) 'Class, race and opportunity' in Jowell, R., Witherspoon, S. and Brook, L., *British Social Attitudes*, [location], Dartmouth Publishing.

Youth Employment and Training Unit (YETRU) (1989) *The Firms That Like to Say 'No'!*, London, YETRU.

Acronyms and abbreviations

AMA	Association of Metropolitan Authorities
AUT	Association for University Teachers
BAPA	Black and Asian Police Association
BASW	British Association of Social Workers
BCC	British Council of Churches
BCS	British Crime Survey
BNP	British National Party
BSA	British Social Attitudes Survey
CAB	Citizens Advice Bureaux
CCETSW	Central Council for Education and Training in Social Work
CCRA	Criminal Cases Review Authority
CLE	Council for Legal Education
CPAG	Child Poverty Action Group
CRC	Community Relations Council
CRE	Commission for Racial Equality
EOC	Equal Opportunities Commission
ESRC	Economic and Social Research Council
ESWI	English, Scottish, Welsh and Irish
FATEBU	Forum for the Advancement of Training and Education for the Black Unemployed
FBHA	Federation of Black Housing Associations
FBHO	Federation of Black Housing Organizations (changed to the FBHA in the early 1990s)
GHS	General Household Survey
GLARE	Greater London Action for Racial Equality
GLC	Greater London Council (abolished in 1986)
HBAV	Households Below Average Income
HEA	Health Education Authority
ILEA	Inner London Education Authority (abolished in 1990)
IPPR	Institute for Public Policy Research
IRR	Institute of Race Relations
JCWI	Joint Council for the Welfare of Immigrants
JRF	Joseph Rowntree Foundation

LFS	Labour Force Survey
LEA	Local Education Authority
LPN	Low Pay Network
LPU	Low Pay Unit
LRC	London Research Centre
MHF	Mental Health Foundation
MORI	Market and Opinion Research Institute
MPF	Metropolitan Police Force
NACAB	National Association of Citizens Advice Bureaux
NACRO	National Association for the Care and Resettlement of Offenders
NAO	National Audit Office
NAPO	National Association of Probation Officers
NCWP	New Commonwealth and Pakistan (the New Commonwealth includes all Commonwealth countries except Australia, Canada and New Zealand)
NF	National Front
NFHA	National Foundation of Housing Associations
NUHT	National Unit of Headteachers
OFSTED	Office for Standards in Education
OPCS	Office of Population Censuses and Surveys
PCA	Police Complaints Authority
PCAS	Polytechnics Central Admissions System (now UCAS, see below)
PFA	Professional Football Association
PRT	Prison Reform Trust
PSI	Policy Studies Institute
RSRG	Radical Statistics Race Group
SCF	Save the Children Fund
SHSA	Special Hospitals Service Authority
SRB	Single Regeneration Budget
SSA	Standard Spending Assessment
THHFC	Tower Hamlets Homeless Families Campaign
UCAS	Universities and Colleges Admissions Service
UCCA	Universities Central Council for Admissions
UNICEF	United Nations International Children's Emergency Fund
UU	Unemployment Unit
YETRU	Youth Employment and Training Unit

List of useful addresses

Asylum Rights Campaign
3 Bondway
London SW8 1SJ

Black Mental Health Group
The Playtower
Ladywell Road
London SE13 7UW

Board of Deputies of British Jews
Woburn House (4th floor)
Upper Woburn Place
London WC1H OEP

Campaign Against Racism and
Fascism
BM Box 8784
London WC1N 3XX

Campaign for Anti Racist
Education (CARE)
PO Box 681
London SW8 1SX

Centre for Multicultural Education
University of London
Institute of Education
20 Bedford Way
London WC1H 0AL

Centre for Research in Ethnic
Relations
University of Warwick
Coventry CV4 7AL

Centre for the Study of Islam and
Christian Muslim Relations
Selly Oak College
Birmingham B29 6LE

Child Poverty Action Group
1–5 Bath Street
London W1V 3DG

Commission for Racial Equality
(Head Office)
Elliot House
10–12 Allington Street
London SW1E 5EH

Commission of the European
Communities
Directorate-General Information
Rue de la Loi
B–1049
Brussels

Citizen's Advice Bureau (Scotland)
26 George Square
Edinburgh EH8 9LD

Commonwealth Institute
Kensington High Street
London W8 6NQ

Community and Race Relations
Unit
British Council of Churches
Inter-Church House
35–41 Lower Marsh
London SE1 7RL

Equal Opportunities Commission
Overseas House
Quat Street
Manchester M3 3HN

Equal Rights Department
TUC
Congress House
London WC1B 3LS

Ethnic Minorities Development
Unit
35 Vine Street
Hillfields
Coventry CV1 5HN

Family Policy Studies Centre
231 Baker Street
London NW1 6XE

Greater London Action for Racial
Equality (formerly LACRC)
St Margaret's House
21 Old Ford Road
London E2 9PL

Home Office
Immigration and Nationality
Department
Lunar House
Wellesley Road
Croydon CR9 2BY

Indian Workers Association
346 Soho Road
Handsworth
Birmingham B21 9RL

Institute of Race Relations
2–6 Leeke Street
London WC1X 9HS

Local Authority Race Relations
Information Exchange
35 Great Smith Street
London SW1P 3BJ

Joint Council for the Welfare of
Immigrants
115 Old Street
London EC1V 9JR

Minority Rights Group
29 Craven Street
London WC2N 5NG

Liberty
(formerly National Council for
Civil Liberties)
21 Tabard Street
London SE1 4LA

NACRO
169 Clapham Road
London SW9 0PU

National Association of Citizens
Advice Bureaux
115 Pentonville Road
London N1 9LZ

National Antiracist Movement in
Education (NAME)
41 Strawberry Lane
Carshalton
Surrey SM5 2NG

National Association of Racial
Equality Councils
8–10 Coroner Street (1st floor)
London N1 6HD

National Council for Voluntary
Organisations
26 Bedford Square
London SE13 7UW

Newham Monitoring Project
382 Katherine Road
London E7 8NW

Office of Population Censuses
and Surveys
Census Division
Room 823
St Catherines House
10 Kingsway
London WC2B 6JP

Refugee Council
3/9 Bondway
London SW8 1SJ

Refugee Forum
54 Tavistock Place
London WC1H 9RG

Runnymede Trust
11 Princelet Street
London E1 6QH

Searchlight
37B New Cavendish Street
London W1 8JR

The Unemployment Unit
9 Poland Street
London W1V 3DG

The 1990 Trust
The Chandlery
50 Westminster Bridge Road
London SE1 7QY

Trade Union Congress Equal
Rights Department
Congress House
23–28 Great Russell Street
London WC1B 3LS

Acknowledgements

Grateful acknowledgement is made to the following sources for permission to reproduce material in this book:

Figures
Figure 1.1: adapted from Fothergill, S. and Vincent, J. 1985, in Kidron, M. *The State of the Nation*, Pluto Press Ltd. Copyright © Pluto Press Ltd; *Figures 1.2, 1.3, 1.4 and 1.5:* adapted from Office of Population, Censuses and Surveys, *Labour Force Survey Reports*, 1981, 1986–88, reproduced with the permission of the Controller of Her Majesty's Stationery Office; *Figures 1.6, 1.7 and 2.1:* Central Statistical Office/Office of Population, Censuses and Surveys 1990, *Social Trends* **20**, reproduced with the permission of the Controller of Her Majesty's Stationery Office; *Figure 1.8:* Office of Population, Censuses and Surveys, *Labour Force Survey Reports*, 1985–87, reproduced with the permission of the Controller of Her Majesty's Stationery Office; *Figures 1.9 and 1.10:* Haskey, J. 1989, 'Families and households of the ethnic minority and white populations of great Britain', *Population Trends* **57**, Office of Population, Censuses and Surveys, © Crown Copyright. Reproduced with the permission of the Controller of Her Majesty's Stationery Office; *Figure 1.11:* 'Households: by ethnic group of head of household, Spring 1994', *Social Trends* **25**, 1995. Crown copyright 1995. Reproduced by the permission of the Controller of HMSO and the Central Statistical Office; *Figure 1.12:* Average household size: by ethnic group of head of household. 1991', *Social Trends* **24**, 1994. Crown copyright 1995. Reproduced by the permission of the Controller of HMSO and the Central Statistical Office; *Figure 2.1:* adapted from Central Statistical Office/Office of Population, Censuses and Surveys 1990, *Social Trends* **20**, © Crown Copyright. Reproduced with the permission of the Controller of Her Majesty's Stationery Office; *Figure 2.2:* Published by permission of *The Guardian*; *Figure 2.3:* 'UK entry refusal rates, 1992', *Guardian*, 24 December 1993; *Figure 3.4:* 'And you get annoyed about junk mail', *Independent* 3 October 1994, © Commission for Racial Equality; *Figure 3.1:* Published by permission of *The Independent on Sunday*, 13 February 1991; *Figure 3.2:* John Sturrock/Network; *Figure 3.3:* Denis Doran/Network; *Figure 3.5:* Stephen Lawrence, *The Independent*/John Voos; *Figure 4.1:* Frayman, H. 1990, *Breadline Britain 1990's*, Domino Films/London Weekend Television; *Figure 4.2 and 4.3:* The *Independent*, 29 July 1990; *Figures 4.4, 4.5 and 4.6:* adapted from Oppenheim, C. 1990, *Poverty – The Facts*, Child Poverty Action Group; *Figures 4.7 and 4.8:* Ormerod, P. and Salama, E. 1990, 'The rise of the British underclass', *The Independent*, 19 June 1990; *Figure 4.9:* Amin, K., Coleman, P. and Richardson, R. 1995, 'Ethnic group and age by income group', *Runnymede Bulletin*, **282** February 1995, Runnymede Trust; *Figure 5.1:* Britton, M. 1989, 'Mortality and geography', *Population Trends* **56**, Summer 1989, Office of Population, Censuses and Surveys, © Crown Copyright. Repro-

duced with the permission of the Controller of Her Majesty's Stationery Office; *Figure 7.1:* David Hoffmann; *Figure 7.2:* 'Households in worst housing: by ethnic group of head of household', *Social Trends* **24**, 1994. Crown copyright 1994. Reproduced by the permission of the Controller of HMSO and the Central Statistical Office; *Figure 10.1:* Reproduced by permission of *The Guardian*; *Figure 10.2:* Department of Employment 1991, *Employment Gazette*, February 1991, © Crown Copyright. Reproduced with the permission of the Controller of Her Majesty's Stationery Office; *Figure 10.3:* 'Unemployed rates by ethnic group, Spring 1994', *Social Trends* **25**, 1995. Crown copyright 1995. Reproduced by the permission of the Controller of HMSO and the Central Statistical Office; *Figure 10.4:* 'Trends in ILO unemployment rates by ethnic origin; Great Britain, Spring 1984–Autumn 1994 (not seasonally adjusted)', *Employment Gazette* June 1995, HMSO. Crown copyright is reproduced with the permission of the Controller of HMSO; *Figure 11.1:* Cohen, N. 1991, 'Racism: someone else is to blame', *Independent on Sunday*, 7 July 1991.

Tables
Table 1.1: Office of Population, Censuses and Surveys 1981, 1986–88, *Labour Force Survey Reports*, © Crown Copyright. Reproduced with the permission of the Controller of Her Majesty's Stationery Office; *Table 1.2:* Haskey, J. 1991, *Population Trends* **63**, Spring 1991, Office of Population, Censuses and Surveys, © Crown Copyright. Reproduced with the permission of the Controller of Her Majesty's Stationery Office; *Table 1.3:* Amin, K. and Richardson, R. 1994, 'Alternative summary of population by ethnicity, 1991', *Multi-ethnic Britain: Facts and Trends*, September 1994, Runnymede Trust; *Table 1.4:* 'Comparison of ethnic group results from the 1991 Census with the Labour Force Survey (1989–91), Great Britain', *Population Trends* **72** Summer 1993, Office of Population, Censuses and Surveys; *Table 1.5:* Amin, K. and Richardson, R. 1994, 'Districts with largest numbers of black and ethnic minority residents', *Multi-ethnic Britain: Facts and Trends*, September 1994, Runnymede Trust; *Table 2.1:* Central Statistical Office 1990, *Annual Abstract of Statistics*, © Crown Copyright. Reproduced with the permission of the Controller of Her Majesty's Stationery Office; *Table 3.1:* German, L. 1995, 'Reported racist attacks', *Socialist Review*, **185**, April 1995, Larkham P&P Ltd; *Table 4.1 and 6.2:* Brown, C. 1984, *Black and White Britain*, PSI, Gower, 1984; *Table 6.1:* Barn, R. 1990, 'Black children in local authority care: admission patterns', *New Community*, **16**(2), January 1990, Commission for Racial Equality © Carfax Publishing Company; *Tables 7.1 and 9.5:* Central Statistical Office/Office of Population, Censuses and Surveys 1991, *Social Trends* **21**, © Crown Copyright. Reproduced with the permission of the Controller of Her Majesty's Stationery Office; *Table 7.2:* 'Tenure: by ethnic group of head of household', *Social Trends* **24**, 1994. Crown copyright 1995. Reproduced by the permission of the Controller of HMSO and the Central Statistical Office; *Table 8.1:* Courtesy of the Law Society; *Table 8.2:* McDermott, K. 1990, 'We have no problem: the experience

of racism in prison', *New Community*, **16**(2), January 1990, Commission for Racial Equality © Carfax Publishing Company; *Table 8.3:* From *Today*, 2 October 1990; *Table 8.4 and Table 8.5:* Amin, K. 1995, 'Police stop and searches: who, where and why', *The Runnymede Bulletin*, March 1995, Runnymede Trust; *Tables 8.6 and 8.7:* Amin, K. and Richardson, R. 1994, 'Crime, law and justice', *Multi-Ethnic Britain: Facts and Trends*, September 1994, Runnymede Trust; *Tables 9.1, 9.2 and 9.3:* Commission for Racial Equality 1988, *Ethnic Minority School Teachers*, Commission for Racial Equality; *Table 9.4:* UCCA, *Statistical Supplement to the Twenty-eighth Report 1989–1990*, by permission of Universities and Colleges Admissions Scheme; *Table 9.5:* 'Highest qualification level of the population: by ethnic origin and sex, 1988–90', *Social Trends* **22**, 1992. Crown copyright 1992. Reproduced by the permission of the Controller of HMSO and the Central Statistical Office; *Table 10.1:* Hansard, 10 January 1990, Parliamentary Copyright; *Table 10.2:* Unemployment Unit 1990, *Unemployment Bulletin* **32**, Spring 1990; *Tables 10.3, 10.4 and 10.5:* Department of Employment 1991, *Employment Gazette*, February 1991, © Crown Copyright. Reproduced with the permission of the Controller of Her Majesty's Stationery Office; *Table 10.6:* 'Unemployment by ethnic origin', *Working Brief* **57**, August/September 1994, Unemployment Unit; *Table 10.7:* 'People in employment by ethnic group, socio-economic group and gender, Spring 1994', *Social Trends* **25**, 1995. Crown copyright 1995. Reproduced by the permission of the Controller of HMSO and the Central Statistical Office, *Table 12.1*. Amin, K. and Richardson, R. adapted from Geddes 1993, 'Members of local councils in England, by party and ethnicity, 1992', *Multi-ethnic Britain: Facts and Trends*, Runnymede Trust.

Maps
Maps 1.1, 1.2, 1.3, 1.4 and 1.5: Haskey, J. 1991, 'The ethnic minority populations resident in private households: estimates by country and metropolitan district of England and Wales', *Population Trends*, **63**, Office of Population, Censuses and Surveys, © Crown Copyright. Reproduced with the permission of the Controller of Her Majesty's Stationery Office.

Additional illustrations
Page 78: Importation 1793; Deportation 1993, *Independent*, 9 August 1993; *Page 200:* Longsight Youth Club, Manchester, 1987, © Clement Cooper; *Page 219:* Mr Bernard, Manchester, 1986, © Clement Cooper.

Cover photograph
From *Presence*, 1988, Manchester © Cornerhouse Publications and Clement Cooper.